CRISIS OF CHARACTER

CRISIS OF
CHARACTER

A White House Secret Service Officer
Discloses His Firsthand Experience with
Hillary, Bill, and How They Operate

GARY J. BYRNE
with GRANT M. SCHMIDT

CENTER
STREET®

NEW YORK   BOSTON   NASHVILLE

In training we always said, "We don't rise to our expectations; we fall to our level of training." The same can be said of character.

To Genny . . .
For reminding me so sincerely to "just do the right thing," because character is the only thing that matters.

To Elizabeth and Ethan . . .
For reminding me, even before you were born, that character is the only thing that we can hope to pass on after we're gone.

Center Street
Hachette Book Group
1290 Avenue of the Americas, New York, NY 10104
centerstreet.com
twitter.com/centerstreet

First Edition: June 2016

Center Street is a division of Hachette Book Group, Inc. The Center Street name and logo are trademarks of Hachette Book Group, Inc.

The publisher is not responsible for websites (or their content) that are not owned by the publisher.

The Hachette Speakers Bureau provides a wide range of authors for speaking events. To find out more, go to www.HachetteSpeakersBureau.com or call (866) 376-6591.

Title page image: White House Photo

Library of Congress Cataloging-in-Publication Data has been applied for.

ISBNs: 9781455568871 (hardcover), 9781455568888 (ebook)

Printed in the United States of America

LSC-C

20   19   18   17   16   15   14   13   12

CONTENTS

INTRODUCTION

I dreamed of becoming an elite White House Secret Service officer, a member of its Uniformed Division.

Nothing more—and certainly nothing less.

My dream came true. I stood guard, a pistol at my hip, outside the Oval Office, the last barrier before anyone saw Bill Clinton.

The last barrier before *Monica Lewinsky* saw Bill Clinton.

Yes, I'm *that* Secret Service officer.

I saw Monica, and I saw a lot more.

I saw Hillary, too.

I witnessed her obscenity-laced tirades, her shifting of blame, how she berated Vince Foster until he could stand no more, how minor incidents involving blue gloves and botched invitations sent her into a tizzy. It was like watching Humphrey Bogart in *The Caine Mutiny* obsessing about a quart of missing strawberries—and losing sight of the world war raging about him. I saw Hillary scheming with Dick Morris to undermine White House Chief of Staff Leon Panetta. FBI agents confided in me about her emerging Filegate scandal; they were just as frustrated with Hillary's methods as we were.

Life at the Clinton White House careened from crisis (manu-factured or not) to even greater crisis, the participants often unable to catch their breath and certainly incapable of learning from them. The Clinton White House atmosphere alternated from hilarity to bitter anger, lurching from nerves-on-end tension to sheer bore-dom, its most important residents painfully trapped between illu-sion and reality.

When I joined the Secret Service, I knew my body would be put to the test, that my knees would buckle from rigorous training, and I hoped that the extent of my ethical choices would be "Body armor or no body armor?" (Those damn vests weighed down my gun belt and me.) We were supposed to lay our lives—not our consciences—on the line.

But at the Clinton White House, I soon recognized a disturb-ing and pervasive crisis of character. Boots on the ground, the men and women at the lowest part of the totem pole—those who faced death head-on—were measured by the highest of ethical require-ments. Those at the very pinnacles of power held themselves to the very lowest standards—or to none whatsoever.

I saw how the Clinton Machine's appalling leadership style endangered law enforcement officers, the military, and the Ameri-can people in general. And with Hillary Clinton's latest rise, I real-ize that her own leadership style—volcanic, impulsive, enabled by sycophants, and disdainful of the rules set for everyone else—hasn't changed a bit.

What I saw in the 1990s sickened me. I departed first to other White House duties (which didn't take me far enough away) and then to the Federal Air Marshal Service, still working to protect those who can't protect themselves.

Over a twenty-nine-year career serving my country in the military and in federal law enforcement, I've encountered both heroes and villains. I've observed human character at its greatest heights and lowest depths. In any organization, character is defined at the top; it percolates down to the top executives of an organization, to the middle managers, and to the grunts at the front lines. Hillary Clinton is now poised to become the Democratic nominee for president of the United States, but she simply lacks the integrity and temperament to serve in the office. From the bottom of my soul I know this to be true.

So I must speak out.

Though portrayed as the long-suffering spouse of an unfaithful husband, whose infidelities I personally observed or knew to be true, the Hillary Clinton I saw was anything but a sympathetic victim. Those loyal to her kept coming back for her volcanic eruptions.

I witnessed firsthand the Clintons' personal and professional dysfunction: So consumed were they by scandal, so intent on destroying their real or imagined enemies, that governing became an afterthought. The First Couple wasted days obsessing over how to "kill" a forthcoming book (one alleging that Bill Clinton's mother ran a brothel) or in squashing yet another tabloid revelation. Their machinations and their constant damage control diverted them from the nation's real business. Good people like Leon Panetta, Betty Currie, and Evelyn Lieberman had to pick up the slack and bear it for as long as they could.

I have not written a word of this book with a political agenda. Whether the Clintons were Democrats or Republicans, I saw what I saw; I heard what I heard.

Politics do not change unpleasant truths.

Politicians only *think* they do.

I now close nearly three decades of military and law enforcement service, protecting the citizens of a country I love. My sense of service compels me to share with you the real-world, often harrowing experiences that career law enforcement professionals face every day. At the same time, I'm revealing the unvarnished true story of the Clintons, the real damage they inflicted via the presidency and, in my view, the threat they again pose to the future of our nation.

During the Clinton administration, I swore myself to secrecy but not because government lawyers demanded it (though they later did). I kept silent not just because my superiors insisted on it. My own conscience also demanded it. Duty required it. But it was hard. Sometimes I'd trudge home to my wife, Genny, and just hug her without explanation.

"What's going on?" she'd ask.

I'd say, "I'm so glad we aren't like those people." I didn't want to live in their crazy world.

I had no animosity toward the Clintons. Out of a sense of loyalty to our First Family I even secretly disposed of sordid physical evidence that might later have been used to convict the president. The blue dress wasn't the only evidence of his misdeeds. But I could not keep from asking myself how our nation's leaders could be so reckless, so volatile, and so dangerous to themselves and to our nation.

And yes, to *me and my family.*

Only under federal subpoena—and later a ruling by U.S. Supreme Court Chief Justice William Rehnquist—did I reveal to Ken Starr's prosecutors the true story of President Bill Clinton's false testimony and misstatements.

I've retired now from public service, from safeguarding the Bush and Clinton families as well as from protecting passengers at the Federal Air Marshal Service.

Maybe I haven't seen it all, but I've seen enough.

I want you to hear my story. It's about the men and women risking their lives to protect this nation. And more important, it's about how the Clintons must never again be allowed to put them—or you and your children—at risk.

—Gary J. Byrne
March 2016

CRISIS OF CHARACTER

1.

THE VASE

Nobody knew everything that was going on at the Clinton White House.

Not even President Clinton's press guru, George Stephanopoulos. He wasn't there at night, and some of the best (or worst) moments happened after hours. People like George didn't hear and see what we did around the Executive Mansion, so my guess is they didn't know how Hillary battled her husband in the West Wing.

One morning in late summer 1995, I entered the White House to assume my post just outside the Oval Office—officially Secret Service Post E-6.

Things were stirring, and I wanted to know why.

Everyone on post that night, Secret Service agents (SAs), Secret Service Uniformed Division (UD) officers like myself, the housemen, and the ushers couldn't help but hear the First Couple arguing as sounds from their fracases traveled through the old building. Mrs. Clinton had a booming voice, and their yelling matches easily traversed the living quarters' private elevator, vents, and staircase. Many housemen eased away, but the SAs and UD couldn't leave their posts. This was especially a big argument that ended with a *crash*. SAs were obligated to respond and found its cause, a vase on the other side of the room. A houseman picked up the damage. The First Couple couldn't just sweep up and toss out the remains because everything in the White House is logged and recorded, befitting its role as a national landmark and a veritable museum.

I peeked into the curator's small, windowless ground-floor office across from the China Room and the Diplomatic Reception Room. It was cluttered with blueprints and history books on the every detail of the White House: fabrics, furniture, artifacts. Sure enough, there was a box containing a light blue vase smashed to bits. The rumors *were* true!

"Can I help you?"

The White House's official curator looked up from what she was reading, clearly annoyed and already tired of people checking out the box. "Can I help you, Officer?" she said again.

"No thanks," I said.

The president entered around nine. His arrival times fluctuated. I couldn't believe my eyes: a black eye! I was well accustomed to his allergy-prone, puffy eyes. But this was a shiner, a real, live, put-a-steak-on-it black eye. I was shocked. Minutes later, I popped into the office of Betty Currie, the president's personal secretary. Nancy Hernreich, his personal scheduler, was already there.

"What's the black mark on the president's face?" I asked.

I felt *real* tension.

"Oh, uh, he's allergic to coffee," said Nancy, turning toward her office.

"An allergy to coffee shows in just one eye?"

Betty smiled. She burrowed down into her work, chuckling, but looking busy. As I departed, I added, "I'm also allergic to the back of someone's hand."

I *wanted* to send a message. *We* knew what the mark was from, and it wasn't right. *Surely the Clintons must realize how close we are to them*, I thought, *how deeply we feel about our responsibilities for their safety.* Didn't they feel the same? It wasn't just that we protected them 24/7, but we were extremely loyal. We didn't do our job for the paychecks. Each man and woman protecting them had their reasons, but the Clintons were the focal point of every reason. What might happen if she had sucker-punched him? Or if that vase had hit its target? If his head hit a countertop corner, my entire life's work would have been for nothing.

Sure, seeing a president's black eye is strange but standing at my post I couldn't escape the sinking feeling that *this didn't make sense. This wasn't how it was supposed to be.* I loved my job and I believed in it, but I couldn't make sense of any of it.

It was a circus. Yet I never lost a sense of wonder and excitement. Even when the First Lady hollered and cursed and demanded firing thousands of people who protected her—and we spent more hours ensuring the Clintons' protection than we spent with our own families—I loved every minute of most every day. Law enforcement—protecting others—is my passion. Protecting a president is an incredible honor. How, I kept asking myself, did a kid from Ridley, Pennsylvania, ever get to the White House? I wanted to stay for the rest of my life.

Reality destroyed my dream—in ways I never imagined.

2.

THE AIR FORCE
SECURITY POLICE

I'm from Delco, a.k.a. Delaware County, Pennsylvania, born of Irish and Lebanese ancestry, but American through and through. O'Byrne even became Byrne so as to not sound too Irish. The concept of "America first" is in my blood.

My ancestors traveled here for a better life and succeeded in no small part thanks to my father's ability to shake off the bad times and be the strongest survivor of them all. He was a great soul. He aimed to do right and act morally, to have his children live better than he did. That's my idea of the American dream.

My father served as an Air Force mechanic in Japan during Korea. He could fix a rock if it was broken. My brother John was born in 1956, then Lynn, then lil' Gary, and finally Anita. Those were the days! We played, teased, biked, fought, and ran up and down the neighborhood with the rest of the kids playing sports in the streets—never indoors. If you were indoors, you were interrupting Mom, being antisocial, or just plain up to no good. Outside, a whole neighborhood of families looked after each another.

Following the post-Vietnam reduction of forces, we set out for Newport News, Virginia, where the Navy was creating a new class of nuclear-powered aircraft carriers. My father received a fully paid education in nuclear engineering.

The South was a big change for us, yet in typically southern fashion the neighborhood was welcoming and full of all-round good people.

My siblings and I feared that if we did wrong, we'd send a message that we took my parents for granted. When I repeated first grade, I felt as if I was letting my parents down. Most people, my father included, thought I was lazy, though I worked hard at sports and in the garage. In seventh grade I was diagnosed with significant attention deficit disorder and dyslexia. For me, sports were a no-brainer, but academics were a lost cause. Still, my parents set an example of hard work and decent behavior that never left me. A hot-shot life never impressed them. They never let anyone look down their noses at us.

There's something more important, though, than academics or sports. Character is everything. Down the street from us lived an airman. Whenever he came home, his wife and kids ran to him. Confidence, purpose, and respect emanated from his blue uniform.

When high school ended my friends marched off to college, but I knew higher education wasn't my move. I signed with the Air Force, hoping to see the world and feed my adventurous spirit with girls, guns, and things that go *BOOM!* I was full of piss and vinegar.

I thought I was immortal.

The Air Force recruiter's questions got to me. I deeply hated terrorism—it boiled my blood. Air Force Security Police (AFSP) seemed the right fit; I hadn't been west of Pittsburgh. I wanted to protect others and see the world. If America was going to prioritize air superiority, our airpower needed superior security.

In January 1982 I enlisted for less than $12,000 a year, but I was itching to go. A decade earlier Viet Cong and North Vietnamese forces had targeted America's air supremacy via brazen sapper missions, assassinations, and bombings. Terrorists kidnapped NATO general James Dozier, torturing him for weeks before Italian SWAT teams rescued him. The Munich Olympic massacre in 1972 proved it was best to stop an attack rather than react to it.

I had an awful habit of laughing and smiling under pressure. When conflict arises, it's healthy to keep a level head and a light mood, but not during training at Lackland Air Force Base: You get smoked. Laughing equals pain.

Air Force basic training wasn't like the Army's or the other branches. Our style was sit-ups, push-ups, and calisthenics so rigorous we couldn't stand it. We learned that a respect for the chain of command builds confidence. It creates a cohesive unit, like a marriage. That's what Basic was designed to do. How much it sucked depended on how fast a person adjusted.

I adjusted quickly but called my parents every chance I could. I didn't mind the physicality or the stress, but the homesickness was awful. I never imagined what loneliness and isolation from my family would bring. My parents sensed it. Every recruit suffers a devastating epiphany: Enlist to fight for the freedom of others and you forfeit your own. You feel a strange guilt, a mourning for your former self.

My father, in his usual blunt style, shaped me up: "Gary, *you* wanted this, and I told you it was going to be like this."

He was right. I needed to take his advice to "rub some dirt on it" and move on.

Our technical instructors (TIs—the Air Force's version of drill instructors) explained that even as untested "slick-sleeve" airmen, we were all leaders. When leaders did their duty, the potential for pain was less. I absorbed the lesson into my soul. If I didn't ensure my weapon was clear of any rounds or if I neglected its proper handling, a good guy could eat a bullet. Hence the military wisdom: There's nothing friendly about friendly fire. If rigging wasn't rigged correctly, it failed and people died. If we didn't eat correctly, people died. Didn't drink correctly—people died. Didn't wear our uniform correctly—people died. That was the military mentality: Don't make your bed correctly, and pain ensues. Why? *Because!* If you thought any duty could be shirked, you didn't see the big or even the little picture, and people were going to die.

It wasn't our job to understand the big picture. We weren't drafted; we chose this. When my TI showed us videos of planes falling off aircraft carriers and giant buck-ups that took lives, I absorbed the truth. In this life, small actions had severe consequences. A lightbulb flickered on inside me; the TI sounded word-for-word like my father.

I always reminded myself of my oath:

I, Gary J. Byrne, do solemnly swear that I will support and defend the Constitution of the United States against all enemies, foreign and domestic; that I will bear true faith and allegiance to the same; that I will obey the orders of the President of the United States and the orders of the officers appointed over me, according to the regulations and the Uniform Code of Military Justice. So help me God.

The Air Force's act-first mentality turned me on. You couldn't go wrong as long as you acted. Do nothing, and you were f—ed. No matter the question, the answer was act, take initiative! If under fire, the answer was to take cover or fire back, but never hesitate or stand still. We were always encouraged to do first, ask questions later.

But before and afterward, asking questions and thinking *were* the name of the game. This was a fighting man's game. A good fighting man is a thinking man, but when he faces conflict, training kicks in and thinking comes second. Everyone who has experienced violence personally knows the military truism, "No plan survives contact with the enemy." Conviction and character do.

Education was very different in the military, and I responded to it like a sponge. Many of my grade and high school teachers were gems who really tried to help me, but I never grasped what schoolroom education could lead to. Military teaching wasn't just about lecturing and grading; it was about *ensuring* lessons were learned. Success was defined not by letter grades but by results: *Mess up and someone dies.*

I learned that I had incredible muscle memory, spatial orientation, and hand-eye coordination. While most people's IQs nosedive during fight-or-flight scenarios, I kept my cool. My fingers never got fudgy under pressure; I kept both my gross and fine motor skills, never got tunnel vision, or lost situational awareness. I couldn't do calculus, but thankfully I wasn't calling in air strikes. My new mission was to enforce the law and protect myself doing it via a variety of weapons, the most important my brain.

Following Basic and Technical School, I eagerly awaited my first deployment to Murtad Air Base, just outside Ankara, Turkey. Our mission included securing our equipment from the host country. Murtad was a nuclear-capable base. During the Cold War, America had placed nukes in Turkey as a first-strike capability against Russia. Following the Cuban Missile Crisis, John F. Kennedy withdrew them as part of a joint deescalation. Arriving at Murtad, I learned that AFSP there had caught rogue Turkish officers trying to push an American F-104 Starfighter with a loaded nuke onto the flight line so they could steal a nuke and bomb Greece. Many Turks bitter about the Greco-Turkish War of 1919–22 wanted a flash point to ignite a new war. I believe this was secretly why JFK took the nukes out of Turkey in 1962. Turks simply hate Greeks. We joked to each other, "Hey, if you're not careful, I'll tell the Turks you're Greek!"

In central Turkey I expected a scene from *Lawrence of Arabia* with large open desert, but it was moonlike. I often thought of Neil Armstrong's "One small step for man . . ." Terrain featured sharp mountain ranges dotted with shrunken trees. The heat was unbearable. Turkey felt particularly eerie on several bus rides with the mountains literally on fire in the distance. The Turks were just clearing brush after their harvest, but it looked like a vision of hell.

Turks lived up to my expectations as hardened warriors, but I hated their methods. Often I was ordered, "Officer, stand down!" as Turkish superior officers brutally pummeled and beat subordinates. My anxiousness for action paled beside their desire for full-blown war.

International tensions escalated when in September 1983 a Russian fighter mistook a commercial plane for a U.S. AWACS probing Russian airspace. When the Soviet Su-15 interceptor intentionally downed Korean Air Lines flight 007, killing the 269 souls on board, we scrambled into high alert.

We once received "don't drink the water" orders. Supposedly someone put arsenic in our water. I was glad someone in the military checked these things. Every bit of protocol is built on trial and error. We showered with well water for a while but that seemed dicey. We got all our fluids from bottled Diet Coke—the only safe drink.

In my thirteen months in Turkey, I grasped we were allies only because we shared a common enemy. Allies are not friends, nor are they ever to be trusted farther than can be verified. From the Turks I learned to take nothing for granted in terms of security; the enemy could just as well be within our gates as on the horizon.

Next stop: Langley, Virginia, and the Elite Gate Section. Military bases are like cities complete with every aspect of urban crime, such as bank robberies, shady characters, sexual assaults, DUIs, prostitution, drugs, smuggling, contraband, trafficking, career criminals, disgruntled troublemakers, murder, suicide, and so much more. But military crime was "camouflaged." Military style, hierarchy, and outright ego entered every aspect of life, especially crime and corruption. Beyond that, we had an occasional spy, aircraft collision, crash, mechanical failure; we guarded President Ronald Reagan's Air Force One when it touched down, experienced international incidents, and identified potential flash points. I saw NASA aircraft fly into lightning storms to test how new aircraft handled extreme natural occurrences. Those pilots had balls of steel—or whatever else is nonconductive.

As police we took arrests very seriously. They were dangerous. An arrest can destroy a person's constitutional rights. So I knew I'd better have a good reason every time. We worried about being overly cautious and ruining a life unnecessarily, but we also worried that playing it cool could ruin an innocent life. It was a thin line, and we did our best to read people.

Many career criminals have the ability to cry on demand. Some are convincing, some are pathetic, but no cop can predict the future. Most of the time we were dealing with an honestly good person merely reaching for his wallet, but other times . . . There was wide room for discretion. We were human, too. We did our best to keep our own character in check while reading someone else's, balancing constitutional freedoms with the sanctity of life.

The first time I got physical on the job followed a base bank robbery—yes, on a military base! We shut down every exit. Some guy freaked out about traffic exited his car and threatened me. I went with my gut, put my gun back in my booth, and punched him right in the chest, knocking him to the ground. I was racked with doubt. Had I used enough force? Or too little? *Oh, shit*, I thought, *I'm in for it now.* But a written commendation backed my play. It meant the world that my superiors trusted my instincts and discretion. Cops fight two battles: the actual one and one against a desk jockey's second-guessing—no one likes the latter. Second-guessing someone else's split-second decisions in hindsight is coward's work.

During this time of "peace," Russian bombers and U.S. bombers routinely patrolled each other's coasts fully loaded with nuclear ordnance. Each side border-checked the other by dispatching fighters to keep the bomber in international airspace. Military police monitored runways to ensure they were clear for the fighters to border-check the Russian bombers as they flew by.

On May 30, 1983, while I served at Langley, President Reagan convened an economic summit at nearby Williamsburg, Virginia, meeting with such world leaders as Britain's Margaret Thatcher, West Germany's Helmut Kohl, and France's François Mitterrand. It was my first chance to see the Secret Service in action, and it was a great thrill. The Klaxon sirens blared, the threat alarms signaling everyone to get the fighters in the air.

But today something was different. The aircrews and pilots were spooked. We turned up our radios.

"Russian bombers five miles off the coast!"

At the same time Reagan's economic summit remained too close for comfort at Williamsburg.

Our fighters took off, full afterburners pushing them so hard and fast that my buddy Levi was catapulted off the ground and trapped in an irrigation ditch next to the taxiway. Jets took off like rockets. We anxiously awaited their safe return but also wanted word that the Russian bombers had been checked and that we were all safe. We held our breath and asked: Was this war?

We cheered our jets' return. Our pilots uncorked their helmets and climbed down.

"Holy shit, the freaking gun port is open and it's all charred. He fired his cannons!" someone said.

"No, I didn't! You didn't see shit!" the frazzled pilot shouted.

I knew better. I knew when a silver hull had its gun port closed and clear and when it returned open and covered in scorched soot.

"He's fired a missile!" I said, noticing that this returning fighter had only three of the four he had departed with. Yes, a U.S. Air Force pilot had launched a missile directly at a Soviet bomber—an act that could have triggered World War III!

"No, it didn't! I took off that way," the airman retorted as he climbed down the ladder.

"Yeah, sure," I mumbled nervously. "Why take four air-to-airs when you can take three?"

Here's the scoop. Somewhere in the communication chain, our fighters from Langley hadn't been notified that these unescorted bombers were dangerously close. The Soviets kept listing closer to our shores—until they were just five miles off our coast. Our jets caught up with them, passing them head-on. Still the Soviets stayed on course. U.S. jets fired their cannons past the bombers' noses.

They only listed away back on course. Our fighters locked on with heat-seekers, giving the Russians a radar warning. Finally, a warning missile flew right past a bomber's nose. The next missile would be right up their tailpipe. Mercifully, the Soviets blinked. Whatever might have happened otherwise was anyone's guess.

Our jets refueled, ready for more action. We nervously awaited Reagan's public response. None came. Total silence. The media never heard of it. Soon afterward Reagan ordered the invasion of Grenada, citing intelligence of a noncommercial, very long runway to be used for Russian bomber patrol. Nineteen Americans lost their lives but the invasion was a success—and made us safer.

Crowds ogle the Air Force Thunderbirds' impressive aerial stunts. They're the Air Force's version of the Navy's Blue Angels. Our job, however, was to eyeball *the crowds*. In one crowd, I noticed a photographer. Everyone else stared skyward at the spectacle. He focused straight at a series of boring hangars. He snapped his shutter with rapid yet steady precision. His bulky professional-grade camera and telephoto lens might have belonged to a serious hobbyist, or a professional journalist or photographer, but I guessed otherwise. This man was not like the others.

Six of us slowly strolled through the crowd, encircling him like lions stalking a newborn gazelle. Drawing near, we checked his reaction. When he tried feigning interest in the jets like everyone else, it didn't work. That was the last clue we needed. He packed his gear and began walking away. We kept on his scent. His head low, he skipped down the stands, hoping to escape. He landed in the hands of another officer.

We cuffed him. Multiple foreign passports tumbled from a small hidden pocket. Each bore a different name and details but had the same damn picture—like in a Jason Bourne movie. We Mirandized him and peppered him with questions. He kept his trap shut. FBI agents whisked him away, but whatever that guy had in mind was averted. *Yes,* spies really do exist.

Some of those aircraft hangars had some nasty crap in them—I'm just guessing, because we had to carry big duffel bags with radiological and chemical protective suits in them everywhere we went. After a radiological, chemical, nuclear, or biological attack, we had to don this gear in thirty seconds, respond, and fight.

I got stuck with a new partner. She was obviously hired to fill a quota. That wasn't speculation—I was told so point-blank. Political meddling had struck again and was going to get someone killed. I just hoped it wasn't me. Again the Klaxons blared and the radio sounded: "Make ready for two-star admiral to fly in. This is not a drill. Make ready for missile launch."

My new female partner and I, as part of Elite Gate Section, were watching over a hangar. We got *the* call, the one we trained for but never wanted to get. The runways had to be cleared and cordoned off. No one except necessary personnel was to go in or out. A 707 Boeing EC-135, a very large jet engine cargo plane, started blow-starting (they couldn't wait for the engines to normally warm up) to get the hell out of the way of the chief of staff's incoming aircraft. My clueless partner sprinted past me to avoid the 707 but forgot her NBCR (Nuclear, Biological, Chemical, and Radiological) gear bag. I turned. It lay on the runway in the way of the aircraft. I couldn't yell over the engines, but if that small bag was sucked up into the 707's engine, it would trigger complete engine failure *and* a fire *and* a giant hazard. It would endanger the chief of staff's incoming aircraft *and* a missile launch.

I ran back, threw my bag down next to hers, and flung my body atop both bags. The engines passed over me as I hugged those bags.

I thought I was safe. But then a back blast threw me off the ground. When I landed, I knew I was messed up. Her tool bag (different from the NBCR bag that I smothered), *which she also forgot,* had blown into the plane's blast deflector, sending debris everywhere— and inflicting me with a concussion. I looked like a complete fool to the other personnel, but there would be time for explanations after. Later I pled with the attending physician to omit my head injury from my record; otherwise my Air Force career would have ended right then.

I reminded myself, feelings don't count.

Lives do.

3.

CLUB FED

I left the Air Force in February 1986 to live in Pennsylvania, where I worked as a composite assembler at Boeing from 1987 to 1991. My paycheck felt like a million bucks compared to military pay. A part-time backdoor bouncer gig at a local dive bar, the Bebop Café, provided my action fix. Life was pleasant but not inspiring.

I had money in my pocket. My hair grew out. One day when I was having a pre-work *cerveza* at the Bebop Café, fate intervened. *She* was stunning from across the bar and damn near overwhelming up close. I quickly attained her number and her name, Genny, short for Genevieve. I soon knew I was going to marry her. She was just so damn cool, down-to-earth, a lady, a princess, my best friend, a hard worker, affectionate, strong, book smart, and street smart, and I've spent the rest of my marriage having my instinct proven right.

Oh, yes . . . and a few months later, she saw an ad in the *Philadel-phia Inquirer* for the SSUD.

Before heading off to work, she asked, "Hey, Gary, you ever heard about the Secret Service Uniformed Division?"

I hadn't. I thought the Secret Service was all agents. Genny and I talked it over. Boeing was laying off. Secret Service life—and pay—

seemed promising. Her sense of service for her patients as a nurse was as strong as mine to my job. Demanding careers didn't faze us.

I sent in the application and found myself in a Philadelphia Center City hotel for an SSUD seminar. A hundred candidates all wore suits. I wore my Boeing security uniform. Not a good first impression, perhaps, but when a long-haired blond teenager skateboarded in late, I realized I wasn't *that* far out of place. A written five-hundred-question psychological and IQ test followed. It seemed like five hundred accusations. I swear each question asked if I hated my mother. I finished and vomited in the corner trash can. I was sure not only that I failed, but that I somehow hated my mother! I felt terrible.

And adding to my worries was a series of misadventures, in which the Secret Service kept losing my paperwork—and even confusing me with another applicant. Maybe not only wasn't I right for the Secret Service, maybe the Secret Service wasn't right for me.

Imagine my surprise when two weeks later they told me to come in. I said, "No thanks." I'd stay at Boeing. But I quickly changed my mind. The next morning I walked in to 600 Arch Street at Philadelphia's federal courthouse for the first urine test and polygraph interview. Was I a subversive? Did I embody the Service's oath to be "worthy of trust and confidence"? Had I ever stolen anything? I had: some nylon rope as a kid once for the thrill. No question, even of a sexual nature, was off-limits to them. It was incredibly invasive as they asked about crimes, thoughts, sex, childhood. Nothing was sacred.

I left feeling I was a criminal, a sexual deviant, and worse. I was embarrassed and again racked by a feeling of sure failure. I questioned whether I was really a good person at all. I'm fiercely competitive, and I was *so* angry. Today I still feel I failed that test.

But as the legendary UCLA basketball coach John Wooden said, "The true test of a man's character is what he does when no one's watching." In hindsight, I don't think they were looking for the man who passed the test; instead the real test was to see *how* each of the applicants failed. That's my theory.

I made it in. Training commenced—and so did the mind games. "Train as you fight" was our religion. The instructors turned up the pressure and set individuals and entire classes up for failure. Failure in training identifies weaknesses so as to prevent them in the field, because as the common saying goes in the tactical community, "We don't rise to the level of our expectations, we fall to the level of our training." We live by that code.

My favorite drills were attack on the principal, countersniper, and attack on the White House. Some drills bordered on the bizarre and were designed to get recruits to think adaptively. The instructors knew from experience that real life isn't textbook; it's stranger than fiction. Instructors also knew our bad-guy counterparts were taught the same manner of thinking, and we needed to be ready. They used their knowledge for different means but it all came down to this: means, motive, opportunity, and intent. The instructors concocted drills from situations they had confronted in the field.

Our finale drill was a demonstration for President George H. W. Bush. We incorporated all of the major attack scenarios at a little fake village set in Beltsville, Maryland's James J. Rowley Training Center. The center's major building has one side designed to look like a grand hotel and the other side to look like an embassy. I stood in awe of being so close to the president.

The drill was a dog-and-pony show typical for the president, but my UD class got to be a part of the mock convoy procession. The president shook hands with role players posing as rope line greeters.

Then someone pretended to pull out a gun and the president was removed from the kill zone while we went behind the mock hotel entrance to giddily watch the mock-rocket or improvised explosive device attack on the convoy. Someone put a little too much sauce on the last explosion. The blast nearly shattered a nearby window, threatening to spray us—and the president—with shards. Bush *loved* it!

Replacing my classmates and me wouldn't be too much trouble, but the president being hurt in a Service training accident would have been *very bad*. Life in the Service always seemed a few pounds of trigger pull away from a funny story—or a massive shit storm.

Each drill was designed to make lessons stick. They say, "Amateurs train until they get it right; professionals train until they get it wrong." That may not sound right, but here's what it means. When you train until you "get it wrong" it means you've trained until you've discovered new, out-of-the ordinary situations that you might have to deal with later on—and which might get you or someone else killed. If you've already encountered them in training, you'll be prepared for them. If you encounter them for the first time in the field, well . . . good luck . . . because you'll need luck at that point.

One such lesson put us in a position that tested decision-making skills even when we thought the drill tested only reflexive firing and marksmanship. Because it was a live-fire exercise, our perception was that when the target appeared, we were supposed to shoot. At the end of the drill, each student, seeing their shot placement and reaction time, would high-five their partner. Then when we saw the target up close, our eyes widened as the instructors asked why we chose to shoot an innocent, a crazy person, someone trying to commit suicide by cop, someone falsely accused, or a now-deceased victim of miscommunication.

"Oh shit," we'd mutter, staring down at our feet.

We felt terrible, stunned, embarrassed, and racked with self-doubt, but it was a valuable lesson. It wasn't only our blood we were worried about. If that were so, it would defeat the whole purpose of our being posted in the first place. Sweat in training saves blood in real life.

Right after shoot/no-shoot drill, they'd tweak the scenario. The recruit didn't shoot but got shot by the "innocent" from the previous drill. Whoops again. I realized that I had to accept the risks of my job; there were scenarios in which I might not live. I had to be at peace with death so as to survive the mental burden of the job. Winning didn't necessarily mean getting out alive or unscathed. If I couldn't accept that, the job wasn't for me.

The Secret Service Uniformed Division ranks among the nation's most powerful law enforcement agencies. Title 18, Section 3056 of the United States Code bestows upon an SSUD officer more arresting power than any other agency's agent or law enforcement officers (LEOs), including the Secret Service agents. Trained in situational investigation, we're licensed to carry our firearms and arrest anyone anywhere the United States flag flies. This includes U.S. territory, even abroad. Agents can't give so much as a parking ticket. And as for SSUD, we, by law, don't need a warrant to make an arrest or invade someone's privacy. From our many "death-by-PowerPoint" classes, we knew the constitutional authority in making arrests. That's especially helpful when suspects try to lawyer their way out of cuffs by spouting legal jargon to intimidate officers.

At my June 1991 graduation, my parents, siblings, and my Genny had such pride in their eyes. I hoped I was finally paying them back for everything they'd given me. My new badge seemed to weigh more than I would ever be able to carry. I saw the words "U.S.

Secret Service," "Uniformed Division," and my name on the back, my own ID number, and maybe most important, the words "Worthy of Trust and Confidence." Responsibility hung heavily on my shoulders but my sense of accomplishment and purpose was uplifting. With that badge against my heart, I absorbed the oath that I had taken—to protect the people, the Constitution, this nation—*and* its president.

4.

TO THE WHITE HOUSE

I started at the White House in late July 1991 with Officer Leslie Coffelt on my mind; he was the only White House policeman to die in the line of duty, sacrificing his life to protect President Truman while the president resided at Blair House, across Pennsylvania Avenue from the White House during its renovations. His story demonstrated how one minute things are fine and in the next second two assassins can turn everything to complete shit and a giant gunfight. I felt that I was standing in big shoes.

Yet any Uniformed Division (UD) officer or special agent (SA) will bluntly tell you, "You know what it's like to be in the Service? Go stand in a corner for four hours with a five-minute pee break and then go stand for four more hours." That's the "action"—99 percent of the time. Have Hollywood make *that* movie! But for me it was a dream.

I was first assigned to the White House fence line, the perimeter of the White House grounds, the first defense for ground-based assaults and assassination attempts, but far more likely the key to interdicting intelligence gatherers (people up to no good, casing the joint for future action), fence jumpers, pot-shot shooters, and various troublemakers. For all its prestige and grand history, the White House is a shithead magnet. The UD faces all the crazies who think they can solve the world's problems by running (or flying) into the White House and performing some ludicrous stunt.

When the Executive Mansion was first built it was the president's private living quarters, nothing more. Though visitors need considerably more representative and/or financial clout to see the president, it still remains the people's house in many ways.

Yet the taxing 8:00 p.m. wake-up calls for an 11:00 p.m.–6:00 a.m. night shift and similarly taxing two-shift days never gave me a case of the Mondays or had me in a grumpy mood. The introductory six-month "hell period" had me jumping from bed and doing physical training (PT) before shift start on the White House grounds. By policy, during the first two and a half years, a UD officer could be terminated without a written reason. It was leadership's insurance in case someone wasn't liked, didn't fit in, was talking out of school, or clearly wouldn't be able to hack it in the long term. Our character was constantly tested. Character was the strongest tool in the Secret Service arsenal.

My first arrest occurred when I walked to lunch. Two bums were fistfighting right in front of me. "Come on, guys!" I pled. "I'm friggin' hungry." Bums would often make trouble just so we'd arrest them—and give them the shelter, food, and medical care they couldn't or wouldn't provide for themselves. "Public urination, public intoxication, and fighting is not tolerated here, sir!" That was my new-guy mentality.

But I soon learned from the sour looks and heavy sighs of the District of Columbia's Metropolitan Police Department that my diligence was highly unappreciated. Many of these homeless troublemakers were down-on-their-luck people whose minds had snapped from hard times. They came to D.C. thinking that if only the president would listen, their problems would be solved. But some were not indigent. They simply chose that life. How do I know that? Because the full might of the Secret Service ran background checks on them. Soon, nothing surprised me.

A woman clutching her child's hand ran toward me. "Officer! Officer!"

"What is it, ma'am?"

There was a man in the park, let's just say, pleasing himself in full view of everyone, even children. She was new to D.C.; by now I wasn't. I knew him by name; we'd arrested him many times before, and I wasn't going to give him the satisfaction of arresting him again. Nor was I going to get the evil eye from the Metro PD for bringing him in to add a notch to his already voluminous rap sheet. "We are not bum-catchers," seasoned officers would growl. All we would do was shoo him away as if he was a seagull at a picnic, yelling, "Get the hell out of here! Go on!" Our background check had revealed that he had $40,000 in savings and was a snowbird traveling to Florida in the winter and to D.C. to soak up government benefits the rest of the time. Unbelievable? You don't know D.C.

My energetic enthusiasm and sense of workplace cooperation during the first six months working the fence line and at other posts created a rapport with fellow officers. Our typical UD "action" was to strike up a conversation with, question, and if necessary, detain suspicious characters. We looked for people wearing trench coats in the summertime or the "tourist" taking pictures of our security measures. We would often scare them off, detain them, or inspect their cameras pending an investigation—the more they insisted, the more *we insisted*. The greatest shot a law enforcement officer takes is the one he or she prevents in the first place. We wanted anyone engaged in pre-attack reconnaissance to return to their counter- parts and say, "Security is too tough." Appearing tough saves an incalculable numbers of lives.

I was on a vehicle patrol and we got a call for backup from a K-9 officer. All I heard was her location and something like "crazy man with a knife." Fifty yards across a D.C. park, a lady held back her police dog and the man standing off in front of her. I knew I could reach them on foot faster than circling the Jersey barriers by car. I hopped the barricade, drew my pistol, and sprinted. The dog was ready to engage, to tear flesh. The man was within the rarely discussed "twenty-three feet rule"—if he sprinted at us he could potentially plunge his knife in, no matter how many times we shot him. There simply wouldn't be enough kinetic energy to push him back. With each stride I closed the gap on my own effective shooting range. I yelled out to let her know that I was in her field of fire. If he charged and was on drugs we had to shoot until he stopped advanc- ing. I yelled. She yelled. Her dog was pulling, snarling, demanding to tear into the man. I got to within twenty feet of him. The sight of three officers (admittedly, one four-legged) and two guns pointed at him made him freeze. His eyes met mine.

"Put the weapon down, motherf—er!"

I didn't have to shoot. No one died. We won. He *wasn't* holding a knife, but it *was* a rigid foot-long oil dipstick sharpened to a shank and duct-taped with the crudest of handles. It was nasty! The K-9 officer, Bell,* observed that her assailant wore so many layers of clothes that

---

* Because of the sensitive nature of law enforcement work, in the case of this officer, I have shielded her real last name. I will often be following that practice in the pages to come, not only for law enforcement personnel but for certain White House staff as well.

he could have wiggled free to stab her dog before the K-9 took him down. If Bell had shot, it would have been justified, but she bided her time, hoping for a better solution. Together we defused the incident.

It didn't make headlines—but these events ride a thin line. Any small change and anyone could have been seriously injured or killed. Such was life. A year later, a similar incident occurred. A man had taped a knife to his hands and refused to back off. This time the officer shot, fatally wounding his attacker.

Such incidents don't happen every day—but they happen. My most frequent service to the community was looking tough and giving directions to some government building, just as Officer Coffelt had done. Our most common arrests were for bum fights, disorderly conduct, suspicious activity, or fence-jumping.

The White House fence is clearly scalable by loonies and potential suicide bombers. It's never been raised or made more secure because of the White House Historical Association—a testament to bureaucratic bullshit. Instead of a simple fence fix, more manpower gets deployed, and the Secret Service take over more of D.C., making streets pedestrian-only or closing them off from public access entirely. But I wasn't worrying about that in 1991.

Local university fraternities thought it was funny to haze newcomers by making them hop the White House fence, touch the fountain, and run back. The Secret Service discreetly informed nearby colleges that the pranks needed to stop. It removed some pressure, but people will keep trying until we send a clear message: *There is no chance of success.* Electrify the top rung, make it two feet higher, or put up another fence behind the other.

Fence-jumpers have been increasingly successful at penetrating deep into our secure area. On September 20, 2014, a knife-wielding fence-jumper successfully ran into the Executive Mansion; he was tackled by an off-duty agent walking through the mansion at the time. A creeping liberal mindset fueled the problem. Old-timers warned me of it when I first came on board: an odd balance of ensuring protection and not offending anyone's feelings. But we need to empower the warrior mindset, not the liberal one. The White House isn't a kindergarten in which to teach grown people about the value of no trespassing, and private property.

Every federal agency's solution is "more" and "grow." More manpower. Bigger budgets. Expand the secure area. Close off parks and streets to the public, traffic, or make streets pedestrian-only. Why do people jump the fence at the White House? Because it's climbable—that's why! Whether mastermind terrorist or idiot criminal, they all think success is possible.

I've had many men and women look me dead in the eye and try persuading me they needed to see the president. You'd better believe I stopped them. When someone came to us at the fence and said, "It's vital I see the president immediately—a matter of national security!" we *knew* they were crazy. "If the president would only say a prayer—I'll personally tell him that prayer—and say it while holding three rocks in his hand, all the world's problems would be solved!" a lady exclaimed to me, holding up three normal-looking rocks. She believed it so fervently!

To such persons we nodded and said, "I understand, sir [or ma'am]. You want to head over there." We'd radio it in and direct the person to special entry control points ready for their arrival and any sort of suicide or attack they might attempt: lighting themselves on fire, drawing a weapon, slashing their own wrists. It bought time to study their movements, survey the surrounding area for other activity, and check for unnatural bulges or weights in their clothing. Officers employed thick, flame-resistant, stab-resistant wool blankets to rush and tackle such wackadoos. It's a method that had been tried and retried often. Simple, thick wool blankets work too and require zero hesitation on an officer's part.

By the time any seriously mentally ill person came in contact with police, it was a systemic failure. We'd take the seriously mentally ill to St. Elizabeth's Hospital, a psychiatric facility, where they'd be committed, treated for a day or three, and then released. When we saw them again, they'd be less trusting, bitter, and off their meds. I underwent a hell of an education in the real world in our nation's capital.

In October 1992 I was patrolling the Ellipse park to the south of the White House in an unmarked van. Three long-haired, bearded guys dressed in blue jeans and green surplus Vietnam-era fatigue jackets were moving calmly and purposefully in tandem, cleaning out a white van and throwing bagged items into a trash can. The van was labeled as a telephone company vehicle but the men obviously weren't in company uniform. I ran the plates over the radio to our headquarters, Bandbox.

They radioed back "stolen"—and routed backup vehicles. Our three suspects moved like us—like military. One was scanning, the way we do, and spotted me. Silently he signaled to his associates. They boarded their van calmly but rapidly. As the spotter entered its rear door, I spotted his dagger, a fighting knife, pointed upward under his shirt. Only someone trained in knife fighting would conceal it that way. Reachable by both hands, it was placed where he could deploy it lightning fast.

They headed east on E Street toward Fifteenth. I followed closely. They knew the jig was up but I hadn't hit the lights yet, and they hadn't bolted yet. We silently maneuvered. I wanted to stop them at the construction barriers surrounding the yet-uncompleted Reagan

Building. The radio net was clogged with officers closing in, but we were running out of time. I had my short 12-gauge shotgun out and hidden below the dashboard and hoped another police car would box them in on the other side. We were in the perfect location for a gunfight, but only if we could block the intersection. And if I could ram the rear doors of the van, they'd have only two points of exit, and I'd have an ideally narrow field of fire.

If I had to exit my vehicle while shooting through my window, sure, I'd enjoy some cover in the concrete Jersey barriers, but no cover stands up forever. We were stopped at the light, each biding our time. They watched for traffic to grow so as to run the red light, dart through an opening, and hamstring my pursuit.

They ran that light and bolted down Fifteenth, snarling me in traffic. I put pedal to the metal across the Fourteenth Street Bridge, to I-395, and then to I-95. I radioed my position to Bandbox: I was in Virginia.

Bandbox relayed my watch commander's orders: "Break off. Turn around, and come back."

The hell with that, I thought, but it *absolutely* was an order. I couldn't be insubordinate, but I knew these guys were up to something seriously evil. The presence of the combat knife solidified that assumption. My watch commander should have trusted my instincts. Twice I pretended I didn't hear the order. Suddenly I saw Virginia police closing in on my tail and was immensely thankful. I looked down at the speedometer: 120 miles per hour. Weaving between cars, we swerved from lane to lane. Our vans wobbled and shook.

My prey changed lanes once more. A UD K-9 officer following me called over, "Watch out, Gary, they're gonna lose it!" I took my foot off the gas so I wouldn't run into their van as they flipped. But that driver knew his stuff. He just wobbled—and then accelerated again! The chase was still on. Each lane change lurched our vans and every bump rocked our suspensions. The state trooper was still catching up, and I wasn't letting up. I passed a sign for Kings Dominion amusement park. Hell! I was near Fredericksburg—*way* past my zone and in the weeds with my watch commander. I gritted my teeth. I planned to jackknife them into spinning their car into the median but my little Dodge Caravan couldn't close the gap fast enough. Just fifteen miles from Richmond, long after that K-9 officer had bowed out, I had to bow out, too. Furious, I raced back to D.C. just as fast because Bandbox kept asking for my location and I kept stalling.

Later when I returned the car to the Washington Navy Yard the mechanic said, "G-damn, Gary," and he informed me the car needed a pint of transmission fluid and a quart of oil and was almost completely empty of gas.

My watch commander tried to write me up. Why was our leadership so risk-averse? *Those guys* had been *up to something bad.* For what other reason *would three trained guys have stolen a van and run with such reckless abandon?*

Officers need leadership that backs them up, but our superiors' trepidation was only getting worse. Our revolvers were swapped for the extremely formidable SIG Sauer 228 pistol, but some posts were issued nickel-plated Remington Model 870 shotguns meant to shoot beanbags an abysmal twenty feet. Many guys openly refused to use them. As a new guy, I didn't have that clout, but I silently shared their opinion. The Service wanted to issue Tasers, too. It was all tactically prudent and politically meddlesome.

Luckily, every day didn't include a car chase scene from *Bullitt* or *The French Connection.* We got to deal with some very nice people too, such as President George H. W. Bush and First Lady Barbara Bush.

One day on the South Lawn, when I first walked past First Lady Barbara Bush, she said, "Good morning, Officer." I nodded and walked on. Per my JJRTC training, I was taught not to engage protectees in conversation. An agent rushed up to me.

"Excuse me, Officer. Is there something wrong with you?" he scolded.

"No, sir," I replied, mortified.

"When the First Lady says, 'Good morning,' you stop and say, 'Good morning' back. Otherwise they consider it rude."

I apologized profusely. I didn't know! It was just one of those things you have to get a feel for on the job. I was extremely loyal to the presidency, not because they were the Bushes but because they were the First Family, and in doing so I forgot that they were normal folks and regular Americans at heart.

The second time the First Lady passed me, they were heading to a vehicle to run an errand. She said good morning, and so did I, which was a relief—the new guy was finally adjusting.

"And Officer, do tell them to turn down the humidity, please!" she said pointedly.

I nodded, turned, and picked up the phone on my post.

"What is it, Gary?" said the no-nonsense call center.

Then I realized we were outside. I looked over. Barbara Bush and the staff were giggling.

"Gary, what is it?" the voice snapped.

"Uh, never mind," I replied and hung up the phone.

She got me again! But her humor kept tension at bay around the White House. Mrs. Bush was famous for it. Executive life was constantly stressful and it can consume everyone who works at the White House. She knew it and appreciated us, and it meant the world.

When I finally finagled a White House tour for my family, one of the Bush grandkids ran down the Executive Living Quarters steps and bumped into my mom. Arthur, a residence houseman, was not happy. He and Mrs. Bush sought us out. Practically dragging two of the Bush boys by the ear, she made them apologize to my mother—and then Mrs. Bush *apologized to me* for their behavior. I never thought I would hear the end of it from colleagues. I was horrified. I just hoped it wouldn't get me in trouble, but it was how the Bushes operated—100 percent class.

The Permanent Executive Residence Staff is extremely loyal and exemplifies quiet character. They run the White House. Their dedication keeps everything in check. Maybe it's ironic, but I know it's true: Though seemingly at the bottom of the White House hierarchy, the Residence crew set the standard for character. Presidents come and go, they stay—thank God.

Part of our job was to create a welcoming environment, not a prison, for the First Family: A smile, a "Good morning, sir," and simple gestures go a long way in tough times. It took a long presidential history and relationship with the Secret Service to find a balance, and with each president and staff that balance has to be reengineered and tailored again. President George H. W. Bush knew what it was to be on the front line, part of the sword and shield of this country. When he enlisted in the Navy his nickname was Skin because he was so lanky. He piloted an Avenger torpedo bomber against Japanese targets. Taking flak, his engine caught fire yet he still hit his target before parachuting into the ocean. Defying death again, Bush was picked up by a submarine and spent the rest of his time with that sub on a mission.

We all respected him because, in a way, we felt as though the president was one of the guys, albeit of a salty older generation.

When he issued orders for a national fight, he understood the consequences of sending people into harm's way. Everyone in the Secret Service respected him for that. He had no Hollywood notions of combat or politically correct ideas of wartime grandeur. Anyone in our shoes, doing our job to protect others, just wants to look back and see the commander's hand still at the helm.

The West Wing Staff, also known as the Political or Presidential Staff, run the president's policy. But no other group is more committed to the White House and the First Family than the Permanent Executive Residence Staff. Many families, like Arthur's, had served for generations. To Executive Residence staffers, the First Family was royalty. Or maybe these staff members simply understood the burden of the office. I had immense respect for the Residence Staff's quiet resolve and work ethic, especially during the Easter Egg Roll and Christmas events. People say the Secret Service would take a bullet for the president, but I tell you that many of the Residence Staff would, too. Yes, the feeling is contagious. The more time I spent working around the president, the more I was hooked.

I was being trained for the post outside the Oval Office when we started heading into the election cycle. I witnessed how impeccably the president's morning briefer arrived at 6:50 every single morning, ten minutes earlier than scheduled. He waited and made small talk until Papa Bush walked into the Oval Office at exactly 7:00 a.m. Both were incredibly punctual. We joked that we could set our watches by their morning routine. They looked us right in the eye, smiled, and said, "Good morning, Officer." They often knew us by name. Such basic actions were so profound.

President Bush would say, "Good morning," even if it wasn't a good morning. Stress didn't faze him. He didn't agonize over walking into his office because he knew firsthand of things much worse.

He carried a briefcase, as did his briefer. I always wondered why the president needed a briefcase. Everything he wanted could be provided, but it spoke to his work ethic. Seven a.m. wasn't their time; it was the people's. Timberwolf (Bush's code name) understood. He understood what it meant to be presidential.

I also watched Papa Bush and his advisors when a group of Uniformed Division Emergency Response Team members congratulated him on being chosen by *Time* magazine as person of the year.

"Hey, guys," the president called over to them, stopping them in their tracks.

He signed the magazine and gave it to one of the guys and thanked each profusely for what he did. Things like that—simple, respectful actions—endeared Papa Bush to us. The president's mind was constantly being bombarded but he thought of us, and some lucky guy was recognized by the president to whom he had dedicated his life and efforts. That guy, whom I knew well, went home to the wife and kids, with whom he had spent less time than with the president's family, with a signed copy of *Time* magazine (which he framed) and a great story to tell.

But we knew better than to confuse the president with the man. He was not our friend, nor should any superior be so misconstrued. Respected? Absolutely. Feared? Certainly revered. The president is never a buddy, though Timberwolf made that hard. He even ordered the creation of horseshoe teams of servicemen and Executive Residence staffers to compete with, and though he was extremely competitive, he wanted everyone to bring their top game. Politics aside—he was great to us.

I served a rotation near the White House Press Lobby. A Presidential Protection Division (PPD) agent walked up to me to shoot the shit. He anticipated that the president was walking out from a different entrance from the one called in over the radio. Without warning, someone touched me on the shoulder from behind. Startled, I swung around—ready for anything.

"Whoa, big guy," said Papa Bush, realizing he'd spooked the hell out of me.

"Sorry, Mr. President. You got me good!" I said, my heart rate coming down.

He smiled and asked me to let out Millie and Ranger, the two First Family dogs, as one of them had been peeing on a couch.

"No problem, Mr. President," I said.

He kept smiling as he walked away.

"Jesus, Gary," said the agent.

I shrugged, winced, and made a face as if to say sorry; he'd just startled me severely! Papa Bush was stealthy. His footsteps were inexplicably silent in such a creaky old building. The anxious dog was ecstatic when I let him out to the lawn.

Timberwolf's light-footedness—and friendliness—kept us on our toes. One day George, the White House butler, and Papa Bush came by the South Portico with a silver platter stacked with sizzling sausage, burgers, and hot dogs. The Bushes loved to barbecue.

By policy, we were not allowed to eat on post but we weren't supposed to refuse presidential orders. I refused politely, saying something about policy. I, a very fair-skinned oaf of a guy, was stark red in the face. George, a very dark man, turned white. He wanted to teach me a lesson right then in manners: When someone as nice as the Bushes offered me something, I should graciously accept. George also relayed to me a strict direct presidential order to disseminate all these fantastic meats, which were *soooo* good, to the rest of the guys on post. George was a font of good information; he even showed me a spot in which to hide food in a utility closet.

I phoned my fellow officers (if I put it over the radio, it would have been a mob scene) that if they sauntered over to the edges of their posts, I would walk to the edge of mine to pass out the meats. I was in a trance with a mouth full of presidentially prepared cuisine. As luck would have it, however, the watch commander swung by, welling with fury, but I had my excuse: "Oh, good, you're here. Watch my post. The president ordered me to take this platter and give it to the guys, sir. I can't refuse a presidential order. I'll be right back and you can have some too." I got the hell out of there, tray in hand.

The staff used to say, "When the president eats, everybody eats." That kind of leadership is real. I figured the saying applied to every president but really the saying came from Bush 41's years. He appreciated the lowest on the totem pole because he'd once pounded the Navy pavement.

I assumed every president would follow Papa Bush's example. The work ethic, love of country, work environment, and respect for the people serving would be constant, and politics would never matter. Soon the late-night phone calls and special assignments came; we were moving into the election cycle—hold on to your butts. Protection was never the same twice, especially with candidates. They had no idea what they were getting themselves into.

And neither did I.

5.

MEET THE
NEW BOSS

A brief, to-the-point conversation at a 1992 Bill Clinton campaign rally rocked our procedures.

A man walked up to an agent. The agent looked the man over. No normal person addressed an agent with the protectee less than a stone's throw away, but the man had a bone to pick. He had the agent's attention.

"Do you guys have any idea what you're doing?" he sneered, gesturing to the agents surrounding Clinton. "I'm a sheriff's deputy and while I am legally allowed to carry, no one screened me. I've got a loaded 1911 [pistol] on my hip, and if I had a mind to, well, I'm within ten, fifteen feet of your boy. Anyone here could be like me but less inclined to be nice, and there's not a damn thing you could do about it. Now, you sure you guys have your act together?"

Alarm bells sounded throughout the Service. Bean-counter Service leaders had dismissed magnetometers as too expensive, and campaign staffers wanted the Secret Service to screen crowds superfast—in reality, in appearance only.

There was an open call that day for volunteers to run metal detectors at campaign events. *Emergency* was an understatement. I signed up.

It took Robert Kennedy's assassination to spur assigning Secret Service protection to candidates, just as it took Jack Kennedy's assassination to finally grant us a countersniper detail. Secret Service vets told stories of unboxing the new on-the-road metal detectors straight from Italy after Ronald Reagan's assassination attempt. A special detail had sped to Italy—with a big bag of taxpayer cash—to buy the metal detectors directly from the manufacturer. My 1992 trip wasn't as frenzied, but it *was* stressful.

The Secret Service couldn't hire personnel for every election and then not retain them. It's not feasible and it wouldn't garner quality personnel. Most agents don't guard POTUS (president of the United States), FLOTUS (First Lady), or the vice president. As Treasury Department employees, they investigate currency crimes out of nationwide field offices (FOs), but when the election cycle arrives, protection is all-hands-on-deck priority. Yet we could stretch election-level personnel only so far. Occasionally we called upon agencies like the Drug Enforcement Administration to fill gaps— but never the FBI because of long-standing interagency pissing contests. Sure, local police forces can provide perimeter protection, but even they have trouble protecting at large events.

Travel duty agents stay at four- or five-star hotels closer to or at the same location as the event and/or protectee; *we* stayed a few miles out in roach motels—a slap in the face, but not worth getting excited about. I was at the center of the political action. As long as we, the Secret Service, weren't in the news and the candidate was— mission complete. As a new guy I was Teflon to stress.

A sudden late-night call, a plane ride, a two-star hotel, ensuring some crazy event went smoothly (in terms of security), another hotel stay, another plane, and I was back home to Maryland and then back to outside the Oval Office. Each special assignment unfolded like that, a dream, a nightmare, a whirlwind, and then back to our normal grind. I was on complete autopilot.

I always feared being so exhausted that I might do something incredibly stupid, like accidentally leaving my pistol in a restroom stall—unforgivable—but stuff like that happened. If you have a healthy fear of screwing up, you're fine. Lose the fear, careers or lives are over. Thieves once broke into a countersniper Secret Service Suburban parked next to a diner (and a *strip bar*, but they were in the *diner*—they swore!). Guns disappeared. So did the agents.

I admit I'd grown sentimental regarding Papa Bush and his family. But I knew we protected the president, not the man. I quickly grew to love the routine and the atmosphere and to sometimes even read the White House morning news briefings, a mosaic of all the major paper's headlines assembled for the president for his morning read. Seeing how candidates and pundits critiqued the president wounded me. Didn't they realize how soul-sucking the presidency was? This was how the political "game" was played. But didn't candidates realize such vitriol would soon turn on them if they won?

I knew Clinton would beat Papa Bush. I read the papers. I worked at his events. Candidate Clinton would become President Clinton, and that person would be under my protection and I had to adhere to "You elect 'em, we protect 'em," 100 percent.

Scandals have often plagued candidates, but the Clintons exceeded any politician's call of duty. Mrs. Clinton coined her "vast right-wing conspiracy" phrase a few years later, but back in November 1992 I chalked up the hype that surrounded them as just that—hype. As the Clinton scandals accumulated, however, in the months and years to come, I kept recalling being on detail at a Clinton campaign event, small-talking with an Arkansas sheriff. When I asked about the Clintons' latest rumors, he gave me a thousand-yard stare.

"Let me tell you something, Gary. Everything—*everything* they say about them is true. The Clintons are ruthless. And [the media] don't even know the half of it."

I didn't know what to make of that.

"From what *I've* seen," he continued, "there's no doubt in my mind they will secure the presidency—you watch."

"How can you be so sure," I asked, "especially with all the scandals, the allegations of affairs, bribery. . . ."

He just waved me off, saying, "It will never matter. Officer, I'm telling you they can spin shit into gold."

He spoke with great conviction, looking me straight in the eye, as if knowing that what he said was stranger than fiction. He spoke from a profound well of personal experiences with the Clintons, and it was eerie.

Sometimes it seemed as though the Clinton campaign staff could get nothing right, and they blamed us for many scheduling problems, among other issues. Many campaign staffers were bushy-tailed unpaid college kids eyeing future administration jobs. Woefully undisciplined, ideological, naïve, inexperienced "sophisticates," they tried to "college" their way out of any problem. The campaign pushed event volunteers ragged, treating them as disposable. The Clintons' young blood didn't mix with ours, and when those volunteers graduated to campaign staffers, their egos skyrocketed.

They still had to cooperate with us to guarantee Clinton's protection but were pissed to ask permission at every step. They complained it slowed them to a crawl and jeopardized their chances at success. Even more, they suspected we would enact sabotage on behalf of President Bush. They even voiced those conspiracy theories around us! It all set the groundwork for a very bad working relationship between the Clintons and the Secret Service. Their staffers wanted the candidate to succeed; we wanted him to *live*. Previously they had free rein over events; now they played by a different set of rules—and they didn't like rules.

For a campaign event, they had purchased a very large banner with the new slogan. We vetoed it—it blocked one of our countersnipers. Later when Clinton was president, they had scheduled a classic photo op descending Air Force One's staircase. Its pilots nearly panicked to see some staffer had placed a set of audience bleachers near the taxiway. Air Force One jet engine exhaust would have blown people right off them!

I feared I'd have to helplessly witness a presidential assassination. Some events resembled a Black Friday sale opening, with Clinton's enthusiastic fans mobbing him. The Clintons embodied their fans' wants, dreams, and political desires. At Clinton events, it was hard to separate fanatics from lunatics—really, what's the difference? I passed it off as being my first Secret Service election cycle. I thought I'd get used to it.

We at the Secret Service UD had plenty of redundancies on our end to ensure safety. If a metal detector malfunctioned, we funneled people over to the next one or used our wands. But if for whatever reason—and it had happened—the generators failed from overload or ran out of gas, what then? The Service didn't want to let in unscanned people. The campaign staff insisted on it, ordering us to "speed it up."

We placated them, but I was thinking, *Can you speed up stitching a wound?* Sometimes they ordered us to "just let everyone through" because we looked too authoritative and intimidating. They had no clue that was how behavioral screening worked.

On some events, we had campaign staff run up to us archway by archway, yelling, "The event is about to start, shut it down now! Just do it!"

Those were awkward and dangerous moments. With gritted teeth, we would explain that we took our orders only from Secret Service hierarchy. Unless my superior gave the order directly, I wouldn't change course. Once, the other UD officers gave in, turning off the metal detectors and "just letting 'em through." I was so angry I chose to keep my post on and screened each person. The people already in my line were not happy, and the staffer insisted, "What do you not understand? Shut it down!"

"Are you Secret Service?" I asked.

"No, but I'm working this event."

"I don't take orders from you. I take orders from the Secret Service. You want me to stop doing my job, go get someone I take orders from."

Sometimes I'd get backing from a superior. Sometimes not.

"Just like she said, shut it down, Byrne."

If I really wanted to push it further I'd say, "Then give me a name."

"What do you mean, 'Give me a name'?"

"I want to know where this order is coming from," I said as I flipped open my notepad.

They didn't like it, but I needed a name to fall back on if I was ever charged with dereliction.

Once I was working a White House metal detector and a nondescript, middle-aged guy halted before the table, eyeing the detectors. His hands entered his pockets—such a simple gesture—but such a red flag.

Also on duty was a UD officer whom I'll call Yolanda. We had incredibly different backgrounds. I grew up in Pennsylvania and Virginia. She was from the "real" D.C., the "ghetto," as she said. She was very crass, and like me never had advanced education. I wasn't sure what to make of her.

Anyway, back to that guy at the metal detector.

"Um, I have a gun," he said quietly, "in my pockets," he said, his face white, his body rigid.

I grabbed his hands, keeping them (and his gun) in his coat pockets. "Do not take your hands out of your pockets!"

Yolanda's arm flashed over my hunched shoulder, her SIG pistol so close to his eyeballs, he probably saw the bullet inside its barrel. He certainly saw dark nail polish.

"I got you, Byrney!"

Everybody froze.

"Listen!" Yolanda barked. "You move, and I will kill you, motherf—er."

Mission accomplished. People didn't complain about screeners after that! A million things could have gone south at that checkpoint, but she had my back, and our training kicked in. Yolanda was great—a top draft pick for any partner. She read people like a human polygraph machine and wouldn't freeze up in the clutch.

And *that* incident occurred at 1600 Pennsylvania Avenue. Just consider the risk at *campaign events.*

6.

THE BOY FROM HOPE, ARKANSAS

The new presidential staff was in, and the old was out. I found myself saying, "Good morning, Mr. President," to a new person, President Clinton. The transition was exciting. I spent much of those shifts answering questions like where the coffee machines were, how the White House AT&T telephone system and the fax machines worked, how to navigate the offices, and of course, the location of the nearest bathroom. Electrical outlets were in short supply in an old building, so I was often asked where to find one.

Most often, I'd pester presidential staff to wear their passes visibly. New staff arrived by the day. We code-named the First Family: Eagle (Bill), Evergreen (Hillary), and Energy (Chelsea). They moved into the Executive Mansion. Mrs. Clinton's office near the Oval Office made her the first First Lady on the West Wing. The media buzzed over her semi-cabinet position, that she could never be fired, how she'd always be first to the president's ear. Should a First Lady to be a social role model or an unfireable, unofficial chief of staff? We were eager to learn that ourselves.

George Stephanopoulos (we nicknamed him Stuffing Envelopes, among other things) and Dee Dee Myers, both key Clinton media people, stood outside the Oval Office, discussing who would get each office. Some had windows or direct access to the president, while some were more secluded and isolated from the annoying buzz of busybodies. They were choosing offices before they knew their exact job positions! I injected myself into their conversation.

"Typically the press secretary's office is over there by the Press Lobby so reporters can have better access."

George turned pale. I wasn't sure how to gauge his reaction.

"Oh, I don't want my office by *those* people."

George owed reporters for his campaign successes, but I suppose even he wanted a break from the spin cycle. George ended up next to the president's study, granting him coveted open access to the president. Nancy Hernreich, the president's scheduler, had wanted that same office but ended up next to Betty Currie, the president's personal secretary. Dee Dee Myers, who became the press secretary, ended up with that far office by the Press Lobby.

Many staffers were stalwart professionals. Some sprouted massive egos upon stepping through the White House door. I was on break when I heard a call over the radio.

"Bandbox to any available West Wing officer."

"Byrne here."

"Byrne, proceed to the pool and check on an unidentified male in the pool. Someone needs to go check this guy out immediately."

"Byrne: copy," I said as I jogged over.

The First Family has its own private pool. Once when First Lady Bush swam there, a rat—the White House has all sorts of wildlife—

dove into the pool. President Bush rushed over, beat the rat with a pool net, scooped it up, and flung it onto the walkway nearby. Their English springer spaniel Millie finished the job.

No rats swam today. But an unknown man in a suit and tie had his feet in the pool, his pants rolled up as if he were on vacation. He was looking around, la-di-da, and kicking his bare feet, leaning back and gawking at the sky.

"Hey, how you doing?" I asked, sincerely curious.

He looked at me bright-eyed. "Isn't this great?"

"Sure is," I humored him.

"We made it. We did it," he said, astonished by his own success. "We're going to change everything." He talked and talked. Some of these new Clinton hires were really something.

"Mind if I see your pass?" I interrupted.

It was in his desk, he told me. I asked his name and he told me we could be friends, but when I radioed Bandbox to check his name the man's tone changed. He waved me off saying he didn't need a pass. I informed him he did.

He responded, "We run the place now. You're going to have to get used to that."

I responded with a flat "Yeah, no."

My colleagues arrived, and his feet left the pool. He blustered that we had it in for him, launching into a "Do you know who I am?" routine.

He never got his White House pass back. Good riddance.

Another day, I was outside the Oval Office. A portly gentleman strutted in with another gentleman as if they were a two-man marching band. The plump conductor and a tall, hovering young guy marched in lockstep, scrutinizing the West Wing. I assessed them as nonthreats, but they had my curiosity. The conductor was brightly dressed, tieless, but wearing multiple brightly colored Mardi Gras beaded necklaces. He got right up in my face.

"You see this?" he said, presenting his necklaces the way I'd hold up a badge.

"Yes, sir, I do," I said, smiling, being as professional as I could. Inside, I was cracking up.

"This is my gay pride necklace! You got a problem with that?" he steamed, eyes locked on mine.

"No problem, sir," I replied. He seemed stunned.

He trundled off, almost disappointed that I didn't have more to say. I didn't have a problem; he had his pass and wasn't posing a risk, so what did I care? The guy seemed to want to lock horns just because I was a law enforcement officer. He must have figured that anyone wearing a badge must be homophobic.

He couldn't be more wrong.

My Air Force roommate was a bit of a shut-in. Only when I stopped in a dive bar far off base for a rest stop and heard, "Gary?" did I grasp why. It was he, and only then did I realize where we were. The joint had a motorcycle theme but in a Village People sort of way. A gay bar! *My roommate!* I waved good-bye and speechlessly peeled out of there. This was before "Don't ask, don't tell"; active homosexuality could result in a dishonorable discharge. Even the suspicion of homosexuality could destroy your career.

Suddenly, his awkwardness in the showers, why he never chased women, joked about porn, or made crude military talk made sense. He must've chewed his fingernails worrying whether I would spread the word or inform a superior. Gut-wrenching fear must have weighed on him from the start.

I drew the big picture. His sexuality had no impact on his competence, honor, or integrity. I respected him more for his committing to the military. Back home, I gave him a slap on the shoulder and never mentioned it again.

Back to 1992 and seeing this oaf saunter down the White House hallway with his beaded necklace. Mr. Mardi Gras had only just begun having his tall, young sidekick slap Gay Pride stickers on the walls and furniture, yes, the priceless historical furniture and walls of the White House.

"Sir! Sir!"

Careers were on the line, so I needed backup. The duo pivoted toward me and got the fracas they wanted, a pointless quarrel with those whose job it was to protect them.

"I don't care what's on the stickers! Do not disrespect, disregard, or vandalize the White House! This isn't your dorm room. It's a living monument to the greatest leaders this country's ever had!"

"Oh no, this is our house now!" they squawked.

They accused us of homophobia. We focused on decorum, protocol—and vandalism. I never expected such behavior from anyone capable of even potentially being appointed to work in the White House. Imagine that after clearing every background check they'd demonstrate such willful, unthinkable incompetence, unprofessionalism, and contempt. The West Wing cleaning staff painstakingly removed the offending stickers from the walls, straining not to leave marks. *They* were angrier than we were. We escorted those clowns out as if we were club bouncers. They never got their passes back, and we never saw them again.

Staffers entered through the Old Executive Office Building (the Eisenhower Building), and it was a magnet for various and sundry weirdos. A polite, well-dressed, and impeccably groomed guy got in line. No problem. Secret Service checked his bag. A-okay. He chitchatted with the officers. All was normal. Yet the staffer was sockless on *one* foot. For some reason, he handed an officer the missing sock.

"Oh, and I guess I give you this," he said, shrugging and smiling as if he was hot shit, as if nothing were wrong.

"Sure, do," the officer said, taking the sock.

The other officer instinctively drew his sidearm and issued orders: "Keep your hands where I can see them! Hands up!"

Next I heard over the radio: "Officers have just apprehended a staffer trying to enter with a pistol!"

That sock had a Glock pistol in it. The District of Columbia ranks among the nation's most anti-gun locations in the country, and this new staffer was blatantly committing dozens of gun-related felonies just by possessing a handgun. He was fired, arrested, and prosecuted. He basically told UD that the rules didn't apply to him. Idiot! But it takes one to hire one, I was learning. The incident was especially incredible knowing the Clintons' anti–Second Amendment sentiment.

"Beware the Glock in a sock," we'd say to remind each other to keep an eye on staffers as much as anyone else.

The word was out on the new staff and the Clinton way of doing things. The hippie generation was anti-authority and disdained us. But now they were *the* authority! The UD quickly grew wary of being in the sights of the Clintons and, later, especially of Mrs. Clinton.

One time when the president stayed at a West Coast hotel, a group was scheduled to meet with him. It's no secret that Mrs. Clinton and their staff created very tight schedules to enable President Clinton to meet a multitude of groups. But President Clinton was a schmoozer, wanting to give each group due time. Schedules got pushed back and squeezed. Staffers made up time where they could.

Downstairs in the lobby, the staffer swore to the agent that she knew each person, but he insisted on verifying each visitor. She pressured him, and he trusted her. Upstairs, people entered completely unscreened: no metal detection, no ID checking—nothing.

One guy rushed right up to President Clinton, gave him a hearty handshake, and exclaimed that he was his biggest fan. Clinton asked who he was, but nobody knew. The agents rushed him out. The staffer responsible for this fiasco turned to the agent and to her credit surrendered her radio, ID, and credentials, resigning immediately. Wrapped up in the president's schedule, she had left his life completely in God's hands, taking it out of the Service's.

Our mystery man informed agents that he didn't even know the president was staying in the hotel, was simply inquisitive about the group gathering in the lobby, and joined in on a whim. A guy curious about a crowd pierced the most protective security blanket in the world because of a frazzled, overzealous, power-tripping staffer. John Hinckley did pretty much same damn thing with the press corps.

Secret Service leadership reminded us not to trust staffers when it came to presidential security. Many, including myself, maintained detailed notes of every staff encounter in our post logbooks: Cover Your Ass notes to guard against possible mishaps or claims of libel, sexual harassment, unprofessionalism, or partisanship.

Unlike their predecessors, this administration didn't focus, pace themselves, or even delegate. Staff wore jeans and T-shirts and faced each problem with grand ideological bull sessions. Rival foreign powers could influence the situation and change it before the Clinton administration could mold a plan and implement it. Their helter-skelter approach had deadly consequences abroad.

Somehow the administration selected Somalia as a scene for international engagements. There were plenty of wars and genocides around the world. They ignored the Rwandan genocide and let the situation in Bosnia-Herzegovina escalate. I guess Somalia seemed more marketable than the others—better for the Clinton brand.

The incident at Mogadishu resulted from their dithering and from their constant insistence that we (LEOs, military, and so on) had to look like their perception of good guys. The administration never got over the idea that the Uniformed Division, the agents, and the military didn't look like what they had envisioned. What was that vision? I don't know. The administration was constantly trying to get uniformed UD officers to resemble plainclothes special agents while on the road. They wanted us to be "user friendly," which translated into, "Do what we tell you, when we tell you to do it." They wanted us to look unintimidating. Appearances really came to a head on Mrs. Clinton's detail. Eventually, personnel assigned to it regarded the "honor" as a punishment. It was a transfer no one wanted because of its constant stress and negativity.

I vividly remember Secretary of Defense Les Aspin, George Stephanopoulos, advisor Rahm Emanuel, and others convening about an operation in Mogadishu, the Somali capital. Though all of this was way over my pay grade, I couldn't believe what I was hearing. The three walked outside the Roosevelt Room into the hallway in front of me at my Oval Office post to reiterate what they had just discussed.

"They don't *need* tanks," Stephanopoulos insisted, as if the request was absurd and excessive.

"Yeah, they don't need . . ." they agreed, listing the military's supposedly excessive requests for AC-130 gunships, armored personnel carriers (APCs), and other equipment.

"We don't want to look too militant," someone said.

I was stunned.

How does a military look too militant? It was bizarre. Some-where in the chain of command the decision was purely political, they agreed based on "branding," and they were meddling heav-ily with the military. I knew from my Air Force days that no one would even see an AC-130 gunship in the sky—it'd be too high. I had no idea what caused their resistance to armored personnel car-riers or if some even knew the difference between an APC and a tank. Their nonchalance in disregarding a military request made me very uneasy.

"Yeah, there's no reason for that," they kept reaffirming.

"It's just a simple in-and-out."

Meanwhile, President Clinton was riding (and still rides) in an armored limousine that rivalled any APC. It just enjoyed the fund-ing to make it *look* like a Cadillac.

In early 1993 military brass suddenly started scurrying in and out of the West Wing situation room. A Sit Room (Situation Room) operative alerted me, "We got major troops in contact in Somalia. The first reports are that we've already taken some casualties, so there's going to be a lot of guys coming and going around here. It's bad."

Only then did I realized the context of Les Aspin's briefing and what George, Rahm, and others were discussing.

"Shit," I said with a sigh as he walked off. "Well, where the hell is Somalia?" I said to myself. I was working so many hours I couldn't even tell what day of the week it was.

A coworker and I wheeled some globes into the Roosevelt Room and located Somalia in eastern Africa. My heart ached for the guys there. Whenever there's a terrorist attack or "troops in contact" (jar-gon for our soldiers being engaged by the enemy), every veteran's adrenaline and anger spike.

Tension ratcheted up around the White House. Sundays were usually very slow and popular with tourists, but dignitaries and higher-ups from all over descended in droves. All tours were canceled, and nonessentials were sent home. The atmosphere was silent except for the grinding of teeth and biting of nails.

The Battle of Mogadishu on October 3, 1993, was part of Operation Restore Hope. We remember it now as "Black Hawk Down" from the novel (and subsequent film) of that name by an on-the-scene journalist, Mark Bowden. Army Rangers paid a heavy price for not looking "too intimidating" or "like invaders," valiantly fighting while stripped of the equipment they requested. Had the administration not ignorantly meddled with events, the 160 Special Forces operators of Army Rangers and Delta wouldn't have taken so many casualties. And here is what the Clinton Machine didn't comprehend: Our guys wouldn't have had to *inflict* as many casualties either, shooting their way out against 4,000–6,000 Somalis with an entire city of civilians trapped in the crossfire. The Rangers became a legend that day but lost eighteen fine men and suffered seventy-three wounded.

Years later, I realized why this always bothered me so. The Clinton leadership style had conflicting ideologies: They wanted to help but never hurt, like a doctor wanting to heal but never use a scalpel or draw blood. He misses both goals abysmally.

Randy Shughart and Gary Gordon, two Delta operators, won posthumous Medals of Honor for taking the initiative to secure one of the Black Hawk helicopter crash sites until Rangers could reinforce them. They knew the risk. They saw the enemy closing in before they even landed.

At the White House during their Medal of Honor ceremony, the father of a Delta operator became unglued, furious that he was to receive the Medal of Honor from President Clinton, who in the father's words was too cowardly to accept a draft to the Vietnam War at the behest of the president at the time, Lyndon Johnson. He believed President Clinton unworthy to bestow the award on his late son. His wife apologized to me and the other officers for her husband. But we felt the same way.

"Ma'am, you don't have to apologize. We completely understand. Take as much time as you need," I told her as I allowed them a buffer of privacy from the press.

Yes, we totally understood, and we were getting choked up, too. Their anguish was a horrendous sight and started to change the way I looked at things. It struck me so profoundly. That father wanted his son back—and I knew this ceremony was merely part of the administration's political strategy to tamp down its Somalian "scandal." Little did I know that a few of the guys who knew Shughart and Gordon—and were present that day—would later become so important to my life and influential in the tactical world as well.

Black Hawk Down never really left me.

7.

"BILLARY"

As soon as Mr. Clinton became the president, Mrs. Clinton and her staff sought to repair the Clinton brand among groups they thought had been damaged during the campaign, scheduling galas, balls, and dinners. They hosted open house tours day and night, especially around Christmas and for the military. What she and her staffers failed to realize was that the White House had a budget like any other government entity. Each shindig still had to be paid either from the Executive Residence budget or the Democratic Party's purse.

Event planners dropped the ball on costs. One Rose Garden event required big, rented, air-conditioned tents that ruined the lawn. Landscaping crews and the National Park Service tore up all the dead grass, installed new sod, and sent them the bill. That's expensive. But you can't just have a whole White House lawn muddy and looking like crap. "Just get it done," staffers would say.

Party rental companies refused future events until they were paid. The discussions were plain embarrassing, but when I heard them I wasn't eavesdropping. They were shouted in the hallway. The Clintons believed that a magic royal pot of money somehow existed for their every whim.

The Bush administration had upgraded the White House tele-communications system. It wasn't easy. Imagine an elaborate phone system wired into a building built when the only common utility was plumbing. The Clinton staff upgraded it yet again. The catch: The Clinton administration hadn't anticipated that it had to *actually pay for things*, and the bill blindsided them. We heard about this both from the West Wing staffers talking or yelling about it and from the AT&T technicians we escorted about the building. These technicians further revealed to us that the new administration believed that Republicans in the Bush operation had tapped the White House system to listen in on them.

The Vice President's Residence is at the Naval Observatory on Massachusetts Avenue, a few blocks from the White House. Technicians at the Control Center of the Technical Service were surprised to see alarms going off at the house. First carbon monoxide, then heat alarms, then other alarms. Even the radiation alarm! Something was seriously amiss. SAs and UD officers immediately responded, letting themselves in. They found Vice President Al Gore standing on a chair, pulling an alarm out of the ceiling, looking for hidden cameras and listening devices.

Early on, the staff kept promising payments but it was common knowledge that they had no idea of where they were coming from. But the buck kept getting passed because Mrs. Clinton didn't want to hear "no," and no one wanted to be the bearer of bad news. Evergreen was spoiled. Her doting, barely post-adolescent staffers resembled enabling, weak-willed parents. She threw massive tantrums. As her husband's term continued, those tantrums and her attitude toward us and various White House staff worsened.

Years later I read George Stephanopoulos's memoir, *All Too Human*. I was amazed at how candid it was. It was a page-turner, bringing many bad memories rushing back. He wrote:

> When Hillary was angry, you didn't always know it right away—a calculated chill would descend over time. [Bill] Clinton's anger was a more impersonal physical force, like a tornado. The tantrum would form in an instant and exhaust itself in a violent rush. Whoever happened to be in the way would have to deal with it; more often than not, that person was me.*

While I often saw the president fume, I rarely saw him become irate. Meanwhile I often saw, heard, or heard about the First Lady's volcanic eruptions at UD officers, SAs (especially on her own detail), and all the people who worked at the White House. I laughed at Stephanopoulos's take because it seemed we witnessed opposite things. While the president must have vented his frustrations to the staff, Mrs. Clinton vented on *everyone*, and it got worse the more at home she felt in the White House. Most of us knew to brace for her inevitable eruptions. They didn't happen every day, but behind closed doors we learned about them fast. In public she was everyone's best friend. Privately, she was her normal self.

It was early September 1995. I had seen the news like everyone else. The night before, a Metro police officer had alleged that George Stephanopoulos was in the midst of a hit-and-run when the officer stopped him and administered a Breathalyzer test for alcohol. George's car was usually parked on West Executive, for weeks

---

* George Stephanopoulos, *All Too Human* (Boston: Little, Brown, 1999), p. 96.

at a time it seemed, because he hardly drove. It had dings all around and a busted taillight. The past night, he'd busted another. George arrived in his office, attracting a group of young straphanger female staffers along with his assistant, Laura. According to George in *All Too Human*:

> I had been arrested in Georgetown. The charge was "hit and run"; the truth was that I couldn't maneuver my car out of a tight parking spot on M Street. When I scraped the bumper ahead of me, an excitable police officer who happened by recognized me and made a scene—patting me down as a crowd gathered around. More bad luck, I had carelessly let my license expire. He cuffed my hands behind my back and called in four cars to take me to the station. Although my car never left the curb, I was cited for leaving the scene of an accident. Several hours later, I was released with an apology from the station chief, and the charges were dropped. But the damage was done: Video footage of my arrest was all over the morning news.

"I mean, who does this cop think he is? You know, typical A-hole cop," he continued in the office. "I barely nudged the car. *They* just *had* to call four cars over!"

He was just like all the other staffers we had either kicked out or had an issue with: They had pushed the envelope too far and the LEOs knew it was going to be a political heavyweight battle afterward.

George blustered—which was typical. It never surprised me. The Clinton people seemed to regard police and military personnel as if we had some grand conspiracy on them, as if we had a "most wanted" deck of playing cards with their faces on it. From the way I knew George, I was sure instead of the officer's recognizing George, it was George who played the "Do you know who I am?" game. George kept dragging out the story, talking so loudly that everyone in the hallway could hear him. Laura saw me snickering in the hallway, tensed up, and tried to flag George off the story, which made it even funnier for me.

"Hey, George," I said. "I understand that you had an interesting weekend."

All the girls looked so awkward. He shrugged me off, and I left laughing. He didn't care, and I knew he, like so many others in the White House, had lost the ability to see themselves through others' eyes. Laura visited me afterward, ostensibly for small talk, but probably really to apologize. I preempted her by saying that I thought of George's self-importance as merely comical.

In a way it was almost guaranteed that the president would vent to George, while Mrs. Clinton would vent to whoever happened to pull the short straw that day. Take, for example, the morning of Tuesday, June 13, 1995.

Just another day at the White House. I answered my phone outside the Oval Office.

"Heads up, there's a shit storm coming your way."

"I knew it!" I laughed. I'd grown used to such warnings. "Here we go."

"Evergreen moving toward West Wing," I heard in my ear.

Her detail stormed in. I always avoided eye contact when she was on the warpath. Everyone got the hell out of her way.

Mrs. Clinton was a joke, taking herself and the entire administration's minutiae *so* seriously. Her "brand" was her only concern. She was a faux leader, all bark, no bite, but in a very real power position as First Lady. I thanked God that the Secret Service answered to the Treasury Department and wasn't some private presidential army.

"They f—ed us, Bill!" Hillary screamed.

I stifled a laugh.

The president tried his best to calm her down. He couldn't. Hillary Clinton possessed no perspective.

"We need to get rid of these assholes, Bill!"

She thought she was being tough—in command—but the issue commanded *her*.

She fumed that the Secret Service's Uniformed Division, my branch, disloyal leftovers from Papa Bush, conspired against the administration. "They've had it out for us from the beginning!" she kept yelling.

She continued screaming about how we had treated campaign event attendees, a festering, deep-seated grudge that she and many administration types harbored against us and the entire Secret Service. Members of the Presidential Protection Division and her own First Lady Protection Division agent—as well as I, the UD officer posted to the Oval Office—stood silently by, hearing wave after wave of vitriol wash over us.

The door shut.

We remained outside exchanging chuckles and exasperated looks. It's inappropriate to eavesdrop, but with the old building acoustics and how loudly she yelled, it was impossible not to hear. White House acoustics are very strange. Scream inside a room, and everyone in the hallway hears it. Maybe she knew that, but no one dared tell her.

Hillary's antics made my job *interesting*. She'd explode in my face without reservation or decorum, then confide in some visiting

VIP, "This is one of my favorite officers, Gary Byrne." She'd put her hand on my shoulder for good measure. I'd smile and nod. But we were like furniture to them.

The day of Hillary's screaming, I moved to the edge of my post, not wanting to hear anything or be seen in eavesdrop territory. For forty-five minutes she berated the president.

"Man, she hates you guys," whispered one agent.

"Of course it's *us*," I said sarcastically—it was never their fault.

"I can't believe he's defending you guys," said the other.

I couldn't believe it, either.

"You can't just do that," the president kept repeating. She wouldn't take no for an answer—even from him!

When she left, I poked my head into Betty Currie's office. "So, how'd that go?" I asked.

Betty Currie, the president's discreet personal secretary, did her best to ignore the issue. I ducked back outside.

Neither the First Lady nor the administration staffers possessed any desire to understand our role—or even their own. Mountains of bureaucracy, protocols, and very different American experiences separated us. Name the incident, and instead of trying to understand, she'd yell. But if she'd had her way, we'd have been gone that day.

Inconsequential events surrounding a visit from a forty-strong gay-rights delegation led by openly gay Massachusetts congressman Barney Frank had ignited this morning's rage. They had come to lobby the president, Vice President Gore, and senior staff. During his campaign, President Clinton had promised gays much. Once in office, he delivered "Don't ask, don't tell." They weren't satisfied. The Clintons had to balance their demands with those of the military.

But people like Barney Frank and Bill Clinton discredited their own causes. Clinton was secretive, corrupt, and a womanizer. Congressman Frank hired a male prostitute and sexual partner as an aide and driver, albeit with personal funds, not taxpayers'. His attaché later ran a male escort service out of the congressman's house in Washington. The House Ethics Committee slapped Congressman Frank on the wrist for fixing some parking tickets and lying about knowing his attaché had a criminal record. That didn't prevent Frank's reelection and he kept pushing for his cause. But his notoriety was a lightning rod. That prostitution scandal didn't help his reputation.

Each member of Frank's delegation was listed as usual in my paperwork. The title of the delegation itself was boldly marked: "HIV Positive." Our screeners took note of this, and their usual safety precautions immediately increased.

As a trained first responder, each day I checked my FAT (First Aid and Trauma) kit and had my UD-issued blue nitride gloves designed to protect me. It wasn't for AIDS. Casual physical contact doesn't spread the disease. We needed gloves to inspect visitors' bags. Worker's compensation and Department of Health and Human Services rules required us to use this protection because we came in daily contact with tampons, tissues, and certain personal vibrating devices. People's bags were gross. But we had to search them.

A prick from a syringe hidden in someone's bag could be life threatening—it had happened. UD had tried obtaining ballistic search gloves, but the administrators deemed them too expensive and unnecessary. If they had done our jobs, they'd have been wearing astronaut suits. Some guys bought their own search gloves.

That morning a couple of UD officers overdid it, donning their gloves as if they were about to perform a rectal exam. One (I'll call him Crusty—an old-school Vietnam combat veteran, a great guy) made a show of slapping on his blue gloves.

"Why are you doing that?" a visitor demanded.

"You know why."

So the day started off on the wrong foot. But the delegation's real ire resulted from the Clintons' having made promises they couldn't keep. Representative Frank's delegation *wanted* to make waves; they loved being offended. With the glove incident they got their chance, the PR opportunity of a lifetime.

I knew the guys who had checked in Frank's delegation. I'd worked their rotation myself, checking thousands of bags. Joking kept us vigilant—it's counterintuitive, but somehow it kept us alert. Yes, this time it *was* a bit much. On an outrage scale of 1–10, however, this should have been a 1. But remember: If we didn't check everyone for *everything*, maybe a John Hinckley would get through.

That didn't stop the charge of the Politically Correct Brigade. The *Baltimore Sun* headlined, "Guards Don Gloves as Gay Officials Visit White House." Other papers screamed similar headlines. Careers were on the line. Our UD leadership promised better training. The Clinton administration demanded that the Secret Service be more "user friendly."

Better training? It never happened. Just a big grab-ass in the media, nothing on the ground level. The insinuation of homophobia by the Secret Service as a whole was reckless. And in the push for staying politically correct they nearly jettisoned the funding for the real training we needed, specifically on how to save lives in truly dangerous "friendly fire" situations. That wasn't a joke. We'd nearly lost an officer, Scott Giambattista, to friendly fire the previous year. (See Chapter 9 for details.)

They gave us black gloves instead of blue. Some of us finally got the Kevlar and leather ballistic gloves we wanted, so maybe we won. But it took controversy rather than common sense to get things done.

But the most revealing portion of the blue glove story was not how a Uniformed Division officer may or may not have overreacted. It was how people under Mrs. Clinton's direct command had messed up in the first place, how she exhibited her rage in a truly over-the-top, unprofessional manner.

Let's return to the memo describing the delegation as HIV positive. Somehow Frank's delegation had secured a copy of that document—and it was the violation of revealing their personal medical records that outraged its members far more than Crusty and his blue glove act.

Now, who prepared that memo? It wasn't the Secret Service. It was the White House Social Office—an operation directly under the command of Hillary Rodham Clinton herself. The Secret Service would never have committed such private medical information to a written document. It knew better than to do that—and certainly better than to label the entire delegation as HIV positive.

Mrs. Clinton's own office created the crisis. But who received her obscenity-filled tirades?

The Secret Service.

But some other people suffered far more than we did.

I was working in the East Wing and heading toward the second-floor Social Office to retrieve an event list for the morning's guests. I spied several clearly agitated members of Mrs. Clinton's staff.

"Sorry to interrupt."

"No, problem, Gary," one answered, but clearly there was a problem. "What is it?"

"Is everything all right?" I asked. "You don't have to tell me if it's not my business. I'm just making sure everyone is safe. Is there anything that I need to be aware of? Or pass along?"

They assured me that I had nothing to worry about security-wise. But they had *plenty* to worry about First Lady-wise.

Mrs. Clinton's mad whirl of special events, special tours, and various other functions—all part of her continuing public relations offensive—had never really slowed down. But each event cost money—and, as usual, the White House budget remained at the bursting point. To economize, her staff had engaged several unpaid interns to assist with their functions.

This morning's stir—and there was a stir every morning—involved an intern's having botched a huge order for official White House Social Office invitations, basing the design on a previous draft of copy, not the latest. These were not your run-of-the mill invitations. These were dispatched to royalty, other foreign leaders, dignitaries, ambassadors, and power players all over the world. They were top-of-the-line and had to be completely redesigned and reordered.

I tried advising Mrs. Clinton's distraught staffers to keep the matter in perspective. Surely the White House, the country, had bigger problems than this—even if it was money flushed down the drain. Hey, *nobody died.*

"That's not the problem," I was told.

"Who's going to tell Hillary?" another staffer continued with obvious trepidation.

My eyes widened. It wasn't the actual problem that was the issue—it wasn't the waste of taxpayer dollars. It was facing the First Lady's response. Yes, imagine dealing with mega-wedding invitations for the world's biggest Bridezilla—in this case, none other than Hillary Rodham Clinton.

Her staffers had to cover their posteriors—and fast. They explicitly informed me that careers were made or broken on the whim of her "wrath"—a term I heard often. I backed away much more quickly and silently than I had arrived.

But the question wasn't the waste of tens of thousands of public funds (probably more than my annual salary). The issue wasn't why they had entrusted this task to inexperienced interns—and then not properly reviewed their work.

The issue, *as always*, was "How do we tell Hillary?"

Fear reigned among her staff. It made it impossible for them to say no to her. It paralyzed their decisions, and in the end, it created disastrous consequences.

I mostly saw Vince Foster in the hallways. He was Mrs. Clinton's personal attaché, a lawyer from Arkansas. Word circulated that she berated him mercilessly. The first time I saw Foster I figured he wouldn't last a year. He looked uncomfortable and unhappy in the White House. I knew what it was like to be yelled at by superiors, but Mrs. Clinton never hesitated to launch a tirade. Yet her staffers never dared say, "I don't have to take this shit!" They reminded me of battered wives: too loyal, too unwilling to acknowledge they'd never assuage her. They had no one to blame but themselves, but they could never admit it.

She criticized Foster for failing to get ahead of the constant scandals, for cabinet positions not confirmed, and for the slowness of staffing the White House. Foster eventually took his own life in Fort Marcy Park. In his briefcase was a note torn into twenty-seven pieces, blaming the FBI, the media, the Republicans—even the White House Ushers Office. A rumor circulated among law enforcement types that contended his suicide weapon had to be repaired in order for the forensics team to fire it since it wouldn't function for them. Maybe his final shot misaligned the cylinders and later prevented contact with the bullet primers. But that, along with many other public details of the case (carpet fibers on his suit coat, etc.), made his case spooky. The last lines of his sparse suicide note read: "I was not meant for the job or the spotlight of public life in Washington. Here ruining people is considered sport."

A UD friend of mine, Hank O'Neil, was posted outside of Foster's office as part of the FBI's investigation of his suicide. Maggie Williams, Mrs. Clinton's always well dressed chief of staff, physically pushed her way past Hank into Foster's office, arguing that he had no right to block her entrance. She removed boxes that were never recovered; they were destroyed. Congressmen bashed Officer O'Neil's integrity, but he held firm. He reported exactly what he saw and didn't make any inferences about it, but they were sure he held some smoking gun and was protecting the Clintons.

All I'd been warned of proved true. Working protective details during the election, I sized up the Clinton machine by talking with agents and local police in Arkansas. I wanted to know what to expect. Mrs. Clinton installed her office one floor up, next to the Legal Department's offices. Staffers scurried to avoid her attention. We exchanged "Good mornings" with President Clinton. With her, we used our best judgment and kept silent, but things grew worse.

Around 1993, I befriended the FBI liaison to the White House, Gary Aldrich. Everyone at UD liked Aldrich—even if he was FBI. The Secret Service agents had their normal interagency chip on their shoulder for him, but his stories about interacting with the Clintons were rich. He was basically the ambassador between the lauded and revered Federal Bureau of Investigation and the Clinton's Executive Branch. For the Clintons, the lines between government and politics were always blurred.

"I keep having to tell them," he'd confide in us, "'we're not your private investigative service over here. We're the FBI.'"

Aldrich's hunched posture betrayed those frustrations, as though he'd grown weary of throwing up his arms, shrugging his shoulders, and shaking his head while exclaiming, "We just can't conduct these inquiries and checks on whomever they wish—even if they are working for the president!" He'd look at us, hoping for a shared sense of disbelief. We'd mirror his look of astonishment and humor. If was as if he was asking for confirmation of his own sanity in a crazy world. We knew the feeling all too well.

"They can't just run a check on someone because *they* want more info on them," Aldrich would tell us. "It's not a good enough reason. And then I have to hear from my people that they're going over my head and contacting others at the FBI directly. It's like, 'C'mon guys. [We're] just trying to help you. . . .'"

It was all Standard Clinton Operating Procedure.

In June 1996 Aldrich's predicament became public knowledge when the House Government Reform and Oversight Committee discovered that the White House Office of Personnel and Security had requested the FBI to conduct more than nine hundred illegal background checks on its political opponents, many of them former Reagan and Bush appointees.

This improper peeking into confidential FBI files began, however, on a rather small numerical scale, with the harassing of seven White House Travel Office officials. Hillary wanted these good people fired so their jobs could go to her Arkansas cronies. But it wasn't enough that these employees be fired; they had to be put through the wringer of a series of inquisitorial federal investigations.

Gary Aldrich would later write:

Mrs. Clinton [used] security agencies as a hammer to attack and punish those who stood in her way. The FBI, the Secret Service and the Internal Revenue Service hounded and then prosecuted seven innocent men who worked for the White House travel office simply because they were standing in the way of Mrs. Clinton's political interests and ambitions. She knew federal investigations would destroy those good men, but she wanted her friends in those slots, and that was all that mattered.*

Did Hillary ever tell the truth about this scandal? *Not exactly.* As Ken Starr's successor, Robert Ray, found in 2000, "The evidence was insufficient to prove to a jury beyond a reasonable doubt that any of Mrs. Clinton's statements and testimony regarding her involvement in the travel office firings were knowingly false."**

Translate that sentence into English, and I think it pretty clearly says: She's wiggled out of it again.

Recall also that all improper snooping was accomplished through the White House Office of Personnel and Security. Its director was a fellow named Craig Livingstone, whom Gary Aldrich considered "a joke."*** No one could even quite figure out who had hired Livingstone, and certainly nobody wanted to take credit. His

---

* http://www.washingtontimes.com/news/2012/oct/30/hillary-clintons-abominable-national-security-reco/?page=all.

** *Final report of the independent counsel (in re Madison Guaranty Savings & Loan Association); in re William David Watkins and in re Hillary Rodham Clinton,* U.S. Court of Appeals for the District of Columbia Circuit, Division for the Purpose of Appointing Independent Counsels, Division, no. 94-1 (U.S. G.P.O., Supt. of Docs., 2000), p. 17.

*** http://www.washingtontimes.com/news/2012/oct/30/hillary-clintons-abominable-national-security-reco/?page=all.

security and personnel experience seemed to consist mainly of being a bouncer in a D.C. nightclub. But rumors swirled that Hillary had hired him (though some said it was Vince Foster). She, of course, denied it.

"Some of my security friends," Gary Aldrich, however, would later write, "thought that this [Livingstone's appointment] was Mrs. Clinton's way of showing us that she held no respect for us."*

This scandal became known as Filegate, just another scandal piled onto the other scandals from Whitewater to sexual harassment and others. We were learning: The only thing that pushed a Clinton scandal out of the public eye was another scandal.

One day, UD officers met to review events at their respective posts. A bewildered new officer arrived. "Hey, you'll never believe it, but I passed the First Lady, and she told me to go to hell!"

A second young officer responded, "You think that's bad? I passed her on the West Colonnade, and all I said was 'Good morning, First Lady.' She told me, 'Go f— yourself.'"

"Are you serious?"

"'Go f— yourself'!" He imitated her, pointing a finger.

We were stunned but not all of us were surprised. Our sergeant challenged him, but another officer soon corroborated his story. Our sergeant was speechless. We assured the rookie that this wasn't the job's normal atmosphere—at least, not under the previous administration. The sergeant fumed and called the watch commander, who pushed things up the Secret Service chain of command, who said they'd forward it to Chief of Staff Leon Panetta. The Service circulated a memo reminding everyone to report any "unusual" First Family interaction to their supervisors.

---

* http://www.washingtontimes.com/news/2012/oct/30/hillary-clintons-abominable-national-security-reco/?page=all.

The new guy (who had earned a Purple Heart fighting the Clintons' war in Somalia) got an apology for the First Lady's actions—but not directly from her, of course. Quite a difference from how Barbara Bush once apologized to my family. Staff morale suffered once more.

By now Hillary's behavior never surprised me—I never *let* it surprise me.

Dr. Ruth Westheimer—yes, *that* Dr. Ruth—had just visited the president. She claimed she had been the final voice in getting the president to run. Every time she visited she told us she had been a sniper in the Israeli army's early inception—that's 100 percent true. "If you were an enemy, I could put a bullet right in your chest out at two hundred yards, young man," she boasted, thumping me in the chest. It honestly hurt. She's a tiny old lady but with hands like a vise. *I* wouldn't pick a fight with her.

Later, one of Mrs. Clinton's staffers escorted a group of visiting Arkansas VIPs. She ordered me to keep an eye on them while she scooted elsewhere. I refused. Her request jeopardized security. We weren't even allowed to help with luggage if the First Family was struggling, because it would tie up our hands.

She kept insisting, emulating Mrs. Clinton's behavior like a caricature. She made a call, and soon my earpiece echoed with an ominous, "Evergreen heading to Oval Office area."

The First Lady marched straight up to me. The Arkansas VIPs were still in awe over the Oval Office.

"I understand we have a problem here."

"No, ma'am, we don't. Ms. [the staffer] wants to leave this party unescorted in the Oval Office and it's simply against protocol. Someone has to escort them at all times while in the White House."

Safely beyond the VIPs' earshot, Mrs. Clinton oozed her typical hostility. Fending off her tongue-lashing, I referred again to my official post protocol. I had to be ready for emergency response. Trouble didn't wait for tours. Someone once dropped dead in my area. I had to act. But this wasn't the first time Mrs. Clinton berated me. She simply didn't understand what the UD did, never bothered to learn about her new surroundings or personnel. She wanted things done. I was there to create a secure environment, and escorting her VIPs prevented that. When she finished slinging expletives, pointing her finger up at me (I'm 6'2" and she's 5'4" tops) and openly threatening my career, I suggested a solution.

"What I would recommend is that they go to the Roosevelt Room. That way they can be supervised as long as they stay there and I'm not called away. If I'm called away, they will have to be sent back to the West Wing Lobby. That's the best I can think of at this time, but they simply can't stay in the Oval Office."

"Ugh. Fine." She stormed off.

Her staffer glared at me. I killed their VIPs with kindness, as Roosevelt Room protocol differs from the Oval Office's. I found a framed picture in the president's study and brought it out to them. One of the ladies was in the picture, and the rest were clearly jealous.

When the First Lady and her staffer returned, our guests informed Mrs. Clinton how much they enjoyed their time, the pictures, and the stories "the officer" told of the Roosevelt Room. She grabbed me by the arm, pretending we were the best of friends and that she loved the Secret Service.

Her personality adversely affected those entrusted with her safety. If I noticed that a new officer was as high-strung as she was, I'd carefully hint to him or her that perhaps they might seek another assignment. The sense of high drama she exuded would only burn them out physically or emotionally. Worse, they might overact on the job or be so stressed out that they would start messing up, might even leave an Uzi submachine gun on the bumper of the presidential limo—that had happened once.

It was strange: Hillary Clinton always looked uncomfortable around her husband, let alone anyone else. I can't call her shy, but she was definitely standoffish. She never relaxed. She never allowed herself any off-hours or off-duty candor. I couldn't imagine being like that—always having to say or do the right thing, always calculating. Human beings need confidants, friends, family, people they can relax with, but the First Lady was always wound up, an unhappy captive of her own sense of mission.

Opposites attract. That's why on paper, the First Couple was perfectly matched. But *their* opposites were *too* opposite.

Bill Clinton was friendly and charming with just about everyone besides Hillary. He always seemed to want to give his company extra time. He was very generous that way. Like him or not, share his political ideas or not, find yourself in the same room with him, and you are hooked. You can't help but like him.

But that was not Hillary. She was clearly all business, 24/7. Her private leadership style was based on pure fear and loathing—and I never saw her that turn off. Even in the president's presence, Mrs. Clinton operated at far greater than arm's length—a cheerless grifter always on her scheming way to someone or something else more important than the person directly in front of her.

If you saw them privately, they never seemed to meld at all. But turn on a camera or bring in a fat-cat donor, and the ice suddenly melted. They'd smile at each other, laugh, trade little jokes. They'd move in closer to each other, turn warmer—yes, even romantic. They might even hold hands. They could flip that emotional light switch whenever they had to, then switch it back off again when the crowds and cameras departed.

It was all a business for them: Clinton, Inc.

At a White House event for agents and their wives, the Clintons invited UD officers who worked closely in the West Wing, and I was honored to be included. The agents weren't too thrilled, which made it that much sweeter. It was a big deal to Genny.

As usual, the First Couple posed for a seemingly endless amount of pictures. At receptions, they never got a chance to eat so much as an hors-d'oeuvre. Standing the entire time in the horribly over-heated room and struggling to stay awake, the president would play little pranks on guests he felt comfortable with. I almost felt guilty about getting a picture with him, but Genny insisted.

The four of us—myself, the First Couple, and my wife—posed for a photo. I put my hand behind Mrs. Clinton, and immediately my hand was grabbed by a soft hand that placed it on Mrs. Clinton's rear. I was mortified and just froze. *Snap.* The picture was taken, and we thanked the president profusely but were whisked away so the next couple could get their photo. I leaned over to Genny.

"Uh, I think the president just put my hand on the First Lady's [bum]."

"You think that was funny, the president kept, like, *rubbing* my back!"

Aghast, we didn't know what to make of it. We received the picture in the mail and still laugh about it. Everyone looks awkward—*because we were!* But don't get me wrong, that was classic President Clinton. He was never dull.

The First Lady had a different sort of liveliness. She once threw a Bible at an agent on her detail, hitting him in the back of the head. He bluntly let her know it wasn't acceptable. He told me that story himself. Assignment to her detail was a form of punishment handed down by passive-aggressive middle management.

She hated smokers, even seeing them. In high-stress jobs, even among her own staffers, smoking was popular. One of my UD buddies on the South Lawn always kept a single cigarette, a big long Benson & Hedges, for when Mrs. Clinton walked by. He would step out of his booth and light one up just so she could see him blowing big plumes. Without making eye contact, he would flick it so she saw it.

When her detail passed, Mrs. Clinton expected everyone else to disappear. She didn't want to see anyone in the White House halls, as if the whole place were her *personal* Executive Mansion. It was insulting. People scurried as if in a giant game of hide-and-seek. An agent traveling ahead of her would direct people to disappear, usually into a nearby closet or alcove.

Once when the First Couple stayed at a hotel, the SA ahead of their detail grabbed another officer and me to duck into a tiny, cramped, kitchenette-like area. "This is ridiculous," I complained.

"Just the way it is. Suck it up," said the agent.

"What are we here for? How am I supposed to protect the president, her, or anyone else if I'm in a closet? Are we here to do a job or not?"

I waited for the First Couple's detail to radio when they approached before emerging to stand my post—to perform my duty. They passed. The First Lady ignored my existence. The SAs behind her glared at me as if they wanted me to spontaneously catch fire.

"Big shot, huh?" said the agent, exiting the kitchenette.

"Just doing my job," I said. "It's insulting that I should just disappear because the very sight of us bothers her."

8.

CLINTON WORLD

When Bill Clinton arrived in January 1993, so did a new presidential chief of staff. Mack McLarty was a longtime Clinton friend and political ally from Hope, Arkansas, but he was simply in over his head in his new job, and he quickly lost control of a grossly immature White House staff, whose idea of propriety fluctuated somewhere between that of a political campaign office—and of an empty-pizza-box-strewn college dorm. Sloppy, disrespectful Clinton staffers spilled so much coffee and soda in West Wing offices and hallways that the stains overwhelmed General Services Administration staff. GSA finally gave up on cleaning the carpets and replaced them wholesale.

The president set the tone, wanting to keep his Oval Office door open all the time. That was his style. He'd welcome each colleague or staffer directly into the office, hearing them out directly. He loved granting everyone open access. But his approach destroyed any sense of hierarchy. Soon it obliterated what little sense of decorum had previously existed. It created chaos. Staffers often didn't see the need to go through his personal secretary, Betty Currie, or anyone at all.

How the Clintons even managed to run Arkansas I never knew.

Betty and Appointments Secretary Nancy Hernreich found themselves shooing away his campaign staffers, who massaged their own egos by treating a sitting president of the United States like an old slap-on-the-back pal. Some kept referring to him as Governor or Bill rather than as Mr. President. At first, Mr. Clinton, a great schmoozer, enjoyed the laid-back camaraderie, but it wasted his time and left him unfocused. Staffers from all over the White House loved to loiter in the West Wing because it gave them a sense of being important and *needed*. The atmosphere made our hallways noisy and crowded. When things got tough—as when scandals needed clamping down—there were people everywhere.

Early on, while Mack McLarty remained chief of staff, the president scheduled an Oval Office address to the nation. Cameras and teleprompters stood ready to roll. As the doors behind the president closed, a staffer came sprinting down the hallway. Her surname was Rodham, just like Hillary's maiden name, and she may have been a cousin of some sort. The Clintons seemed to like her. Usually I had no problems with her other than having to remind her to wear her pass and keep it right side up.

Today she was going too fast for me to worry about just her pass. Ms. Rodham was heading hell-bent-for-leather for the Oval Office.

"Whoa! Just stop!" I ordered her, physically blocking her path.

"Move!" she commanded, maneuvering to get past me.

"They're broadcasting. I can't let you in." I couldn't believe she would just barge in at will.

"*This* is the correct speech," she fumed, waving a computer disk. "They have *the wrong speech!*"

I blocked her again. Her story didn't pass the smell test—on any level. "How could that be right?" I asked, and emphasized that by entering now, she'd risk jolting a cameraman and ruining a presidential address—she might even trigger a minor national panic if she knocked the camera over. I steered her over to Betty, whom I trusted to discreetly sort it all out. Thankfully, Ms. Rodham was wrong. It was *she* who had the wrong floppy disk.

I wish that incident was unique. In July 1994, Leon Panetta replaced Mack McLarty. He cleaned house and restored order. The free world was safer—and so was the White House carpeting.

Panetta was widely respected and by reputation quiet, formidable, serious, passionate—neither a blowhard nor an ideologue. Our first interaction sent shivers down my spine. Inside the Roosevelt Room, Panetta conferred with Rahm Emanuel, George Stephanopoulos, and assorted other Clinton heavyweights. It was an informal meeting, and Panetta was getting a feel for everyone and letting it play out as if he were a fly on the wall. I saw someone with their feet propped up on a table. President Clinton entered, and Panetta stood to greet him—the only one to do so. The pair of feet resting on that table remained at ease.

The president departed, and Panetta quietly ripped into *his* staff. I'll never forget it. I never heard him curse or yell, but he certainly had a way of being heard: "The next time one of you doesn't stand when the president enters—I don't care what your reason is or what you did to get the president here—it is unacceptable. And that's all."

The next day the White House was more serious and focused, yet less frenzied, as if it was finally getting down to work! It was great. Someone had dared to issue marching orders. Panetta expected results.

Congressional elections approached. It's strange how command-and-control structures take their cue from the top. The Clintons didn't create the political correctness movement, nor did they invent "noncombative combatant" mindset. But diversity encroached on merit. Professionalism degraded. As these plagues became more blatant, they became more contagious. Office promiscuity, DUIs, unprofessionalism, leadership from behind, and unethical behavior had all existed well before the Clintons. Now they accelerated. After the Clintons arrived, interoffice politics were exacerbated—not because of Panetta but because of the president.

On September 13, 1994, the federal Assault Weapons Ban became law. It accomplished nothing beyond humoring gun control advocates. It protected no one. What difference did it make (to borrow a phrase from Mrs. Clinton) if the month before that a potential assassin like Francisco Duran attacked the White House with a regular SKS or with a 1911? None. But what did I know? I was only trained in firearms by one of the most elite federal agencies.

Leon Panetta walked up to me outside. "Hey, Officer. They're about to sign. You want to come in and see? Come on in."

"Thank you, Mr. Panetta, but I'm fine out here. It's not really Uniformed Division policy."

"Oh, come on." He waved me into the jam-packed Oval Office.

"Thank you, sir. I appreciate that, but to be honest it's not really my cup of tea."

I was honored, however, that he asked. He knew my name and thought to make small talk. He is a great man, and you bet I shared that story with other UD officers. I believe Leon Panetta genuinely placed America's well-being first and foremost. I never took his politics personally.

While I did my job and kept my head down, a series of scandals tarnished the Clinton brand and presidency. They weighed on the administration, but they were never (at least, then) *my problem.*

They commenced, of course, long before Inauguration Day 1993. During the preceding election, a cabaret singer and former Little Rock TV news reporter named Gennifer Flowers revealed that she had been candidate Clinton's mistress for twelve years. Other women quickly emerged from the woodwork, stirring a media frenzy. Some were mistresses. Some alleged they were victims of sexual harassment—even rape. There were actresses, career businesswomen, and former employees. It seemed too strange *not* to be true, but not everyone believed them. The Clinton pattern was deny-deny-deny. Behind the scenes, the Clinton Machine slut-shamed accusers, impugned their integrity, and supposedly even paid them off and intimidated them.

The major scandal emerged in 1994. Paula Corbin Jones, an Arkansas state clerical employee, sued now-president Clinton for sexual harassment. It all seemed like unpresidential celebrity news gossip. Again, this didn't involve me, so I didn't care.

And then there was Whitewater, with a lot of money moving around in unethical ways. The Clintons had invested about $200,000 in Arkansas's Whitewater Development Corporation, losing $67,000 of it when the feds shuttered Whitewater for cooking its books and acting as a money-laundering front for local politicians and favor-seeking businesses. How the Clintons could invest so much money while wallowing in $50,000 of campaign debt still mystifies me.

Operating Whitewater was Jim McDougal, an Arkansas power player and former congressional candidate with ties to the Clintons, though supposedly he never involved either Clinton in his illegalities. To defend himself against federal charges, McDougal engaged Mrs. Clinton's former law firm, Little Rock's Rose Law Firm. Afterward McDougal, out of the goodness of his heart, hosted a fundraiser to erase Clinton's campaign debts. Authorities finally convicted McDougal of multiple felony conspiracy charges. Other scandals followed.

Meanwhile, a real under-the-media-radar, tough-on-corruption judge, Ken Starr, a man I later learned to both respect and loathe, took up the Whitewater investigation. I'd never heard of him before, but Starr's name soon was in every newspaper. He was a bloodhound, locking on the Clintons' scent, though I still shrugged everything off as mere tall talk.

Nothing revealed President Clinton's lax attitude toward his personal security more than his jogging routine. Nobody could get a straight answer from him on the Shakespearean question: "To jog—or not to jog?" Nobody could. Not even the armored vehicle squad who would trail him if he did. Not the military liaison who safeguarded the nuclear "football," the satchel enabling the president to launch a nuclear strike when away from the White House.

Each morning PPD and UD hovered near the Executive Residence entrance to spy his attire. Running clothes and sneakers or a suit? A suit and we returned to our normal posts—we knew he was on his way to the Oval Office. Sneakers, and all hands on deck. Agents had to devise ways to jog with enough concealed firepower to protect him and also to adapt to his spontaneous choice of route. Officers and agents had to adjust their PT schedule to his whim. We struggled to avoid endangering or snarling regular D.C. traffic while covering him as best we could. The Service's version of SWAT teams stayed as close as possible, but it was a shit show.

Once, UD officers stationed on the lawn spied President Clinton heading out for a jog, but his PPD wasn't in sight. A friend of mine on entry-control duty pursued the president in full gear at breakneck speed until the PPD finally caught up with both of them.

UD personnel made arrests, questioned suspicious people, and occasionally, when President Clinton outpaced his motorcade and his protecting agents, also sprinted after an essentially isolated and completely unprotected chief executive. He just didn't care. In his book, *Within Arm's Length,* Special Agent Dan Emmett even detailed a frightening near-assassination attempt during one of these reckless jogs.*

If, however, the president wasn't jogging, we hurriedly stowed our gear, redressed, returned the motorcade cars, PT'd if possible, and hiked back on regular posts all in a manner of minutes—*a freaking nightmare.* Finally, someone donated money for a private jogging track on the South Lawn's circular roadway.

The First Lady also jogged. I was posted on the South Roadway and she emerged from the Executive Mansion wearing a ball cap, gloves, gray sweatshirt, and black jogging pants. She was clearly fuming about something.

"Evergreen walking down South Lawn looking like she's heading to the gate," I heard in my ear from the officer at the gate. It sent the signal to me: *Where's her SA detail?*

"Be advised, FLPD [First Lady's Protective Detail] is aware. They are on their way."

I can't forget the look on one of their faces—he was a big muscular guy still wearing his suit—as he looked at us, rolled his eyes, and flung his hands up in the air, as if to say *Here we go again!* He sprinted across the lawn to catch up. A few more agents, still struggling to don jogging attire, followed his lead. Meanwhile, Mrs. Clinton neared an exit gate. The officer manning it agonized over what

---

* Dan Emmett, *Within Arm's Length: The Extraordinary Life and Career of a Special Agent in the United States Secret Service* (Bloomington, IN: iUniverse, 2012).

to do if she demanded that he open it. Or whether he should abandon his post and fall in behind her if he did!

Some agents literally went mad. Many turned to alcohol, drugs, performance enhancers, affairs (sometimes at the workplace), and even prostitutes and other dangerous habits. A "f— it" mentality trickled down.

Our intel briefings provided us with no-nonsense intelligence agency data on international and domestic terrorism developments. They always referenced Osama bin Laden. We also learned which morons had tried to hop the fence, attempted suicide at entry posts, or swung at a Secret Service agent, a Metro police officer, or a UD, and how each incident had unfolded. We discussed suspicious types snapping photos and the like. All of our national monuments and, of course, the president were top terrorist targets. That's public knowledge. But much more remains classified.

I can, however, disclose details of two very well-known events. I wasn't on post either day—for which my colleagues never ceased giving me crap.

It was the evening of September 12, 1994. A good friend of mine, a Secret Service Emergency Response Team (ERT) officer I'll call Keith, guarded the South Lawn. He spied a single-prop Cessna plane swooping just over the tree line, heading straight for him. After shitting his britches, Keith sprinted and hopped over some bushes to reach some safety alongside the building. That was all he could do. *BAM!* The Cessna crashed, wedging itself, contorted and mangled, against the doctor's office in the Executive Residence. Keith was the first to arrive at the crash. He yanked open the Cessna's door. The pilot's head had rotated nearly 180 degrees! He was obviously dead. Fuel poured over the lawn, but duty—and training—compelled Keith to check for a pulse.

Posing as a tourist, the dead pilot—Frank Corder—had conducted a pre-advance, reconnoitering the grounds from the South Lawn fence line. Corder calculated distances, what dotted the ground, clearances, and so on. He wasn't trying to crash the plane or pull a suicide attack; he was trying to land the plane safely for an international stunt, copying daredevil German pilot Mathias Rust, who had taken off from Finland and landed in Red Square, Moscow, to expose Soviet vulnerabilities. Rust had been promptly arrested. Corder promptly died.

Ironically, Corder posed relatively little immediate threat to the First Family. With the White House undergoing renovations, the First Family was temporarily residing across the avenue at Blair House.

On October 29, 1994, a trench coat–clad man loitered by the North Lawn fence—a definite red flag. UD eyed him, but he hadn't yet reached "reasonable suspicion" level. Meanwhile, a political office staffer (instead of the usual Tours Section officer) detoured a special guest tour from its typical route to view the North Lawn staircase—a rare privilege and clearly outside of protocol. The UD officer manning the moat area warned that staffer against taking the tour through there. The staffer insisted. A tourist beyond the Pennsylvania Avenue fence line pointed at a tall, gray-haired man who was a part of the tour group and screamed, "Look! There he is!"

Francisco Martin Duran, the man in the trench coat, thought the gray-haired man was President Clinton. From under his coat, he whipped out a Chinese-made SKS magazine-fed rifle, spraying twenty-nine AK-47 caliber rounds over the lawn and hitting the West Wing Press Lobby, where an officer scrambled to prevent the journalists from jumping out the window for a better view.

"You can't stop us. We're the press!" one shouted as he tried prying himself through a window.

A bullet struck that window. A moment sooner, it could have struck him.

Duran kept firing from the hip while jogging backward—there's a YouTube video of it. It was a panic. Even Duran wasn't sure whether to continue firing or to escape. With *any* tactical training he could have easily gunned down several of the officers or even the president—*if* that gray-haired man really were the president. Officers didn't have a clear shot. What you can't see in the video are civilians near Duran freezing and running after the shock of the gunfire. Out of ammunition, Duran dropped his magazine on the sidewalk and retrieved another from his coat pocket.

Three civilian bystanders tackled him. Watch the YouTube home-video vacation footage turned impromptu assassination evidence, and you'll see a man in a comically tall and wide cowboy hat tackle Duran exhibiting zero regard for his own life and safety. What most people don't know is this: that Texan was ironically well known to us as a frequent White House "caller" who demanded to see the president. I'd dealt with him before, but that day he rose above and beyond the call of any civilian's duty.

Officers cornered Duran, their guns pointed squarely at his head. Among them was a UD ERT officer who had vaulted the fence—we called him Flying Harry, and he was a workplace friend and later an SA. Instead of returning fire through the fence, Flying Harry bolted headlong *over* it to isolate his own field of fire and to safeguard White House visitors. He, along with the three civilians who reacted without any training to run toward the fight, were heroes.

Secret Service higher-ups told Congress that the Duran incident resulted from a lack of funds and from not being permitted to secure a wider perimeter. But what the UD did that day was exactly what it was trained for. There was no friendly fire. No deadly mistaking civilians for assassins. Everything went according to plan—well, mostly—according to plan.

It was, however, a massive learning experience. The lack of a common radio network cost us a few seconds of reaction time. In a perfect world we should have checked Duran sooner, but we weren't there to check everyone with a bulge in their pocket and a big belly, though some in the Secret Service wanted it that way.

Another acquaintance of mine also hopped the fence that day and ended up holding a bystander at gunpoint. That wasn't a mistake. That was actually necessary diligence. We can't assume just one shooter. The bystander later told the FBI that he could hear and see the hammer de-cock on the officer's SIG pistol. You can bet there were a lot of itchy trigger fingers at the White House that day. Yes, days like that shatter complacency—until things settle down again.

Following Francisco Duran's failed attempt, everyone submitted his or her own report for evidence. A UD officer on the portico (I'll call him Henry) raced toward the gunfire, ending up near where officers collared Duran. When Henry submitted his report to his lieutenant (henceforth known as the Editor), he was pressured to change his statement—*to lie*. The Editor absurdly believed that Henry should have remained at his post and not chased the gunfire— an absolutely ridiculous idea. He handed Henry a doctored report. Henry refused to sign it.

Later, when prosecutors were preparing their case against Duran, they requested that officers review their reports. Again, that's just routine due diligence. Henry reviewed his. "Yeah, I thought this might be a problem," he responded.

"What do you mean?"

"That's not my statement. *This* is my statement," he said, producing his original, *undoctored* report.

Henry had anticipated that the Editor would proceed with filing a falsified report. Higher-ups reamed out the Editor. Word of his offense traveled as high as the director of the agency. Had federal prosecutors presented a falsified statement, their whole case could have been questioned.

As strange as it seems, Duran could have gotten away with it. That's why the quality of being "worthy of trust and confidence" remains pivotal for the Secret Service. The Editor kept his job and even filed a lawsuit a few years later for not being promoted. The Service should have shit-canned him immediately. But it wanted the story squashed and couldn't if it had fired him.

On the presidential staff side, the scandals never ended. Staffers remained on high alert, but facing a constant barrage of daily headlines, they failed to focus on clear priorities. I almost felt bad for them. Many were good people trying to do right. They didn't seek the limelight—I can empathize with that. They just wanted to serve their country's leadership and implement their common vision. I can respect that, too.

Once the president's national security advisor emerged from Betty Currie's office after presenting a briefing. Making a sharp left turn, he looked distinctly off-kilter. Proceeding gingerly down the hallway, he shifted his papers to his left hand, touching everything with his right: the furniture, the walls, the door to the Roosevelt Room, the table, the plant on it, the credenza, and the next doorjamb. He looked as if he was losing it. I did not envy him.

Conversely, President Clinton's cool-cucumber personality impressed me. Nothing seemed to get him down. He was pure Teflon, always displaying a good positive humor. It helps explain his incredible magnetism. He just had a magical way about him. Maybe it was his radio voice or his James Bond–like demeanor. My father could *fix* a rock. President Clinton could *charm* a rock.

"If the president told me my name wasn't Gary Byrne, I'd have to check my name tag," I told people. If I had only one way to describe President Clinton, that was it.

I once needed to write up an incident that occurred in the fence line area. It was the midnight shift, and I asked the control clerk, a UD officer, if she could type the document for me. I confided to her how nervous I normally was about writing or typing anything, how I certainly didn't want my dyslexia to screw up a legal document. She was glad to help. When she handed me the finished document, she advised me that our watch commander was still at his Old Executive Office Building office. If I hurried, I'd catch him right in time.

I was still a new guy to the job—so naïve!

I raced to his office and knocked twice. Not waiting for an answer, I swung his door open—and froze. What I saw was *not good*. His office lights were off, but hallway lights allowed me to see what I didn't want to see: him screwing a female sergeant on the desk!

"Uh, I'll come back later." I closed the door much faster than I opened it.

Taking into account their, er, position and his office's dim light I hoped they didn't recognize me. But the hallway light silhouetted me, and my height and build were fairly noticeable. I later passed the super in the hallway and made small talk. I made a mental note to remember to forget what I saw. But I never forgot the look on that control clerk's face when I next saw her: It was an expression of pure satisfaction. She had placed me in an incredibly difficult spot with both my watch commander and my sergeant, severely damaging team dynamics. Every grievance I might have had in the future, I very well might attribute to their character flaws—a pretty easy case to make when you see management screwing other officers on their desk.

I came to believe that that control clerk hoped I'd spread the word: "Hey, guys, I walked in on . . ." I didn't dare. I didn't blab.

Power corrupts, as they say. Leon Panetta pondered such matters in his book, *Worthy Fights: A Memoir of Leadership in War and Peace*. Ninety percent of the personalities who get into the White House are hotshot types. They're overzealous about everything they do: relationships, sex, money, nightlife, and power. And everything gained *by* power can be used *to gain* more of it. I didn't catch on quickly enough that sex was a part of that. But I caught on enough to know it was trouble and to abstain. People got transferred. Careers got ruined. Most important, favoritism, drama, and distractions hampered the mission.

I was serving on post during a photo op for an SA who was leaving the PPD. Before retiring or being transferred, agents (but not UD officers) could pose for a photo with their families and the president. It meant a lot to them.

This agent, however, was being transferred to what might as well have been Siberia, punishment for his general office drama and for various other behavioral issues. The Secret Service was saving itself an embarrassment.

Being the genius that he was, this hotshot asked me to ward off So-and-So—his mistress! What the hell was I supposed to do, sweep a broom at her feet? Coldcock her? She had a White House pass and was even part of the Arkansas Mafia!

I spent the next half hour or so nervously watching the members of this unholy love triangle eye each other with open scorn. I just prayed, *Please, don't let this blow up in front of the president's face!*

Stuff like that happened far more than it should. Why? Because superiors told us one thing and did another. Leadership—in both the Service and the administration—often conveyed the message that bad behavior was truly bad only if it made headlines. I called it the Caesar mentality: Do as I say, not as I do, or off with your head.

Who could take the orders seriously when rumors flew that even the president was having midnight calls of his own?

Increasingly, I had reason to pray.

Please, don't let this blow up in front of the president's face!

9.

OKLAHOMA CITY

April 19, 1995: Betty Currie waved me into her office. A few staffers stared at her small television set. President Clinton hadn't yet arrived, though I was sure he'd already gotten the news.

We didn't need CNN to tell us what we saw: a massive bomb had exploded at downtown Oklahoma City's Alfred P. Murrah Federal Building. Only half the building remained. Half was smoking rubble. We all thought, *Somebody seriously screwed up*, but hardly anyone spoke. This was an attack on the federal government. This was an attack on *us*.

Maybe I shouldn't say it, but the ugly, bitter truth is that whenever a tragic, horrific attack happens, I feel vindicated. All of those like me do. We signed up to stop people like these monsters. We think about that every day. Most other people go about their lives and forget. Incidents like this remind them of the terrible risks society faces.

That April morning, 168 persons were murdered just for doing their jobs. Each casualty was someone exactly like us. I just happened to be in D.C.; they just happened to be in Oklahoma City. I recalled the 1993 World Trade Center bombing.

The White House sprang into high alert. So did every military and federal installation. I tried to keep a good humor. "Some Middle Eastern country's getting bombed tomorrow," I let slip.

A voice behind me said, "Well, not so fast, young man. It could be domestic. But we'll get this sorted out," said President Bill Clinton.

I was mortified. "Sorry, Mr. President," I said, turning to keep my head low and dismissing myself.

I asked a nearby PPD agent if we had a field office there.

"Yeah." He bit the side of his mouth and added, "There was also an all-agency day care on the bottom floor for any agent to drop off their kids for free day care, too. Perk of the job," he added sorrowfully.

We later learned our field office was the attackers' target.

Every UD officer checked their gun box and FAT kit and made ready. Secret Service closed Pennsylvania Avenue, Fifteenth Street, and Seventeenth Street. Everyone asked "what if?" and came up short on answers.

Concrete barriers on a portion of Pennsylvania Avenue created a permanent pedestrian-only area. But D.C. streets were never designed for this, and the move bewildered and frankly scared visitors and tourists.

After Oklahoma City, the value placed on our warnings increased, if only for a time.

A month later, May 24, 1995, and the day was coming to a close. It was dusk, and the White House spotlights switched on, illuminating the South East lawn and . . .

"Crash-Crash!"

Every serviceman couldn't help but hear it. A Bandbox radio report blared that a fence jumper was sprinting toward the White House. Hindsight is close to 20/20. Only later do you know "something" was really nothing. But we had been trained and engrained to think Benghazi, long before Benghazi. We knew of the siege of the Iranian embassy in London, the U.S. embassy in Tehran, the 1993 WTC bombing, the Japanese embassy takeover in Peru, Beirut's U.S. embassy bombing, and 1992's Israeli embassy attack in Argentina. You hear "Crash-Crash" and you don't know what's next.

Following *this* "Crash-Crash," UD Officer Scott Giambattista sprinted toward a fence jumper (who, by the way, *wanted* suicide by cop). They raced uphill through the pachysandra and toward the mansion, passing a set of floodlights. Another UD officer, Dave Levine, fired a single shot at the fence jumper. *Bull's-eye!* But his bullet passed through the fence jumper's left arm, seriously wounding Scott in *his* left forearm as Scott tackled him. Dave and Scott were friends and both were top-notch guys. It wasn't fly-ball gazing that screwed them over—they had each lived up to the level of the Service's training for such incidents. It was, however, a result of miscommunication in an incredibly fast-moving situation. White House lawns aren't open fields. They're a maze of booths, roads, paths, trees, hedges, and bushes. There's even a moat. It's invisible from the fence line, but trust me, it's there.

The Secret Service simply lacked the budget, time, and leadership to support training that properly dealt with intersecting fields of fire, sprinting fence jumpers, *and* adaptive light situations (that is, at dawn and dusk when light sources are shifting and make pursuit difficult). Fence jumpers pose an extra hazard because they sprint. Shooters, at least, take a fixed position, landing themselves in our kill zone. Hunting fence jumpers is like hunting quail—birds that wait in the brush and once spooked, spring out and fly past you. Quail fly up five feet and then travel laterally—just like fence jumpers. Get a bead on a sprinter, and your field of fire can trap a teammate. It's why we drill, drill, drill: *Know what's behind your target*. Mistakes can happen to complacent or inexperienced quail hunters, just like what happened to Vice President Dick Cheney when he shot his pal. Another happened to Scott and Dave, both highly trained, great guys.

The incident highlighted one of our major weaknesses in dealing with these damn fence jumpers. Dave and Scott did everything right; they just did the right thing *at the same time*. It's a hazard of the job. But let's not forget: They stopped the bad guy. Had Dave or Scott been an agent, the White House staff would have erected statues on the lawn, but they were UD.

Scott underwent surgery at George Washington University Hospital. The president phoned and thanked him profusely. What the president didn't know—certainly no one was going to delay a call from *the* president—was that Scott was a little wonky having just come out of surgery. "Hey! Hey, Bill," Scott babbled, "we should have a barbecue up at Camp David! It'd be great."

"Well, that's an idea, Scott," said the president, chuckling.

That cracked us up and became a running joke. Obviously nobody was going to have a barbecue to celebrate an officer's getting shot. Still, there were times when the administration did convey its appreciation (and the president's call meant *a great deal* to us all). From then on whenever someone tried saying something serious, we'd interrupt: "Hey! Let's have a barbecue!"

One of my greatest honors—and I knew it at the time—was when the First Couple vacationed on Block Island, Rhode Island, in August 1997 and were doing something as a family, getting ice cream with Chelsea. Maybe it was all for show, or maybe the First Family really did want some normalcy in their lives.

I worked the rope line. Even a simple ice cream run is a celebrity event for a president. Presidential Protection Detail agents singled me out to screen people inside the store before the First Family entered. I remained inside as the Clintons purchased ice cream. The agents remained outside. For a few minutes, as the president paid, it was just the Clintons, shop employees, and myself. No agents—just me. It was a profound honor.

Soon the spectacle moved outside. As the Clintons walked, every PPD SA spied a shirtless drunk fast approaching. "That's my girl!" he shouted, "Hillary! Hillary! That's my girl! Hillary!" Agents closed in behind him as he weaved through the rope line. Fathers shielded family members from this buffoon. He kept yelling, caring nothing for rope lines—hell, he didn't even care to wear a shirt.

"Hey!" I addressed him loudly, amiably, and disingenuously. "Can you do me a favor? Squat down for a sec."

He probably thought I was going to let him under the rope line. Crouching down, he looked up at me with big gullible eyes. I shoved him in the chest—maybe his head—and he plopped on the cement sidewalk. I fretted about using too much force, but the Service backed me up.

One day I felt the same heebie-jeebies I had in catching that spy years before at the Air Force Thunderbirds air show. Two CIA officers mysteriously arrived at the Secret Service training center with no purpose listed for their visit. I requested their IDs. Everything checked out.

"Well, how about this one?" one said, plopping down a different driver's license and passport on the table.

I ran the new documents, and they checked out, too. "Are you serious?" I said. They just laughed.

"What about this one?" the same guy said. "And this one?" He kept plopping down credentials with different *names*—but the *same* face.

His passports and driver's licenses came from different countries and even different government agencies—but were all valid, at least as far as I or anyone else in my position could tell. He smiled at me, and I knew this guy was the real-deal Secret Squirrel or Jason Bourne, operating far beyond the front lines for his country.

I just kept thinking, *F— me, these guys really do exist.* Every foreign country, whether friendly, enemy, or less-than-friendly, employed its own off-the-book types. Each eyed the White House and our security installations. As for this CIA operative, he just gave me a pat on the shoulder and walked right in for his meeting.

International intrigue—and real security issues—don't stop at the president's door. Special Agent Dan Emmett's book, *Within Arm's Length,* describes a tense moment when Syrian president Hafez al-Assad conferred in 1993 with U.S. leadership. Emmett was fully ready—on a hair-trigger—to draw his SIG P229 and protect the president against Assad's bodyguard's Czech-made, fully automatic Škorpion machine pistols.

My hold-your-breath moments occurred in 1993 when I interacted with the staffs of Israeli prime minister Yitzhak Rabin and Palestine Liberation Organization head Yasser Arafat at the White House for the signing of the Oslo Peace Accord. Everybody feigned amiability, but I couldn't help but feel that at any given moment, everyone in the room with two hands (let alone a firearm) was going to be at each other's throats. I had never felt such a feeling emanating between anyone, and I can only describe it as pure hate. The president literally had to coax the two sides to shake hands. His vaunted charm and charisma really did break the ice between intensely wary adversaries.

One Palestinian delegate looked just like my mother. I broke my own ice with their group by mentioning it. That was my two seconds of diplomacy as I mentioned that my mother was Lebanese. Looking beyond each delegation's smiles and surface formality, the Service reported to us that they believed that both diplomatic staffs were actually highly trained operatives. The Palestinians, we were told, were crazy enough to try anything. As far as I was concerned, they'd made it to the negotiating table by having their henchmen explode suicide vests. I wouldn't put anything past them. Each person maneuvered through the rooms and hallways as if they were just finding a spot. All of us were thinking: *Who will my partners kill? Who I am responsible for putting down?*

My stomach always twists when I get nervous, but my palms don't sweat anymore after those meetings. I've never since had reason to sweat as much as I did watching those sessions. I knew two things really existed from then on: pure hate and spies.

This was the West Wing; the country was run from here. The most sensitive information in the world passed through it. Confidential, Secret, Classified, and Top Secret documents were commonplace. The UD helped create a secure environment. We had to ensure that sensitive documents stayed "eyes only." Just because someone enjoyed a clearance level didn't mean that person was deemed "need to know." This is why UD personnel needed to be impeccably trustworthy—trusted to secure documents, not to read them, and especially not to leak them.

Staffers might lack maturity, but it wasn't as though we could surveil them. When Clinton's administration gave way to George

W. Bush's, we knew—and I even saw—that some staffers were stealing the antique brass caps on the ends of the stairwells in the Old Executive Office Building. The administration dismissed this as office pranks, but lunches and even an agent's gun had been put in the incinerator burn bags.

What are burn bags? After a document had been left in the open or after a staffer was finished with it, it was locked up in a safe or placed in a burn bag. To newcomers, burn bags looked odd. They were the size of fall cleanup leaf bags, but marked with bright white and orange letters and stripes. A UD officer would swing by (I had that duty occasionally), make small talk, and load the bags onto a flat cart, take them to another location, and destroy them in a custom incinerator.

All classified documents had to be in a properly cleared person's immediate possession or locked in a safe—in other words, handled pretty much like firearms. Some documents were so hush-hush they had no electronic duplicates. Some staffers, usually policy makers, had the nasty habit of placing sensitive documents in their safes but not closing or locking them, or of leaving them in places that, while still in the White House, were vulnerable to the hundreds of other staffers, employees, visitors, tourists, and other people who worked there or simply passed through. At each shift start or when the president left the room, I ensured that safes were locked and their latches turned. If a classified document was left in the open—let's say the president dashed out for a quick photo op—a UD officer like myself secured it in our weapons locker until Betty Currie or the president returned.

Military men hardly ever left items unattended. Some of Vice President Al Gore's staffers—though not Gore himself—were notorious for such behavior, as well as for not closing or locking their safes. Per protocol, we'd secure these documents and report any infraction up the chain of command. Early on, I was even asked by my colleagues to talk to one staffer to reiterate the importance of closing up the office. Afterward staff really got on board, even checking with UD to ensure security.

The secretary of the Treasury notoriously abandoned materials on the Oval Office couch, in bathrooms, the Roosevelt Room, the Cabinet Room, and elsewhere. I secured his dossiers in my gun box a few times. That was our job. We were his safety net. A great deal weighed on high-level staffers' minds, but while they were in the West Wing, we were there to protect their sensitive materials. Each document—down to each page—had its protocols.

But soon the nation would witness the most sensational leaks—ones never anticipated by *any* protocol.

10.

MOLE

The November 1995 federal shutdown was great, at least for me. The White House was empty; our jobs were cake. We read or even snacked in plain view because no one saw us—though we never sat down. Well, maybe we sat just a little. You try standing for hours on end. Being able to sit at times felt like a gift from God. It is!

The shutdown meant that that nonessential federal workers temporarily hit the bricks—and temporarily lost their paychecks. None of this applied to White House interns. As unpaid labor, they were welcomed with open arms. Moreover, they now received greater responsibilities. I hoped they wouldn't be trusted with anything important, but they were.

Unfortunately, President Clinton, to his detriment, was left to his own devices. His wife was always the business partner, never the supporter. Before the shutdown, President Clinton was a complete opposite of his wife; he was unwaveringly jovial, a true extrovert. But once the shutdown arrived, he found himself surrounded by fair-weather friends or those who for professional reasons had to keep him at arm's length.

President Clinton had no support group. I always had my friends and my family. Even better, I never mixed family and friends with my profession. The president had clearly sacrificed whatever real friends and family he might have had. I've mentioned that I never saw the First Couple so much as hold hands without cameras present. Once in the spotlight, they were warm. But that was a lie. Portraying the Clintons as a warm, middle-class family was a calculated marketing ploy, mere political theater. And that was never clearer than during the shutdown.

Without his cheerleaders, President Clinton was alone and looked it. Every president gets gray, but the president's salt-and-pepper hair turned white. His eyes—the windows to his soul—aged even faster. I wished so badly, as a man to a man, to give him a pat on the back. But he wasn't our friend, and surely he wasn't mine. He needed to find his own bootstraps.

Pre-shutdown, interns were no strangers to us, though I rarely interacted with most of them. Because of necessary security clearances and the sensitive things being decided, they had no reason to be in my sector nor elsewhere in the West Wing.

Unauthorized personnel and classified materials don't mix. As for the interns—*especially one of them*—we knew their ways. They pretended to be more important than they were. To gain West Wing access they'd stretch the truth, claiming they were delivering staffers' messages as a favor or were "just seeing a friend"—or my favorite, they were "just looking for a bathroom."

We called them straphangers and loiterers. Some tried to befriend us, even date or seduce us, to gain access to restricted areas and to power players. They were gold diggers as much as power diggers. They got their jobs thanks to political connections—that's all. I was suspicious of the whole gig.

One in particular—just a nobody, another pretty face to us—
quickly became a series of UD red flags. Monica Lewinsky thought
she was slick, but man, she was *obvious*. She played dumb to make
friends with White House staffers, Navy stewards, and even UD
officers—anything to get closer to her target, President Clinton. I
was often her biggest hurdle, but other officers also stood in her way
and soon wearied of her weaseling.

During the shutdown, Monica visited Betty Currie's office, and
because of the president's own failings, Monica gained the access
she coveted. We soon figured out her motives. *So did he*, and soon
they were having private "mentorship" meetings. He took her under
his wing—grooming her for politics.

Sure.

Some dismissed her as young, naïve, and "chatty." She even
invited one officer to her family beach house. She had often been a
straphanger when we were on break, but only for people in the president's path despite officially working nowhere near us. On break,
officers would remove their earpieces, unplug their mics, and crank
up the volume on their radios. UD and SAs knew the president's
every move (well, maybe not *every* move) and location, so Monica
hung around us batting her eyes until she overheard the president's
position or direction of travel, then bolted to maneuver into his
path. She lived for even his passing glance.

What (if anything) she did all day as an intern mystified me.
Some days she seemingly had nothing better to do than play I Spy
the President. I didn't care for her games but couldn't fully anticipate where they'd lead. Still, I knew this: Monica Lewinsky was serious trouble.

Nobody had the right to move about the White House on
his or her volition. The building revolved around a high-security,

compartmentalized system coordinated down to each individual. Monica was probing each avenue toward the president, and each UD officer in the rotations knew it.

"Ms. Lewinsky, without a specific reason or on the task of a staffer, you *cannot* be in the area," we'd lecture her.

She'd keep playing dumb, drawing from her well-thumbed playbook of lame excuses:

"I'm just here to use the bathroom."
"You mean I have to walk all the way around?"
"I just thought I'd check in on Betty."
"They asked me to deliver something here."
"I'm just here to see Nel [a White House steward]."
"I'm just here to see a friend."

She was maddening. Her excuses were insulting. Still, I tried never to take my work personally. Working the fence line I'd grown a thick skin against crackpots demanding to see the president. But did she really think her sorry pretexts would work? She was supposedly a smart person—hey, *someone* let her have her internship. But she was initially stationed at the East Wing or Old Executive Office Building—on the opposite side of the complex!

"Unless you have one of these [blue White House passes], you cannot be here," I scolded her, as if she were a misbehaving child. "Monica . . . Monica, you know you can't be here."

Eventually she would catch sight of me and swing a quick U-turn. That's how I *knew* she was probing the West Wing. Never knowing who was on shift, she was always scheming for a way in. If I was there, she'd just try again some other time. Or she'd try sneaking in via neighboring offices and corridors—a real red flag.

Mostly by word of mouth, through radios, post meetings, and brief-ings, UD officers communicated her actions, yet she persisted. A few UD officers besides myself (particularly a female officer named Sandy) butted heads with her.

A UD officer would block her. She'd go around to another hall-way. A different UD officer would check, and she'd give them a dif-ferent excuse for her presence—as if we didn't have radios. I made my notes but couldn't do any more than that. Meanwhile, she was establishing ties with the presidential staff, other White House staff, and Navy stewards.

Pre-shutdown, Monica and I had numerous awkward run-ins but apparently not enough for her to back off or for me to realize just whom I was dealing with. Then Monica—and other women—kept appearing even more. Initially I assumed it was all work, though with Monica that was very hard to believe. Eventually I didn't.

A new guy entered our rotation, and we didn't fill him in on anything beyond what was official. A White House switchboard operator would phone our post to have us get the president for an important call. On such a mission, he discovered Monica and the president in a compromising position, *as we by then all had*, either unprofessionally close, embracing each other, making out, or on the Oval Office desk. He was furious that we hadn't warned him. But we played matters *very* carefully. Everyone's post notes were as cryptic as mine. We feared for our careers, and with good reason.

It was incredibly awkward to be roped into the president's cheat-ing. I was a married man; many of us were. Professionally this was just very bad. The Clintons had enemies; Ken Starr was honing in on Whitewater. How could President Clinton so willfully involve us in his sordid games? What a far cry he was from his predecessor.

Why would a supposedly brilliant Rhodes scholar like Bill Clinton embark on such risks?

Once Monica appeared wearing a borderline unprofessional dress, a bit *too* short, if you asked me. I could only think, *Who does she think she is?* She was straphanging around George Stephanopoulos, and I shooed her like a stray cat. She hissed another lame excuse. I was fed up with her games, but at this moment the president arrived, easily catching her sight (or scent—I don't know which). They made small talk. She walked away. Her mission was complete; she had caught the president's wandering eye. She turned back to ensure she had his attention—and flipped up her black-and-white print dress to reveal her blue thong.

The president laughingly exclaimed something to the effect of "Hey, there!"

I wanted to vomit but ended up nervously laughing myself once the president disappeared into George's office. Were we *invisible* to them? Or did they feel *they* were invisible to *us*? Was all of this nonsense worth destroying his image? His very presidency?

And where was Mrs. Clinton? I couldn't be sure. PPD and FLOTUS detail agents coordinated their respective protectees' movements so as to avoid one another. They carefully communicated when the president was "with company."

I was sick of being put in awkward positions.

One weekend, the president was alone in the Oval Office. Monica appeared—*on a weekend*—with a stack of papers she claimed the president had requested. I snatched them from her hands. It was just a copy of his morning briefings, a collection of news articles. I informed her the president already had a set on his desk and that she had no business there. I handed them back to her. Her lying pissed me off. She departed, but about five minutes later, President Clinton emerged.

"Hey, Officer."

"Yes, Mr. President."

"Did someone come by here with some files for me?"

He wasn't asking. I knew the game. *Let the girl through, idiot!*

"No, sir, but if I see someone I'll let them know."

"Thanks," he said in his charming accent, adding a thumbs-up and a nod. His door shut.

"Was that as obvious to you as it was to me?" I asked another agent.

"I told you. That's how it is with them," he answered.

Soon I saw Monica peeking out from the nearby Roosevelt Room. The room had a phone, and she had clearly used it to call the president and alert him that she had just failed on her mission to reach the Oval Office.

But people *don't* just call the president. If she, as an intern, picked up the phone and said to a White House operator, "This is Monica the intern, I'd like to speak to the president, please," they'd hang up in disbelief. Most likely, they would inform their superior that some arrogant intern should be reprimanded for thinking she was worth even a second of the president's time.

So, something was going on . . . something *ominous*.

The White House Communications Agency (WHCA) maintains a top-secret phone line connecting senior military brass directly to the president. On Sundays, the WHCA calls to test it, and the officer on post, like myself, answers to ensure that it works. I usually answered, "Pizza Hut," and the WHCA guy would laugh.

But this was no laughing matter. The only way Monica could

have reached the Oval Office from the Roosevelt Room phone was to dial that same secret number.

The president had provided Monica Lewinsky with access to his direct line. He had given her a number so secret that it required not only a four-digit pass code but a rhythmically coded one, that is, one not just depending on the right numbers being entered but also for how long each digit key is depressed and even how long the pauses between digits last.

A PPD agent advised me to leave the matter alone. I should have listened, but I didn't. Why should I? I had a job to do. I was supposed to protect the president!

"You have no idea what it's like on the road," the agent would say with a smile. Was he warning me?

Every time I stopped Monica, I stuck my neck out. What the president did in the privacy of the Executive Mansion was his private business, but workplace ethics were involved here. Simultaneously, a new PPD agent bragged to me that he was "seeing" Monica. That stunned me, and I pulled him aside.

"She and the president have a behind-closed-doors kind of relationship," I warned him.

I was learning. Our mandatory, nauseatingly boring HR sexual harassment courses taught us that people like Monica were trouble. They cautioned that unless males and females worked together, they should avoid-avoid-avoid prolonged contact. They advised us to make notes of everything. Seemingly mundane matters might later prove vital. Make that note! Write down the date and time! Cover your ass, dammit!

Matters only got worse. On the behest of the other officers—and to cover my own ass—I approached a staff member for White House

Deputy Chief of Staff Evelyn Lieberman. Evelyn was not only the first female in her position, she was top-notch.

I didn't dare reveal to her staffer the nature of my concern. I could only tell her that I needed five minutes of her boss's time for an off-the-record talk. Lieberman and I conferred the very next day.

"What can I do for you, Gary?"

It was just me and her. She had work to do, and her tone said to cut to the chase.

My shoulders rose as I stammered, "I'm gonna ask you to do something, and I need you not to ask me why—I can't give you any details. If you want to do it, fine, but please don't ask me why. I think I'm overstepping my position, but I'm going to ask this anyway. Do you know the intern Monica?"

Arms folded, Evelyn responded, "Yeah?"

"You need to get her removed from here. She shouldn't be here. And it's not personal. But you should just get her removed from the West Wing. If you think I've overstepped, and you need to report me to the Secret Service, that's fine, too. But you should know I believe I have your—the administration's—best interest in mind."

I couldn't continue without providing details—"privileged information"—that I should neither have possessed knowledge of nor disclosed to others. It was government gossip, only the kind that could end my career, maybe even land me in jail. Trying to protect the president, I was professionally torn. The irony of my doing my government job and worrying if I might end up in jail was never lost on me. I think Evelyn realized this. I emphasized to her that I didn't care about how she did it (she could fire Monica, transfer her, or whatever), just that she safeguarded the president. I emphasized protecting the administration.

Lieberman was smart. She could read people. She read me enough to know that I knew what I was talking about. She trusted what I said because professional career women like Nancy, Betty, and Evelyn *could read President Clinton, too.*

The next day Monica was gone—transferred to the East Executive Building as a Social Office intern under the First Lady. She now had no way of getting near the West Wing. I had protected the president from himself and wanted the whole mess dead and buried.

Once the gossip died down, I felt I'd made the right decision, but I never told anyone that I had talked with Evelyn. I'm sure the president was perturbed by Monica's removal, but he wasn't supposed to interact with interns anyway, whether mentoring them or not. He should have honored the mission he had sworn to protect.

And where was the First Lady in all of this? I wasn't yet sure. What if she ran into the president with Monica or with another mistress? Would I have to protect the president from his irate wife—or even from a mistress?

It was nerve-racking. If FLOTUS came by while he was "with company," was I supposed to refuse her entry? But the Clintons didn't care for *us,* making that abundantly clear by placing us in such precarious positions. I do believe that Mrs. Clinton knew of the affairs, but how did she feel about an affair with someone of her own daughter's age? And in the Oval Office? In plain sight of us? Still, I don't think she knew of Monica.

The First Couple had blowout arguments when alone and while at work. The blue-glove scandal told me that. She would berate anyone, whether her personal attaché, lawyer, brand management people, all the way to regular White House Residence Staff and ushers or security like me. I had been reamed out before by her over mere protocol, which begged the question, what if she walked in on the president *with a mistress*? Would she finally become unglued? What the hell am I supposed to do during a FLOTUS-POTUS domestic dispute?

Ask any police officer and they'll tell you that next to shootings or stabbings, domestic disturbances pose the most danger for police. Previously normal people suddenly turn rabid and recklessly impassioned. Responding to a domestic dispute, I nearly had my skull split open when an angry Air Force captain's wife flung a giant cast-iron skillet down the steps at me. That wasn't unique. You have to get bad-breath close in those disputes. *You* try holding two fighting exes or a crazed parent trying to kill their own kids. Somebody retrieves a knife, a bat, a screwdriver, a lamp, a paperweight, or the phone on the mantel in the Oval Office, and the next thing shots are fired at point blank, a box cutter slices off your thumb, or someone gets blindsided by a piece of furniture. Things get really nasty. The Clintons were our top protectees. Thank God the president didn't fall or hit his head on a mantel or countertop in the course of a yelling match or when she had thrown a vase at him.

11.

WILD BILL

I wanted to block Monica's path but couldn't. "Look, I have a *blue* one now," she said, mocking me. Her pass was faceup this time; she finally got that right. She was now a paid presidential staffer. I was stunned.

"Sure is blue," I said.

She wanted to send me an unspoken message. She was heading for the Oval Office—her ultimate goal.

I was sunk. Evelyn Lieberman and I had stuck our necks out to short-circuit an insanely dangerous marital affair. And now the situation was even worse. It was completely on the government dime. The president had pulled strings to get Monica back. I'm sure she must've made a show of it when they talked on WHCA's top-secret line. How they got in touch with each other in other instances, only they know. But paying a mistress with taxpayer funds and giving her a security clearance? These were new lows.

"I told you so," said a PPD agent. It wasn't the first or the last time I heard that.

Did this agent suspect—or somehow even *know*—that I had dropped a dime on Monica to Lieberman? I just prayed no one would ever point the finger at me. I was a federal officer, not a babysitter, and no one's left-hand man. But if FLOTUS surprised the Blue Pass Princess at an awkward moment, I might not be a federal officer much longer. We all worried about the danger.

And we had more to worry about than even Monica. I worked the evening shift during a Christmas season. The president was in the Map Room. I'd grabbed some food in the East Wing and was headed back to the West Wing. A PPD friend and I shot the breeze. A Navy steward pushed the Map Room door open with his butt. In retrospect, we might have advised him to knock first. We didn't.

There before us was E! Network host Eleanor Mondale—former vice president Walter Mondale's daughter—and President Clinton in a compromising position, that is, making out on the Map Room table. The steward hurriedly put his head down and departed. The doors closed.

"Am I the only one who saw that?" I asked.

I wasn't. *I clearly wasn't.*

We tried laughing it off, returning as nonchalantly as we could under the circumstances to our posts as if to say, "Nothing to see here." The steward, however, went off in a mad dash. I'm not sure how he took it. The Secret Service has a work-hard, play-hard mentality. The commander in chief took it to the next level. A PPD agent shared some stories of the road and how agents dealt with "Clinton time," the president's habit of being late for everyone—except his mistresses. To him schedules were *recommendations.*

Nel, short for Nelvis, came to me damn near in tears, distraught, and that was not his style. He was a Filipino-American, and more important a Navy steward, a senior chief petty officer, the equivalent to an Army sergeant major. He was, by the way, *not* the Eleanor Mondale–Map Room incident steward.

We had become work friends. He knew that by serving the president even a simple cup of tea to ease his mind, he served his nation. Whatever the president needed, whenever he needed it, Nel was up to task. He wrapped gifts and ironed his shirts. Stewards remained on call 24/7 and were *expected* to respond 24/7.

Nel was kind to everyone. On hot days, he'd bring us water and in true White House fashion, in a tall, stunning crystal glass with a lime—and atop a silver platter. We'd have been content with a crinkly old plastic water bottle, but a steward like Nel wasn't just bringing water; he brought with him the dignity of his job and that of the whole White House.

But let's back up a bit. Monica was again straphanging in the hallway. Again, I moved to shoo her back to where she was allowed.

"I'm just here to talk to Nel," she said defensively.

That's when I heard him say, "Be careful, you don't want to end up like that Paula Jones girl."

"Oh, don't worry, I'm smarter than that."

Feeling very awkward, I retreated to my post, not wanting to hear any more and giving Monica a stern glare, maybe even grabbing her by the arm and giving her some office-friendly yet choice words to make her go away.

Weeks passed. Nel was now distraught. In late 1996 or early 1997 he informed me that despite all his years of service and all the presidents he had such pride in serving, he wasn't sure what to do next or who to turn to. He couldn't get his words out.

He nervously showed me a towel, asking, "Does that look like semen to you?" I could not imagine dealing with that as a UD officer. But I was. Any boy lucky enough to live past his high school years could identify the stains, translucent and white, half gooey, and already absorbing into the fabric.

"Yeah, that sure looks like it," I replied. "What the f— and who would?"

Nel explained that he'd been finding—and cleaning—semen- and lipstick-stained towels for weeks. I was shocked. If the stains didn't rinse out, he'd carefully remove them by hand. He was terrified that if he passed them on to other Navy laundry personnel downstairs he'd not only reveal Bill Clinton's affairs, he'd embarrass the presidency itself. Sure, they might have missed the semen stains—but not the lipstick.

A Navy senior chief petty officer was washing those towels by hand: that's how much Nel cared for protecting the office of the president.

Upon seeing the fluid, I instantly thought, *"F—ing Monica!"* But that lipstick . . . no.

Among White House women, fashion and especially lipstick were like trademarks. This *wasn't* Monica's lipstick. Someone else was entertaining the president late at night. As I testified in the Ken Starr investigation, I believed that this particular lipstick belonged to the current West Wing receptionist. I just knew it. I sighed. But I kept it to myself and didn't tell Nel or anyone else. I mentally filed that piece of knowledge under *"Please* forget."

You might ask why the lipstick was so significant. That receptionist wasn't using those towels to clean smudges off her mouth. *She* hadn't used the towels. The president wiped the lipstick that wasn't just on his lips but that remained on his own skin near the semen. That's why Nel and I were freaking out. That was the key to the towels.

The White House engages in a lot of pageantry. Those towels, if not silk, were something like the softest materials I've ever come across. The towels were emblazoned with the White House seal. I'd

think twice about even just drying my hands on them—but for anyone with any sense of decorum, they were for nothing else. Many,
like President Reagan, and like myself, never even walked across the
Presidential Seal on the Oval Office carpet (the same seal is on the
ceiling). It just didn't feel right. The White House was where kings
and queens, sheikhs and ambassadors met the world's most powerful leader. Pageantry was a business expense and SOP, Standard
Operating Procedure.

I understood why Nel felt belittled. He was well respected by
many previous administrations, yet here he was confiding in me,
reduced to picking up after the president's affairs, literally dealing
with his dirty linen. Nel asked if he should just throw them out,
maybe even dispose of them in burn bags. Neither of us wanted
another scandal to keep the president and FLOTUS from their real
work.

I knew what I had to do. But I had to get it right. The president was priority number one. If this scandal leaked, his presidency
would be at stake.

I calmed Nel, reassuring him that I'd take care of this myself.
He wouldn't have to worry about it. He brought me the rest of the
linens. From a nearby trash can, under the liner, I knew there was
a roll of more trash can liners. I grabbed a new one as I scanned
the hallway, already preparing an excuse should another officer ask
what I was doing. I placed the offending linens in the trash bag and
hid them in a furniture drawer near my post. I didn't let that drawer
of my sight until my very long day was done.

Getting the trash bag to my gym bag to my car involved some
risky moments, but I made it. In D.C. traffic I worried, *Have I just
illegally destroyed evidence? Can you dispose of evidence if there's no
investigation yet?* Ken Starr was investigating Whitewater, and the

Paula Jones case proceeded. Starr never went away, never stopped. Had I done the right thing? I'd protected the president, but why? And had I just jeopardized my entire career, my pension, my future, or even my kid's future? Our first child was on the way! There was no protocol for *this*! I was improvising, big-time.

I now felt things I never conceived that I'd feel: a sense of betrayal, and a real disdain for the man I protected.

I pulled into the driveway and tried greeting my wife as if this day were just another *normal* crazy day at the White House. I now realized that if I could exit the premises with such a sensitive item, so could others. And someone *would*.

Yes, the big shots could shut everyone up, but they couldn't stop someone from strolling out with the little blue pass and worse, the same damn blue dress she walked in with.

But that hadn't happened—*yet*.

12.

USSS WORK ENVIRONMENT

While I remained intensely loyal to the institution of the presidency of the United States, by 1994 I no longer felt that allegiance to the man who now occupied that office. As if that were not bad enough, I felt that I was developing the same attitude toward the U.S. Secret Service (USSS). It seemed I was starting to experience a war on two fronts.

For me, the USSS was nothing but family. I never had an issue with the men and women who served within the UD. To this day, they remain my closest friends. What disturbed me the most was that the Clintons were trying to change the very structure of the Secret Service. The Clintons mandated change upon their arrival in 1993 that exacerbated the defects within the SS and in particular accelerated the friction between the special agents (the suits) and the UD. Hillary's ambition—given her deep-seated dislike of the uniformed military and of uniformed law enforcement—was to get rid of the UD that she so loathed.

Diversity initiatives drew mixed feelings within the UD. This affected me personally when I was told that a job for which I qualified had to go to a woman because of her gender. Under this administration, the Diversity Club was created. The hypocrisy of the weekly meetings was that they were limited to nonwhite males. I informed my superior that I was a minority and wanted in.

"Gary, c'mon," he said flatly.

I asked him to find me another Irish-Lebanese person of Arabic descent in the White House—*just one*. Just before I put my signature to an official grievance, they allowed me to attend Diversity Club meetings.

When I walked in the door I felt the stares—no surprise there. Most of that meeting was ridiculous. One guy wanted to speak Spanish over the secure radio and thought it was discriminatory that he couldn't. Management squashed that one. Two black officers explained that someone had changed their work evaluation scores to obstruct their anticipated promotions and pay increases. They lacked proof. The Diversity Club leaders, the deputy chief of the White House and inspector, quashed that one, too.

"Anything else? Anyone have anything else they want to bring up?" they said, trying to end the meeting.

I raised my hand.

"Yes. Gary. What can we do for *you*?" they asked dismissively, still bent on leaving.

I took a deep breath but didn't miss a beat. "I would just like to add that I believe these two officers are telling the truth—I saw a lieutenant change their scores."

You could hear a pin drop. Now three officers had challenged another officer's integrity. The Diversity Club leaders asked me if I saw it on such-and-such a date. I pulled out my notepad, one of the greatest pieces of equipment an LEO has.

"No. It was actually the day before."

I had witnessed the two black officers' interactions with this bitter lieutenant. From my years of reading people, I knew he was passive-aggressive and had a chip on his shoulder. But I didn't make anything of it at the time.

"Well, that doesn't prove anything, Gary," said one supervisor.

"Let me finish. A buddy of mine is in the radio room. I visited to chat with him while I ate lunch. In the radio room were the evaluations. They're kept in two file bins."

"We know where they're kept, Gary."

"Well, I saw the lieutenant come in. He looked around, and the lieutenant said, 'Are those the evaluations?' My buddy responded, 'Yeah, but those are marked "Sergeant's Eyes Only."' The lieutenant said, 'It's fine' and took the evaluations and erased where the scores were and wrote in something else. I'm telling you, that's what I saw. I was sitting right there eating my lunch."

All eyes were on the Diversity Club supervisors. The two black officers swelled with vindication. The deputy chief of the White House and the inspector knew they had a pile of shit to deal with. Even though the incident in the radio room had felt mundane and outside my ballpark, I still noted it. It just hadn't felt right.

"Well, did you see exactly what the lieutenant did on those forms?" a superior asked, implying he could have changed something innocuous.

"Was it the scores?" the other reiterated.

"Here's what I saw: I didn't specifically see what the lieutenant changed—I saw him walk in, ask if those were the forms, say it was fine; then he took out a pencil, erased something, and wrote in some-thing else. He's not supposed to have access to those forms at all."

I knew those two officers were telling the truth; I had seen it firsthand. They didn't have the evidence, but as it turned out, unbe-knownst to me, I did. I could mind my own business, but silence would have been absolutely wrong, and I couldn't have lived with myself. These two black officers were good men, and some A-hole lieutenant had a bone to pick with them for a reason beyond me. Was it racism? I don't know, but I couldn't help but laugh at the ridiculousness of my predicament. Initially I objected to the diver-sity meetings, and now I realized how it enabled me to vindicate two great officers and question their superior, a guy no longer "worthy of trust and confidence."

The Clinton administration had major problems . . . and, I was sad to say, so did my own Secret Service.

13.

TOURS AND JJRTC

The Tours division, a part of Secret Service Special Operations Section, allows everyone from American tourists to Arab potentates to see and experience the White House and to inhale its storied history. I wanted in. Even if it wasn't my original career goal, it was the next best thing and a promotion and honor in itself. Most important, it would get me away from the Oval Office.

Absorbing the incredible amount of history necessary to become a competent tour officer is daunting—and it seemed impossible as far as my capabilities went. The UD officers who ran Tours knew every factual smidgen about the White House. They could tell you fascinating stories of great leaders and world wars or get into details as seemingly minute as who made the floors, where the wood came from, why it was chosen from other kinds of woods, and more. They could go for hours about a specific set of drapes (and each window has drapes!), how they were chosen by which FLOTUS, and how some important decision was made "right there on *that* spot." They were walking encyclopedias of our presidents, First Ladies, First Families, First Dogs, the whole sweep of American history, and how it flowed through those hallowed grounds.

How could I ever master that? My dyslexia and ADD were things I couldn't keep secret for long, I knew. I worried that failing my initial Tours testing and training (if I ever got that far) might reveal my learning disabilities to other placements.

But Genny never gave up on me or let me give up on myself. She was my savior. Each day when I came home, she grilled me on what I needed to know. Fortunately for me, the test was oral. The final test was two hours of stress and pain but simple, and it reflected whether you could do the job. You'd give a tour to the other White House Tours officers, answer their questions as if they were expert visitors, and if you did it right, you passed. Quite the novel idea: If you could do the job, then you could do the job.

That being said . . . I failed the Tours test more than once. Things grew tense but the guys could tell I was a people person and how much I wanted this, so they gave me another chance at passing their very high standards. They didn't want me to fail, but they were not about to compromise the Tours' mission either. To them it was about preserving American history; the White House depended on it. With each test tour and practice with Genny, I found that she had engrained herself into every detail of the White House. When I saw whom I was giving the tour to, it was as if I were giving the tour to half a dozen Gennys.

That helped to keep my nerves from pouring out of my stomach and having to replace yards of carpet—particularly historic White House carpet. I have a strong constitution but not a strong stomach. Suddenly everything clicked. It seemed that as soon as the tour started, I blinked, opened my eyes, and we were at its merciful end. *I had the job.* Finally I had largely escaped from the Oval Office, departing my full-time duties there in autumn 1997. My American dream was evolving. I looked forward to my new normal.

Around Christmastime 1996, I was officially transferred to Tours. Such a grand feeling. The White House staff outdid itself just as it did for all major events: the White House Easter Egg Roll, New Year's, Thanksgiving, Independence Day. Its members never slept. They knew how important they were to the White House and how important the White House was to the nation. For me, the Christmas celebration was almost as giant a cause for celebration as it was when I made Tours. I often found myself standing in front of a window looking out on D.C., the snow falling on the park, seeing our booths covered in snow and the "booth creatures" and marveling at how lucky I was to be one of them, an officer of the Uniformed Division and the U.S. Secret Service, and how lucky I was to be here at Tours. And by the way, with a Byrne baby in the works, the incredible amount of overtime that came with the holidays was very welcome.

Oh, yes, sometimes it was stressful. A simple mix-up of words can set dominos into motion that lead to front-page headlines and national embarrassments, but I wanted to be back under the radar. I readied myself for a very big tour, escorting the NAACP (National Association for the Advancement of Colored People). I was honored that management selected me. As I left the break room, a UD Tours friend of mine warned me not to screw up, but actually he ensured that I would.

Above the fireplace in the State Dining Room on a mantel is a quotation cut in marble, a prayer from John Adams after he had spent his first night in the Executive Mansion. During the NAACP prayer I recited the prayer aloud from memory—just as I had to hundreds of groups. Only this time it came out: "I Pray Heaven to Bestow the Best of Blessing on this house, and on all that shall hereafter inhabit it. May none but Honest and *White* Men ever rule under this roof!"

One of the NAACP members leaned over to me. "Does it really say 'white men' in the White House prayer?"

I stopped the tour. Red-faced, I asked if I had indeed made the mistake. I had. I told them how mortified I was and then explained the story of how a friend had tried to trip me with his joke and how I had actually tripped—and that the term I replaced was "wise men." I stopped breathing, waiting for their response. I could see an avalanche of user-friendly sensitivity training hurtling our way. This was the blue-glove incident on steroids.

I didn't laugh, but thank God they did. Imagine the *New York Times* headline: "Racist Secret Service Guard Insults NAACP Delegation" or "Are All UD Officers Racists?" The big, historic wooden door of the White House would hit Officer Gary Byrne on his way out. Old "friends" would distance themselves from me. The agency would paint me as a bad apple they had promptly kicked out of the barrel.

Fortunately, the NAACP members had a great time and thanked me for my tour; I guess they had their own workplace humor. No "ado" was made of it, although I'd seen much ado made over smaller things. I get goose bumps just thinking of it.

I had seen the NAACP when I had been posted outside the Oval Office. The president, Al Gore, Jesse Jackson, Al Sharpton, and other NAACP officials entered the hallway. The various reverends decided we should all pray together, and before I could weasel away, the next thing I knew we were all holding hands and bowing our heads. Was I supposed to bow my head or stay alert, on guard? An agent too far away to get suckered in snickered at me and later said he knew I'd never stop getting crap for it.

"Dear Lord . . ."

While at Tours, I got a call from a friend at my home from his home phone. "The Oval Office logbook is new, Gary. Just a heads-up,

Ken Starr's investigation subpoenaed the old logbook," he said.

We talked about it for a while. "Thanks for the heads-up," I told him and we knew what we were in for.

We were screwed.

Maybe, just maybe, everything would go away and leave us alone. But the Clintons couldn't help themselves. They couldn't keep their hands out of the cookie jar. Despite having such a great man as Leon Panetta as his chief of staff, President Clinton insisted on having outside unofficial dealings with the shadowy political figure and pollster Dick Morris, whom you now see peddling retirement plans on TV infomercials. After the White House wound down for the day, I and other UD officers on the late night rotation would occasionally allow Morris, a close friend of Hillary, in for unofficial policy meetings. It placed the Secret Service in yet another delicate position.

Morris was essentially a Republican (he'd worked for GOP Senate leader Trent Lott). The Clintons snuck him in by night—never by day when Panetta was there. We didn't quite comprehend that Hillary was undermining Panetta, and we certainly couldn't insert ourselves into these mysterious visits to sort out their true meaning. Morris (the Clintons called him Charlie to hide his visits), Bill, and Hillary met frequently, mostly in the Executive Residence, though once Bill and Morris met alone in the Oval Office. It all translated into Dick Morris's functioning as President Clinton's shadow chief of staff, blindsiding Leon Panetta on issues Panetta thought had previously been decided. "Over the course of the first nine months of 1995, no single person had more power over the president," George Stephanopoulos later concluded of Morris.[*]

---

[*] George Stephanopoulos, *All Too Human* (Boston: Little, Brown, 1999).

Hillary could not readily intrude on her husband's official meetings with Panetta, but she could easily participate at these intimate, secret sessions with Morris. Her true power was of the night—not the daylight. Increasing Morris's power meant increasing *her* power.

But these hush-hush meetings weren't so much about governing as they were about branding and politics and polling—and Dick Morris and Hillary Clinton were masters at that game. I found confirmation of it all in Leon Panetta's autobiography, *Worthy Fights*:

> Unbeknownst to me, Clinton had been secretly reaching out [to political advisor] Dick Morris, in an attempt to take stock of the nation's politics. Clinton surely sensed I didn't like Morris—he was right about that—so even though Morris started doing polling on the very issues the White House staff was working on, Clinton didn't share the results, or even the facts of the polls with me. . . .
>
> It was actually Hillary Clinton who had asked Morris . . . to resume working for the president. The Clintons admired Morris [who] openly disdained the substance of policy. He was about winning.*

So the Clintons were sneaking around the ablest assistant they ever had, Leon Panetta. Then again, President Clinton was good at sneaking.

While at Tours I still felt I needed to put an even greater distance between myself and the debacle the presidency had become. By now I had lost my ability to provide these professional scandal

---

* Leon Panetta, *Worthy Fights* (New York: Penguin Press, 2014).

makers with any benefit of the doubt. Eleanor Mondale and Monica Lewinsky could not satiate the president's horndog sexual desires. There were many others. I saw plenty of awkward run-ins and drama with other officers and staff. President Clinton had difficulty managing where he saw his many mistresses, whether it was at the White House or on the road. It baffled the Uniformed Division as to how he could manage all these women without any of them realizing there were so many others. We wondered how he got any work done and joked that he would have been better at running a brothel in a red-light district than the White House.

And why didn't the president's staff and supporters believe Paula Jones's allegations of sexual harassment? Why did they take the president at his word about his other sexual scandals when they knew he was a cheater? But his luck was bound to run out. He had lit too many fuses, and I knew that at least one was sure to explode in his face. The Clintons had attained the White House by manufacturing an image of being bright, shining stars who cared deeply for the little guy. The truth is they wallowed in mud and were willing to drag numerous little people with them to retain power.

Over the radio around dusk, December 6, 1997, I heard that Monica was at the Northwest Gate. I shook my head. "Here we go," I told myself. The president was having a private session at the White House.

Monica visited on the pretense of seeing Betty Currie to have Betty convey a number of Christmas presents to the president. By this time every single person in the White House, except perhaps the First Lady, knew the deal between Monica and the president. The Northwest Gate officer, a friend of mine, wouldn't let her in. Betty had instructed them to delay her entrance. Everyone had already heard of my awkward run-in with Eleanor Mondale in full display with the president in the Map Room—*and* the Library Room. We knew the score.

"The president is still with another appointment"—or something to that effect was what Betty informed the Northwest Gate officer. Normally, if someone was scheduled to see the president and he was running late (a pretty normal occurrence), they'd be let in to wait in the West Wing Lobby.

But the White House didn't employ Monica at this point. I wasn't involved in her being "transferred" to the Pentagon in July 1996 or swept under the rug by her "mentor," but if I could have dragged or kicked her off the premises, I would have. By now, Betty and the gate officer knew enough not to let Monica on the White House grounds at all. She could stay in the security booth, but she was not allowed beyond that. She was left standing.

Still the president signaled to her that she was welcome, and she visited by scheduling "appointments" with Betty. She would have been welcome that night except for the president's conflicting "engagement." Somehow—whether through the president's top-secret military staff or through trusted employees—Monica had remained in contact with the president and Betty.

It was only around five o'clock on a weekday. A normal person would assume the president would still be working, but it wasn't so.

I don't know how Betty felt about it, but the president put her in a hell of a jam. The Northwest officer's initiative was part smart decision and part unofficial protocol quietly backed by Secret Service upper management; he told Monica she couldn't enter and had to wait. In our minds, Monica never had a job beyond mere busywork; she hadn't been a real employee before and had been "transferred" across the Potomac—and everyone knew why. She was *only* the president's mistress, as far we were concerned, and we didn't appreciate being part of the president's nonsense. Monica, however, still regarded herself quite favorably as *the* president's singular mistress. So now she was pissed off. She pressed the officer about the delay and wanted to know why she was left standing in his security booth. He lashed back.

"You have to wait. He's with his other piece of a–. Wait till he's finished," the officer said—or something to the same effect.

That was not the answer she wanted. She became irate when she heard whom the president was with.

"What's he want with her when he has this?" and she made some gesture to herself.

The officers relayed the story to me after and how incredibly awkward it was for them. UD screens for dangers, but this was a constant hazard of the president's own making. I kept thinking, *Please don't let her up.* Betty, the Northwest Gate officer, and everyone had the right idea. Inevitably the president was going to get his meetings crossed up and there would be a wild domestic dispute. The First Lady was typically either one floor up in the West Wing, in the Executive Mansion, or just walking around.

But that wasn't the only problem. The president and Betty had a different take. The problem to them wasn't that they now couldn't keep his *mistresses* in line and safely separate. Someone in UD had leaked to one of the mistresses (Monica) that the president was meeting with another mistress.

I received a call from my watch commander. He wanted my opinion about how high this incident would blow. But who could tell in this topsy-turvy world of the Clinton White House? One thing I knew: These Northwest Gate officers were protected by a fear of mutual self-destruction on the part of upper management. Management couldn't discipline them without formally detailing the issue in writing—and *nobody* wanted to do that. But that was only half the game. Would the UD and Betty start finger-pointing at each other? Or worse, somehow at me?

Betty Currie wasn't the real problem. The Northwest Gate officers weren't the real problem. Monica wasn't the real problem. The real, the massive, the central problem was Bill Clinton.

That being said, after everyone had simmered down and thought things through, we felt terrible for Betty. I even felt bad for Monica because I knew how powerfully charming President Clinton was. He was the master. That charm can't be fully understood or described unless you've seen it, unless you've been in the same room with the man. He's incredibly endearing. I saw the effect he had on people.

I was glad to have moved off my main posting. Ken Starr turned up the heat. Subpoenas for logbooks and people started flowing like an errant stream.

After just a year at Tours, I put in for a transfer to the Secret Service's James J. Rowley Training Center (JJRTC).

In 1998, my transfer was quickly approved, much faster than I had any right to expect. No doubt Monica and Bill had something to do with that. I was a thorn in their side. Now I was gone.

My commute was much shorter and I was back in Beltsville, Maryland. I had landed a spot on the security detail for the JJRTC, a 660-acre mix of dense woods, swamps, fence line, interstate highway, dynamic firearms ranges, indoor ranges, and office buildings. We secured the grounds and the facility. This even included taking care of the beaver and poacher problems JJRTC was having, in addition to dealing with any infiltrations, police issues, reporters, panicky people, and the like. It was a great job. I immediately fell in with the team. Much of my stress was gone. Life was simple. No burn bags, no special towels, no seedy interns; just the facility, good people, and Maryland woods. It was just like Air Force Security Police.

The year was 1998. I liked my job immensely, along with the woods, the clean air, and no more colds and office bugs going around. My sinuses cleared up. It was as if I could smell for the first time. I was free from all the stress. I didn't throw up anymore. I slept better. When I awoke my sheets and pillowcases were no longer drenched in sweat.

I had put in for my real dream, to become a JJRTC firearms instructor. My life *was* firearms, and what better way to fulfill my dream than by passing on my passion to others? Firearms clicked with who I was. They made sense. It was the one thing I wasn't just good at, I was extremely good at. I should have been a shoe-in, and I waited for a spot to open up.

I'd only been at JJRTC a couple of weeks when my dreams of a new—a normal—life vanished as quickly as they had appeared. My calm wasn't a calm at all: I was in the eye of the biggest storm the presidency had yet witnessed.

It was the night of January 17, 1998, and two supervisors and I had crammed into a Chevy Tahoe for a road trip to a nearby military base, Fort Dix, New Jersey, hoping to obtain some extra ATVs and light vehicles to assist in our patrolling duties.

We had just left the fort's surplus site after tagging some equipment and were flying 85 mph down the New Jersey Turnpike in our unmarked federal vehicle listening to *The Howard Stern Show* on the radio. Stern started talking about a media leak website called the *Drudge Report*. It was a million laughs—until my blood ran cold, and I almost drove off the road. Stern was telling us about a White House intern turned Pentagon intern turned paid White House employee, who had been having an affair with the president. They mentioned oral sex, the Oval Office, *and the Secret Service.*

The *Drudge Report* had broken the story of the president's cheating and lying, his lack of professional integrity, and how he lied on a legal affidavit. *Newsweek* had the original scoop but didn't have the guts to publish it. Everyone knew the *Drudge Report* had credibility.

I knew immediately this was going to be a disaster involving everyone, that it would tear apart the Secret Service—and maybe the nation itself. I knew it would involve many of my friends and me. The public would rip at us the way a dog tears a toy to get at the squeaker. As Howard spoke, I knew that I alone could prove the president had lied on a sworn affidavit and committed an impeachable offense.

I flipped out. I pounded the dashboard. They had to stop the car so I could get out and vomit.

Back in the car, I talked about it with my superior. He brushed it off as not "a big deal." He advised that if I was asked about it I should say I didn't remember; I couldn't recall. We kept listening and we kept talking, and he soon realized how poor that advice was. Cooking at 85 mph on the New Jersey Turnpike, which feels like you're driving down a lit-up runway for miles, he asked, "Well, what do *you* think you should do?" I wanted him to contact the chief and get the ball rolling down the chain of command so that we could get ahead of this thing. The Uniformed Division was a tight-knit group of about a thousand strong, and we had a policy of talking it out whenever possible rather than leaving a paper trail. We rushed back to Beltsville so we could make the call.

Forced by the Starr investigation, the president was to give testimony on the Paula Jones case any day now. Somehow Matt Drudge and his website received a leak. In response the president had signed a subpoenaed affidavit, legally sworn testimony denying any sexual relations with Paula Jones, the low-level Arkansas state employee who had accused him of sexual harassment, *and more so, any relationship with Monica Lewinsky.* He said they didn't have any contact with each other, hadn't even been alone in the same room together. He swore to it and said others could corroborate.

Monica Lewinsky signed another affidavit. Ken Starr had been following the Clintons like a bloodhound. But at each turn of each scandal (Whitewater, Vince Foster's suicide, Travelgate, Filegate, the affairs, the bribes, Troopergate, and more) it all came down to deny-deny-deny and the Clintons' word against everyone else's. Only this time, Clinton arrogantly denied his affair with Monica on a legal affidavit, sworn testimony. The shit was hitting the fan.

Ken Starr now needed to prove Clinton was a liar—a perjurer. He needed evidence. Since they subpoenaed our logbook, I knew I was on Starr's list.

I couldn't listen. I couldn't take it anymore. I couldn't drive anymore. My partner asked me what was wrong. I can remember the feeling, my heart racing, my mind whirling, racked with pain, doubt, remorse, and regret. *Oh my God, Starr, the Clintons, the Service, the FBI, the Justice Department, my friends, my family—no, not my friends and family—but everyone is going to implicate me, my integrity, my professionalism, my ethics, my foundation, my character. What about Genny and my unborn child? I didn't sign up for this! We never signed up for this! Why did the Clintons have to do this to us? Haven't I treated them well, done my best? They just couldn't do the right thing! They couldn't stop themselves!*

And we couldn't help them save themselves. We couldn't stop them from embroiling us, either. They had embodied the hopes of their generation. How do you do that to your supporters, your constituents, your *believers*?

It took me a good hour and a half to finally get home, and when I did I talked to Genny briefly. She had already heard the news. We agreed that we'd have to see how the next day played out. I needed to blow off steam and went for a run. She understood. I returned with my head on straight. The chief of the Uniform Division had called—the chief, I couldn't believe it! I called right back. I had warned my lieutenant that my situation was about to blow sky-high and that the agency had to take the matter seriously. At first he hadn't believed me, but later he went around the chain of command to alert our superiors. I hadn't expected his call to travel so far and so fast, but clearly we were all worried.

"Gary, first off, before you say a f—ing word, don't tell me any information, because they'll subpoena me and it's just going to make it harder on you and everyone else. I don't want to know why you're calling, because then I may have to corroborate later, but I'm going to put you in touch with the Service's lawyers. You're not the only officer involved. Hang tight, and they'll contact you. Got it?"

My chief had been around a long time. I respected him immensely and hoped that he really did care and would back me up. He had been a UD officer, then became a special agent and then head of the UD. He knew the job from the bottom up and led from the top down.

I hung up and looked at Genny. We exchanged blank stares.

My dream of becoming an instructor or even staying and working the security detail at JJRTC, my entire career, my income for my family and our unborn child, were in jeopardy.

I waited in silence for a call back.

14.

MUD DRAG: PART I

I, Officer Gary J. Byrne, received my first Justice Department sub-poena. Word went out that Ken Starr had found fired staffers from the White House and had an ax to grind. Some of them dragged me into the investigation. I've often wondered who gave me up. I believe the reason the Starr investigation targeted me was that they knew I was nobody's stooge. I had my hunch it was a certain Press Lobby staffer whose passes I pulled from him. He was subsequently kicked out of the White House for insulting an officer. I'd had him removed.

What I did surmise much later from both the Secret Service grapevine and from news reports was that because I had knowl-edge of Bill and Monica I had been outed to the papers and to Starr by at least one colleague, the Silver Fox. That's what we called Lewis C. Fox, the first of the subpoenaed servicemen. The Silver Fox was a great guy and in many ways had ushered me into my Oval Office posting. He was a cop's cop. When I first met him he was among the crew's more experienced members. With his mane of pure silver hair and innate charm, he looked like the Most Interesting Man in the World from the Dos Equis beer commercials.

The Fox had retired by 1998 but had served at our postings and was right there for much of Billary's dramas. Being retired and a bachelor, he didn't have the strings others and I did. I found out that the Fox was having dinner with friends at a bar when the TV reported the *Drudge Report* leak, the same story I heard while barreling down the New Jersey Turnpike. The Fox told his buddies something like, "Oh you guys don't know the half of it . . ." and proceeded to tell people what he'd seen. He didn't reveal any secret info, and since he was retired, nothing he said was considered "privileged," as it was for me. His monologue was the talk of the joint. He went on to say that the guy they should see is Gary Byrne, because Gary'd had the most run-ins with Monica and the other women and could blow the president and his cohorts' affidavits wide open. Legend has it that a friend of a reporter was in that bar and used the diner pay phone to call his buddy. It's a small and dangerous world. The papers were hunting the Fox even before Starr was, but the bloodhound soon closed in. Somehow they caught my scent along with his.

It was the Fox who first went on record claiming that he had seen Monica and the president in the Oval Office alone together for forty-five minutes. Hardly stop-the-presses news—*until* the president responded to Matt Drudge's leak by saying Monica and he had never been alone in a room together! President Clinton had exclaimed that all the reports were absolutely false—the ones about her actually being a paid mistress on top of other illegal, risky, and unethical activities that I knew had occurred. The story circulated through TV, radio, the papers—and that relatively newfangled thing called the Internet. I knew shit was avalanching downhill and I was in the valley below it.

Starr sent subpoenas to the Secret Service headquarters' legal counsel's office, and I was notified of mine.

"Hang tight, Gary. We'll deal with this," they told me.

With the Justice Department heading the investigation and filing the subpoenas while playing both sides, I felt legitimately outgunned, the way a lawyer might feel in a gunfight. This wasn't my turf, and everyone might as well have been speaking Greek. I hung tight but worried that I'd be hung out to dry like my fellow UD officer Hank O'Neil.

The lawyers were going to legally stonewall the subpoenas. Though they were addressed to the USSS office, the subpoenas were for myself, not the Secret Service. As far as I was concerned, *Secret Service* meant *secret*, dammit. We were not in the business of telling anyone what we saw while on the job.

Secret Service personnel had never been subpoenaed previously, but I thought if I was I would be granted immunity. It could be perceived that I was committing obstruction of justice, but the FBI was targeting not just the Secret Service but the Clintons. Everything was all very political, and the difference between stonewalling and obstructing depended on which side you were on. While the FBI felt I was illegally obstructing, the Service considered my actions appropriate. The Service's lawyers thought that their stalling tactics would work as they filed endless appeals.

I just wanted to concentrate on my job.

After several subpoenas ended up in my circular file, I was yanked off my JJRTC security detail and told to come in for briefing by the Secret Service's legal heavyweights.

The Justice Department played both sides like a fiddle. For the offense Ken Starr was appointed in August 1994 by Attorney

General Janet Reno. President Clinton had appointed Reno. For the defense, she also appointed Gary G. Grindler to represent the Secret Service against Starr. Grindler and Starr duked it out, with officers like myself caught in the middle.

I spoke often with Genny. Our talks were straightforward and serious. We sorted out our life's goals, what we could expect from the legal process (and that we couldn't avoid it), and how we would go through it. She stuck with me. She was carrying our first child. The legal system was about to slice-and-dice her husband, but she always told me to "do the right thing." She was my rock. I never had to worry about leaving the shit at work to meet the shit at home. Home was sanctuary. I just never wanted to disappoint her—or our expected baby.

JJRTC leadership thoughtfully allowed me to use a federally marked Tahoe so I could avoid D.C. parking issues. I could at least be spared one aggravation. Each morning I drove from the "shit box," what we affectionately called our rental home while our new home was being built for our growing family, to JJRTC in Beltsville. Then I drove to the Secret Service's D.C. headquarters, just a block from the White House, though I couldn't park *there*, nor did I want to.

At first I just wanted to tell my story and get the hell out, but the first week turned out to be a mind-bending experience as the Secret Service attorneys told me how complicated this was going to be. They had no "fiduciary" duty to me—and this worried me. I enjoyed none of the confidentiality privileges normal in an attorney-client relationship. They were loyal to the government, but more specifically to the Service. Anything I told them was going to be shared with the Service and in one way or another with my leadership. They warned me that this was going to be a long, drawn-out process. They explained my rights and I was surprised that my rights needed so much explaining. I felt incredibly demoralized.

I was told that I could never reveal information that might jeopardize the safety and security of the president. That was nonnegotiable. They explained to me that information needing security clearances required separate and individual subpoenas. They advised me that I could never buckle under pressure. Never, no matter how hard the Starr people pressed or insisted, was I to surrender information regarding the president's movements, our standard operating procedures, the secret layouts of the White House, or security protocols. But within those caveats was a wide gap between what was absolutely non-shareable and what could be non-shareable. I was caught in a very tricky situation: I couldn't perjure myself or withhold information gained from my employment, but I also couldn't reveal secret information. That's how it was in Secret Service.

But I knew that if I kept dodging FBI and Justice Department questions, they'd soon believe I was withholding evidence or even obstructing justice. And if I was overly forthright, I faced prosecution for revealing privileged information. I was dead.

Complicating matters even further, our lawyers informed me that they didn't have the same clearances I did, so I had to be careful about sharing info with them. They weren't deemed "need to know" for certain procedures involved in my answering their questions! If I felt it necessary to include an explanation of a procedure in my answer, they'd have to be administratively deemed "need to know" by going to the White House and being given a tour by SAs and UD officers. I couldn't just depend on vetting every potential answer with them first.

My head was spinning. My stomach turned. It reminded me of the scene from *A Few Good Men*. Yes, *that* scene. "You can't handle the truth!" I'd joke, but the truly unfunny joke was that they truly couldn't always legally handle the truth (that is, the facts) of my job and what I had witnessed on duty.

My ADD and dyslexia didn't help in managing the legal mumbo-jumbo. But this legal stuff was never part of our job description. I wasn't just outflanked, I was outgunned and surrounded: I was a captive but hopefully still had a fighting chance.

The second thing the attorneys and I agreed was that I had to keep my job. Being a stooge was a non-option, and I knew in my gut that's why Starr homed in on me. Someone had ratted me out, but at least I could take solace in its being for a good cause. The FBI hoped I'd reveal their smoking gun, but I couldn't do that without violating protocol. I wouldn't be a stooge—I wanted to keep my word, my integrity, my character—but I needed to tread carefully to ensure that no Clinton, congressional, Justice Department, or Secret Service hard-liner packed me off to jail or stripped me of my ability to take care of my family.

I had to toe the line enough to keep my job, but I couldn't live with myself or sleep at night if I didn't tell the truth. My conscience, my sleep, my head, and my stomach were going to take a beating for weeks on end while they dragged me through the mud, but I couldn't let myself be racked with doubt, regret, and inner turmoil for the rest of my life. My unborn child was on the way and I needed to support that child, but I needed to be able one day to look my child in the eye and not only teach, but demonstrate real tough-in-the-clutch honesty. I could have relied on "I don't recall" or "I don't remember," but I would have been a liar. *Plausible deniability* is talk I reserve for criminals. I wouldn't stoop to the Clintons' level to protect myself. I wouldn't have been any better than they were.

It was my epiphany: They couldn't jail me for telling the truth and doing the right thing. I repeated this to myself. It became my inner motto. I needed "Worthy of Trust and Confidence" to mean something. The Service's attorneys assured me that I couldn't be fired for telling the truth when subpoenaed. But doing the right thing meant *doing*. Doing the right thing would never be doing nothing.

After that first week, the SS attorneys started asking. I started telling. Since they were representing the Secret Service, I didn't have to tiptoe so much. But as they made clear in the first week, I didn't have to tell them, nor did they want to know, anything they didn't ask. And as I mentioned, I couldn't readily vet my questions with them. Whatever I told them was trial evidence and to be shared with Starr. But if the FBI, the Justice Department, and the Secret Service didn't think to ask, I didn't have to tell, and that was fine by me.

If you had told me in 1995 that it would be a mistress that would politically assassinate the Clintons, I would have laughed in your face. The Clintons and their people appeared to be way in over their heads with so many other things, but those internal things never got out, things that are still classified today or were swept way under the rug. And I won't describe those things because I know they're still classified. While this situation was overwhelmingly confusing, country still came first, and I'd never let my enemies take that from me.

The headline read, "Starr Zeroes in on Secret Service Guard." The story said,

> The independent counsel cited Gary Byrne by name in his motion to compel his testimony. The hope is that Byrne could shed some light on what led to Monica Lewinsky's dismissal as a White House intern. A former Secret Service officer, Lewis Fox, told investigators Byrne was concerned about the intern's visits to the Oval Office. On the

day before Lewinsky was told of her dismissal, Byrne spoke with Deputy White House Chief of Staff Evelyn Lieberman about the intern. Starr wants Byrne to tell a grand jury why he went to Lieberman. For her part, Lieberman says she doesn't recall details of the meeting.*

Shit.

I liked Evelyn a lot, but the pressure had gotten to her. It had been she and I against Monica and President Clinton when we had tried to kick Monica out. But when I saw that headline, it was my word against *all* of theirs.

I phoned a friend I'll call Mark H., a legal heavyweight and former legal counsel for the CIA and for Pennsylvania senator Arlen Specter. He now worked at a private D.C. firm. I called him from a pay phone, revealing little, but he was interested in my situation and scheduled a meeting. As crazy as all this was for me, this was right in Mark's ballpark.

We quickly established my absolutes: I wanted to do the right thing. I wanted to keep my job. I didn't view those terms as being at odds. Mark wanted in—this was the stuff of lawyers' dreams, his *A Few Good Men* moment. His firm would work pro bono but should the government ever reimburse for their legal fees they'd file for them. That was fine with me.

I knew how lucky I was. Many of my colleagues were on the hook for their own legal expenses, which ran to upwards of $350 per hour. It ruined them financially. That's part of the damage the Clintons callously inflicted on the men and women sworn to lay down their lives to protect them. The Clintons knew that on meager Secret

---

* http://www.wsj.com/articles/SB892699092473349000.

Service salaries they could never legally afford to challenge them, to reveal their secrets. Financially strapped and fearful of retribution, White House personnel found it sensible to fall back on a convenient "I don't recall."

Since the Secret Service lawyers were from the Justice Department, I had a feeling that some of them were playing double or triple agent. "They're all fed from the same trough" was the political saying. I wanted a heavyweight loyal to *me*.

Mark H. may have saved my life.

Yes, I got bogged down in the details and started wringing my hands as my stomach felt as though it would crawl its way out. As much as I liked Mark, I wanted to back out and put my faith in the Service and God. Was it even legal for me to have independent counsel? I'm just a cop. Cops sign up for the action, not the legal aftermath, and it blindsides us *every* time. This was no Air Force DUI bust, this was an impeachable offense against the president of the United States for perjury, bribery, sexual harassment, paying a mistress, and risking national security intelligence. Then there was trying him in the court of public opinion for being a coward, a scoundrel, a womanizer, sexist, and playing political poker at the entire world's expense for his personal pleasure.

My emotions reached the bursting point. Mark, seeing me in my wrecked state, had the decency and sense to phone his firm's constitutional expert in Atlanta. This guy knew his shit front to back—*every* possible Supreme Court interpretation. His manner reassured me. The Constitution was still *my* Constitution, the one I'd sworn to protect. I could rely on the protections under the Bill of Rights. I *needed to know* that I still had my right to be a part of Paula Jones case, to "petition the government for a redress of grievances," to use my freedom of speech, my right not to incriminate myself, my right to independent legal counsel, my right against unlawful and unreasonable search and seizure of my property—to privacy, to due process, and to all the others. I was a born-again man who'd taken an oath in defending and upholding the Constitution and the country.

Now that Constitution would defend me.

After all, it was the president who took an oath to "faithfully execute the Office of President of the United States," and "to the best of [his] ability, preserve, protect and defend the Constitution." I took a similar oath at the Air Force and the Service to protect and defend the Constitution and follow the orders of the president.

I kept telling myself, "Do the right thing, Gary. They can't jail you for telling the truth. You are a good man; that means something. You are and will be 'worthy of trust and confidence.'" In Mark's office that day I was still choking up. My eyes welled with tears. I clenched my hands, then clenched them again. My face reddened.

I would push on. We'd get through this.

Mark and his constitutional expert did me one better. We were getting fired up. I listened in as Mark arranged a conference call between himself, the constitutional expert, and Gary Grindler, the Justice Department honcho Janet Reno had appointed as the Secret Service's counterweight to Ken Starr. Mark ordered me to keep silent.

Hell, I couldn't have spoken even if I had wanted to. Was it legal for me to obtain independent, personal legal counsel? I was going to get the answer right from the horse's mouth. The Expert and Grindler had known each other from college—small world.

"Hey, Gary [Grindler]. It's [the Expert]. How are you?"

"Hey, [so-and-so], I'm fine," says Grindler.

"Good, good. Listen, I've got a Secret Service guy here with me who's involved in your little case and he's seeking independent counsel. I'm calling you as a courtesy to let you know we're representing him, but I'm not obligated to say who, and he's not obligated to say he has independent counsel. But we're representing him nonetheless. That fine with you?"

"Uh, well enough. Yeah, it's probably a good idea to get independent counsel. Sure. Why not? I would."

"You have no issue with it?"

"No. I got no issue with it."

"Great."

"Yeah."

"Okay, see you, Gary."

"Bye-bye."

And that was it.

I choked up again. This was really happening. Someone had my back. Mark was outside the Clinton sphere of influence, outside of their web. His firm wasn't the Service. It wasn't the feds. They weren't political. They were independent, for-profit, capitalist heavyweights, and I believed that they wanted to do the right thing for a law enforcement officer. They also wanted in on one of the biggest legal cases in history. And I couldn't blame them for that. People speculated that this case could overthrow the president.

Mark was my protector. It meant the world to me.

The Treasury Department (the Secret Service's boss) had evoked—hell, it was more like they created it out of thin air—what they called the Presidential Protective Function Privilege. It meant that protectors, specifically Secret Service officers, could not rat on their protectees. It was the extrapolation of case law, a privilege, not even a right under the Constitution, that a protection detail formed a marriage of sorts.

The idea was if the Service ratted on its protectees, the protectees couldn't trust the Service and would duck them. The Service couldn't protect an uncooperative protectee, but that doesn't mean the Service has to collude with misbehavior. Still the Treasury Department evoked the Presidential Protective Function Privilege knowing full well it wouldn't work. I suspected it was a part of Mrs. Clinton's "just get it done" leadership style: She didn't care how, didn't know if it would even work, and didn't get personally involved. She prided herself on plausible deniability, which is how she and her husband gained the presidency by ducking their scandals in Arkansas.

But the Service and Clinton's defense wasn't remotely plausible—we knew better because we had seen the incidents in question! And somehow Starr discovered who exactly knew what and whom he could squeeze. But deny-deny-deny was turning into drag-drag-drag; eventually those pesky FBI agents and reporters would just be worn down over time—so they thought. Sound familiar? Why change the playbook if it worked?

Therefore, presidential protectors couldn't be compelled to testify if they chose not to. No one ever asked me if I would—it was assumed I wouldn't testify—such was the Secret Service way. If the privilege was upheld and I wanted to testify, I would be sticking my neck out and I'd be the only one. One way or another, this side or the other, I'd be a dead man.

The Clintons directed others to lie for them, never in writing (as far as I knew), but I had seen lying firsthand. Their culture of corruption had pushed me out of my post and eventually from the White House. I feared it would push me from the Service as well. Many in the Service just said, "I don't remember," "I'm not sure," "I don't recall," or "I can neither confirm nor deny," or they obstructed justice by constantly standing by privileged information. The spirit was to protect the president and protect the Service. I couldn't do that, but I still had to tread carefully. "They can't jail me for telling the truth," I kept repeating to myself.

In mid-January 1999, prior to my subpoena and unbeknownst to me while I was at JJRTC, Monica Lewinsky had signed an affidavit, a sworn statement, about her affair. In a Pentagon City, VA hotel, Monica also handed Linda Tripp, her Pentagon staffer pen pal, a document ("Points to Make in an Affidavit") detailing what to say on an affidavit so as to protect Clinton from charges of sexual harassment made by White House volunteer aide Kathleen Willey. Where that document originated is a mystery. But it was amateur hour for Monica, as usual. Monica and President Clinton had been subpoenaed by the Paula Jones lawyers and both swore in a public civil case, under penalty of perjury—an impeachable offense for the president—that they did not have a sexual relationship.

The Clintons and Monica didn't know it, but Linda Tripp was no Clintonite. She was feeding information on them all to *Newsweek* and to Ken Starr. Tripp had the affidavit document proving conspiracy, and Starr had his carte blanche. Janet Reno signed off on the Justice Department and FBI expanding their investigations from the Whitewater scandal—in which their main witness, Jim McDougal, mysteriously died—into conspiracy and perjury in Paula Jones's sexual harassment case regarding a government employee. Tripp had taped her phone conversations with Monica detailing her affair with the president, how in the Oval Office she gave him oral sex while he was on the phone with ambassadors and with Dick Morris. President Clinton paid for a White House mistress with taxpayer funds and jeopardized national security with her compromisable and corruptible presence in a secure area, all for little more than on-demand oral sex. We thought we knew what was going on. We didn't know the half of it.

Tripp somehow manipulated Monica into giving her the infamous blue dress. Nel and I hadn't cleaned up everything. The president had "deposited" somewhere besides White House towels. The biggest security leak in history was the one that Monica wore into the White House and then strutted out with—right past us. There was no way to spin it. Either the president had mysteriously gone around the White House ejaculating on people's clothing, or he and Monica had a taxpayer-funded affair for which he committed perjury.

It also proved what I damn well knew, that Monica was easily manipulated, either by the likes of a higher-up like President Clinton or a lower-down like Linda Tripp. She had no business playing in a high-stakes environment within arm's reach of intelligence of the CIA, the FBI, the State Department, and the Department of Defense. I mean, the spook shit that moved and was approved through the White House was the most sensitive intel in existence. Actionable intel is power. How could anyone in the Secret Service be expected to do his or her job if the Americans allowed people like the Clintons to assume national leadership?

People still think the Lewinsky affair was one political party making a big deal over a little extra pie on the side; it wasn't. What Starr proved was that the president had engaged in inappropriate sexually related workplace conduct with an intern/employee, as he had with other women. Some women, such as Juanita Broaddrick, even alleged he had assaulted them. He had zero integrity in this area, and that made everything he did suspect and untrustworthy. It revealed his real character. The president of the United States believed that he was above the law. He perjured himself and convinced others to perjure themselves to try to save his carefully crafted image. He created a spirit of corruption that infected the White House, the Secret Service, the whole government. Bill Clinton endangered us all by serving himself. He dragged me through the mud for it. He raked a lot of people over the coals for it.

Don't shit where you eat. Don't harass and screw interns and staff for the same reason. If someone can't see how they jeopardize the mission by not being able to see past temptation, they aren't fit for the job. I heard my old TI's mottos, "The little mistakes get the wrong people killed!"

At any moment the Clintons could have stopped each scandal; they could have told the truth about his affair with Monica. They didn't. They kept pushing and peddling. Monica was young, inexperienced, and immature. The Clintons weren't. They were just immensely arrogant. They told us explicitly that they weren't used to hearing "no."

Tripp manipulated Monica, but Monica herself had manipulated her way to the president as much as the president schemed to ensnare her. I'd seen it all—or at least enough. But Monica was a pretty, spoiled girl; the president wasn't. He knew damn well what he was doing to her emotionally and physically and to her reputation. He couldn't have cared less.

People like Monica and the entire Clinton Machine should never have had access to classified national security–related intelligence or enjoyed leadership positions. Their irresponsibility had consequences. Good men died from it—both in Mogadishu and Benghazi. We had friends die from exhaustion or from falling asleep at the wheel while ensuring the Secret Service mission of protecting the president. To die for a man of character—I can live with that. Scott Giambattista got shot to protect the president. Everyone watched the Clinton scandal shit show play out in Congress, in the media, and in the Oval Office, and every night in America's living rooms. All the Clintons' successes can be credited to men and women of character like Leon Panetta, Nancy Hernreich, and Betty Currie. The Clintons' failures all point to themselves.

The president and Mrs. Clinton were purely business partners. I believe from their movements and interactions that Mrs. Clinton knew of the affairs. But I do believe she was surprised by her partner's stooping to romancing someone the age of their daughter and was furious that he besmirched the brand. Politically it was unthinkable. How could anyone excuse his womanizing and workplace conduct?

I was drowning in the BS and couldn't see clearly. Walking into the Starr investigation's office for our FBI/UD meetings, I took a deep breath. It was contentious from the outset. They asked the same questions the Secret Service's attorneys asked. I told them exactly what I legally could. But they wanted all the details. They were certain I knew more and was holding back. They wanted the smoking gun.

It went on for days. Finely dressed suits grilled me and accused me of corruption. After each session I trudged to Mark's office (his role defending me was strictly hush-hush and he did not accompany me to Starr's offices), rehashing everything once more. Back home I would just pass out, leaving Genny with little support. The BS wore me down. I didn't want to put it on her shoulders. She had enough to carry with our first child. It wasn't right.

Suddenly I realized, *This must be what Vince Foster felt like—no escape except one.* I never felt as if I had no way out, nor did suicide ever cross my mind. But I was overcome by desperation. It's painful to remember everything even now. I reminded myself of what I still had, what I believed in. But my paranoia festered. This wasn't a fair fight. I felt surrounded.

A couple of nights I couldn't sleep so I placed myself on the couch directly facing the door with my sidearm loaded, a round chambered, ready at the slightest sound to draw and fight. That's what it took to get to sleep at times. Each day, my feeling of no sanctuary, no reprieve, grew. No husband or father wants to feel as though he's putting a target on his family or that his job could compromise their well-being. We discussed some security measures, and I told her that if I ever gave her a call to leave, where she was to go—and how I'd meet her there.

If the Clintons had just told the truth, my wife wouldn't have had to suffer this torture. *Why did they have to operate like this?*

Each day, the FBI/JD squeezed me between a rock and hard place. I couldn't reveal any confidential intel but still tried to answer their questions as best I could. In a small, glass-paneled office at the Starr investigation headquarters, things started to get out of hand.

"Read him his rights!" yelled the investigator. I was being arrested.

"Are you f—ing kidding me?" I yelled in disbelief.

"You have the right to remain silent. . . ."

An FBI agent read me my Miranda rights, but they didn't care if Gary Byrne lived or died. That was clear. Shouting erupted. More Secret Service lawyers rushed in. One pulled me out of the room as the agent and I got in each other's faces. Outside, a Secret Service attorney calmed me down as he explained that they weren't going to let the FBI arrest me—but in the same breath he told me that if the FBI wanted to, the Service couldn't legally impede them.

Some reassurance.

The issue? Nobody could understand how Monica got past me, the president's uniformed gatekeeper. Duh! *Because the staff kept aiding and abetting her and because the president wanted her there—* that last part I couldn't legally say; it was privileged. And every detail had to be mulled over. "Well, how did you know Monica was paid or unpaid?" Because she had an intern pass, and then after I recommended she be removed she appeared back in the White House with the blue pass indicating she was a sanctioned West Wing staffer. Any mention of the president was illegal.

Days later, the bastards did it again. The same agent yelled in my face, "I will come to your house and arrest you in front of your pregnant wife!"

I bolted up and slammed the table. We leaned in across the table separating us, ready to pounce. It was about to tip over—if I didn't lurch over it first.

"F— you! I don't have to take this shit from you!" I yelled, and everyone started shouting again.

Each word drew us physically closer. The Service attorney grabbed my arm, pushing me out of the room as others poured in, and the agent and I were still yelling. Every word from that agent destroyed my ability to process. If the attorneys couldn't keep us apart, we were going across that table and settle it like old-school cops.

Gary Grindler might as well have kicked down each door as he stormed into the office. It was just him, the Starr guys, and that FBI agent. That office was soundproof but I saw it all through the glass. Grindler took a verbal ax to those assholes. He got his point across. They needed to understand that we were all cops. Despite the petty BS, I was no criminal, and they had no right to threaten *anyone's* family like that. They did it to my subpoenaed colleagues, too.

But I made myself another promise: If that FBI agent came at me one more time, we were going to go at it—and I was going to strike first. *If I was going to go to jail, I was going to make it worth my while.* My blood still boils when I think about it.

Grindler came out and sent me home for the night. It was the safe thing to do.

My paranoia was justified. Between the FBI's keeping close tabs on me (too close for comfort, and apparently even on Genny), their intimations of arrest, the Service's pressuring me *not* to remember, and rumors of Clinton intimidations, the stress was mounting. I never called my independent counsel from a White House or Service phone, and I knew all of the Justice Department attorneys "were eating at the same steakhouse," to use a D.C. term. They were from the same damn office and were excited to throw the book at hardworking cops stuck in the worst situation cops can be in, the kind where we have no g-ddamn clue or chance to defend ourselves. I loved Mark and his boys like they were my *family,* but man, I loathe all other lawyers.

A well-meaning pal of mine sent a memo to all posts. He was a bit of a computer wiz and thought it was in good taste. The fax read, "Gary J. Byrne is being transferred to Ft. Marcy Park," *the park where Vince Foster was found dead in a supposed suicide.* It was even taped to my locker. Everyone laughed, but behind the laughter was a lump in my throat. I saw firsthand how the First Couple had lied, demeaned, and manipulated in such an arrogant and gutless fashion. But could they actually be behind so many of the suspicious—or merely coincidental—deaths surrounding their activities? Had they really killed Vince Foster? Was it even possible? It weighed on me.

Every cop knows how to get away with murder, but cops are supposed to be above being targeted. Even the mere perception of it was frightening. Genny tried reassuring me, "Don't worry, Homer [our beagle] will protect me." That didn't help. I thought, "F—ing great, it's even on my wife's mind." I couldn't get the words of numerous Arkansas troopers and PPD agents out of my mind. They all looked me right in the eye and used the word *ruthless*. I kept hearing, "Gary, everything you hear about them is true."

The only thing I could do was commit to a personal operational security regimen. With the heat increasing, I started making plans for what to do if my brake line were cut or someone tried to run me off the road, or if someone tried sneaking something into a beverage. I started planning in case Genny and I had to disappear and go off-grid. It was my word, *and my word only,* against the most powerful people in the world. I'd seen them lie and intimidate. It wasn't a stretch to think that things might escalate.

I knew what I was fighting. I contacted a friend, Richard, who had some rural property in north central Potter County, Pennsylvania, known officially as "God's country." He was a doctor in Philadelphia and he'd saved my mother's life from a dangerous tumor. His family was well known to mine. My mother and father had gratefully promised him and his wife a White House tour—of course, they hadn't consulted me first. (That happens to everyone working at the White House!) Despite being overworked and exhausted around the holiday season, I begrudgingly gave the doctor's family the tour. Their little stroller-bound kid—one who'd grow up to be a fine man—threw a small stuffed animal onto the White House lawn. ERT freaked and nearly called in the bomb squad!

It was now 1998, and the weight of the Clinton circus fueled my anger and paranoia. I confided in Richard that I was in a jam and needed to get out of Dodge. I didn't provide him with any details, and what was great was that he didn't ask for any, not even when I asked him if Genny and I could use his property if I had to disappear.

"Just go and don't stop for anything if I tell you to go there," I told her—something no LEO should have to tell their spouse, particularly a pregnant one.

Around this time the world finally learned about Monica's blue dress. To this day, I believe that that DNA-soiled dress saved my life. Monica had worn it on February 28, 1997, during one of her many "mentoring" sessions.

After I had recommended to Evelyn that Monica be removed from the White House, Monica became friends with White House employee Linda Tripp. Had I never recommended to Evelyn Lieberman that Monica needed to leave, Monica would have never met Linda. Tripp hated the Clintons for reasons I can only guess. Monica had preserved the stained dress as a souvenir and confided this to Linda.

Linda, who had already contacted reporter Michael Isikoff at *Newsweek,* manipulated Monica not to dry-clean the dress and to hide it in Linda's care—for Monica's protection in case the Clintons ever smeared and demeaned Monica as they had Paula Jones and other victims of Bill's sexual adventures. Linda then passed the dress on to the FBI. Hook. Line. Sinker. They used that dress to force Monica to sign for an FBI immunity from prosecution from the FBI to testify against Bill Clinton.

Later my lieutenant came up to me. I told him, "I'm doing fine." He wasn't buying it and could tell I was at wits' end. On top of everything else, I was even losing badly needed overtime assignments. I was strapped emotionally—and financially. I really needed to get away.

He gave it some thought and said, "Gary, here's what I want you to do. I'll work on the OT—no promises. I want you to leave a number, some number where only I can reach you. Take your wife. Go on vacation somewhere where no one can find you, not your usual hangout spot, but where only I can reach you with that number. Got me?" he said.

Genny, Homer, and I absconded to a nearby yet remote lake in Maryland. I hitched my Jet Ski–laden trailer to the car and peeled out on the highway with pedal to the metal.

One sleepless night, I watched Geraldo Rivera talking about me on national television. I just knew my two weeks of Jet Ski freedom were about to be cut short. Sure enough, the next morning, I got the call: "I'm so sorry, but we're going to have to bring you back in. How soon can you be at SSHQ?"

It wasn't an actual question.

If I wasn't back in twelve hours, I was told, I'd be in jail.

15.

MUD DRAG: PART II

I had been called back to answer a subpoena.

In total I received six subpoenas, all of which compelled me to testify truthfully via videotape before a grand jury. I was questioned in a small, simple room containing a few chairs and a single table. Nothing was ornate. It resembled a nicer version of a standard interrogation room. With the videographer's setup, plus the court reporter, her little machine, and the prosecution lawyers crowding inside, the room got even smaller. All eyes, especially the dark eye of the video camera, were on me. All I had for comfort was my conscience and a plastic bottle of water.

The court reporter swore me in. Secret Service attorneys stood outside waiting for me to excuse myself and come to them when I had questions regarding what I had to keep secret. "Do the right thing, Gary," I felt my wife was saying miles away.

A female attorney from Starr's staff counseled me on my right against self-incrimination.

She reminded me that I couldn't lie by saying, "I don't remember." She reminded me that her team wouldn't ask about secret or privileged matters of the White House. But they definitely wanted nonprivileged information. The gray areas between privileged and nonprivileged was my not-so-private hell.

C-SPAN later broadcast the video of my interrogation. But viewers didn't get the whole picture. The Secret Service blacked out details regarding my postings, official names, and details or accounts of the president's movements. (I could finally provide those after Chief Justice William Rehnquist essentially voided the concept of "protective privilege.") Then all the marking, noting, and initialing of exhibits started—just to keep things straight.

My plastic water bottle was my crinkly comfort blanket. I really wanted to feel the reassurance of my firearm against my hip, but that was not to be. They made me hand over my gun before my questioning commenced.

They wanted to know every little detail. I testified to the numerous times I had discovered Monica where she clearly didn't belong, what I thought of her, how she manipulated friendships, how distraught Nel was, and how I'd thrown away those lipstick-smeared towels. I couldn't legally mention semen—because that was the president's.

I wanted to curl up and die.

I made it clear that I never thought I was committing any crimes. I thought I was protecting the president from more rumors—particularly the true ones. They asked if I connected the lipstick to Monica. Surprisingly, no one had ever asked me that before, so I never revealed my thoughts. But Presidential Protective Function Privilege prevented my honest answer. I was on thin ice any which way I moved.

"You thought it could be anyone?" a lawyer asked.

I responded with a heavy fear upon my chest. "Without revealing any privileged information, on the advice of my counsel, yes, I did."

I wasn't lying. Or was I? I was up a legal shit's creek without a paddle. The only one who could un-f— my situation was the president!

"I did not connect the lipstick to Monica at that time."

"At all?" he said surprised.

"No."

"Did you connect the lipstick to anyone?"

"Without revealing any privileged information on the advice of my counsel . . ." I paused before saying, "Yes, I did."

"You connected it with *someone* but didn't connect it with Monica?" he said with some surprise, his voice betraying eager anticipation of what I might say.

"Yes," I answered.

"Did you connect it with a woman?"

"Yes."

"Can you tell me whether it is a White House employee?"

"It is."

It wasn't past tense. She still worked there.

"Well, I'll just ask the straightforward question, who did you connect it with?"

"I connected it with [the Service blacked out her name]. She was the West Wing receptionist at the time."

"What made you connect it with [blacked out her name]?"

"Without revealing any privileged information . . ." and I trailed off.

I tried insinuating that there were other women, what a womanizer and an unabashed cheater the president was, and how crazy things really were at the White House. But that was risky. I had no attorney-client privileges to save me from my own bosses. The Justice Department swore they would never release these tapes to the public. But who trusted them?

They asked me about the towel incident and if Monica was an employee, a blue pass holder, at the time. I told them the truth: yes. She had been an *intern*-mistress who was fired. She returned as an *employee*-mistress despite the intention of many others, including myself. I told them about the West Wing receptionist, and how I believed for reasons that I couldn't reveal that it was her lipstick. The woman had been a flight attendant turned organizer (with her husband) of private flights for people like rock stars or, in this case, for a presidential candidate. ABC News broadcast video of 1992 presidential candidate Clinton with his hand between this future receptionist's leg on one of those flights. Another flight attendant from that series of charter flights later accused President Clinton of sexual harassment and tried peddling that story.

Hailing from Texas, the receptionist had that special Lone Star twang and flair. Actually, she was very charming and a good person. I did not want to reveal her name. But neither she nor I fell under the "Presidential Protective Function Privilege."

When she became a White House receptionist she worked closely with Hernreich and Currie. She'd even fill in for them if they stepped out of their offices. I never doubted her character because I never knew how the First Lady factored into it. The rumors were that Mrs. Clinton sanctioned everything like a grand puppet master, so I never had a problem with that receptionist. I did have problems with Monica, who manipulated us into allowing her into unauthorized areas ultimately to get to the president.

I knew about that receptionist (I even once witnessed her giving the president what looked like a back massage), about Eleanor, and about Monica. Discussing Clinton's behavior (however, tangentially) during my deposition made 1600 Pennsylvania seemed more like a late-night red-light district than a national institution. I never discussed such matters with any coworkers outside of work. The information we shared was always a whispered heads-up, a professional courtesy, but not gossip. I felt like I was gossiping here. In the deposition videotape you can see me slump farther into my chair, not exactly my proudest moment. I felt trapped. I couldn't reveal what I knew about the semen! I couldn't say a word; it was the most "privileged" of information.

I corroborated what I (among many others) had heard of how an officer or a staff person had walked in on Eleanor and the president in the White House movie theater. I also corroborated how Monica had tried to gain entrance to the White House during a congressional visit by befriending some other higher-up. She had her ways. An officer she had once befriended was used to her being "off book" (not officially logged in, as per protocol) when he screened her, and he escorted her through to the White House. Another officer barked at him, "Either you walk her off the grounds and back to the gold rope section immediately—or I will."

I also testified regarding an incident that occurred during the 1996 Christmas season—a black-tie, who's-who event. We were clearing guests in tuxedos and ball gowns when I saw Monica. I stormed over to her, saying indignantly, "You know you're not supposed to be here." But when I checked the list, sure as shit, there she was—as a guest of an invited guest (how strange was that?).

Minutes later, a Social Office higher-up approached my sergeant and me as we screened more visitors. She barked: "You guys screwed up—you let Monica in!"

I just laughed. She stomped off. I got my buddy "Henry" to cover my post for a second while the sergeant and I chased another Social Office employee, whom I'll call Kim. Kim was with her assistant and was also fuming about how "you guys screwed up" by letting in

Monica. Kim pointed at me specifically, getting a tad too personal. I knew I couldn't let Kim get away with that.

At this point in the deposition, the Secret Service blacked out a huge chunk of my testimony. I still can't discuss it. Honest.

Back to the action. I interrupted Kim. "Is this Monica's name on the list?" I asked her like a smart-ass. I couldn't help my bitter undertone. I pointed to "Monica Lewinsky" on the guest list. Flipping to the first page, I pointed to something else. "Is that your signature? Then you let her in, not us. You signed off on it, not us. That was your job."

Ironically, the Social Office was under the First Lady. Technically it was FLOTUS's job to extend the invitations, but the idea that Mrs. Clinton would take responsibility for someone under her command? Laughable. I surely never saw it.

At this point in the deposition, I realized I had roped myself into a bit of a snare. The investigators start asking why Kim would be angry that Monica made it into the White House and why everyone from the Social Office to the UD knew that Monica was unofficially blacklisted. If it wasn't official, yet everyone knew, *what* did they know? What were the terms by which people, including Kim and I, knew why Monica was transferred and blacklisted? They kept asking. I told them how Kim knew that Monica had been transferred to the Pentagon even after being a pass holder, an employee. I couldn't really say *what* we knew.

Why would Kim be so adamant that "you guys had screwed up?" asked the one lawyer.

"Well, she would blame anything on us, to be honest with you," I responded.

I explained to them how Kim and others from the Social Office disdained us, which was absolutely truthful. I didn't dare explain the reason for their animosity: Their boss, Mrs. Clinton, hated us.

The previous administration's Social Office had been very kind and professional to us even if they suspected that we *had* screwed up.

I ducked the lawyer's queries about Monica's exile because I couldn't give him the real answer: that the president had dropped her like a bad habit—which, come to think of it, she was.

I did relate a story of how the president one night had directly ordered a sergeant to rush the Control Center to expedite Monica's screening so she could meet him for a completely off-the-books, late-night session. He had never before called the CQ to expedite screenings for anyone.

I explained to the lawyers, "Whenever I had heard about any of these rumors, I tried to get the hell out of the room. I was just so fed up with the rumors. With the things at the White House, I was tired, so aggravated, that I had to just get the hell out of there. And I still do."

The manpower costs involved in this investigation were massive. I was paid for weeks to do nothing more than answer (or not answer) questions. The Justice Department allocated all its legal heavyweights to the fray. The Service lost dozens of men for days on end to the legal battle of protecting the president. Who could tally the cost of all the men and women who felt compelled to leave their jobs, or those like Linda Tripp who were compelled to work against their boss, the president? Morale descended to an all-time low. The president could have let all these resources return to their normal jobs with a few simple words, but he—they—possessed too great a store of Machiavellian pride for that.

The *New York Times* published a drawing that was spot-on, albeit demoralizing. It nailed the issue of our credibility. It portrayed three cartoon Secret Service agents with their aviator glasses and earpieces. They separately gestured "Hear no evil, see no evil, speak no evil," but the sightless agent had slightly lifted his dark glasses. He was peeking. He saw the evil. While I wasn't an agent, I knew I was among this trio. I wasn't happy about being in the *New York Times*, although with each subpoena, I did request legal counsel to mail me more presentable copies. I wanted something to frame on my wall when everything was said and done. They laughed in disbelief.

My final testimony concerned Monica's arrival at the Northwest Gate on her way to meet with Betty Currie. I revealed Betty's name but once again, not the president's. I related how gate officers phoned Betty to confirm Monica's appointment and how Betty ordered them to delay her since the president was busy.

I testified that Monica called the Oval Office via a checkpoint pay phone (she couldn't have used the president's secret military line as I testified she had inside the White House). If only Nancy Hernreich, the director of Oval Office operations, had put Monica on the "E-6 access list" (that granted The First Daughter, Lady, or Chief of Staff anytime access) as other E-6 UD and I had futilely asked, but there were so many what-if's. With Monica giving the president an earful, and the president fuming to Betty, Betty called me to see how we could sort out the issue of a UD gate officer leaking whom the president was with—and what he was doing. What the president didn't know—and I didn't mention it because nobody asked—was that the gate officer told Monica that the president was with another piece of a– and that she would have to wait her turn. With his cats out of the bag, the president was incensed.

An attorney halted the proceedings. "I'm going to ask you to stop at this point and maybe ask you to step outside. Have you discussed this incident with your attorneys?"

"Yep," I said quickly.

"You have? Have they discussed privileges with you?" she inquired unemotionally.

"Yes. And that's probably as far as I can go. Yeah. So . . . that's what they decided I could talk about."

We all started to begin every sentence by saying, "Without revealing any privileged information . . ."

I testified that the incident had traveled up the chain of command to the sergeant and the watch commander. I informed them that even in discussing the incident among ourselves within UD, we remained circumspect. An attorney asked why. The real answer, which I also couldn't say, was to save ourselves from being dragged through the mud like this. The less you knew, the safer you were. Not to mention, we simply feared the Clintons.

They asked me to disclose the name of the officer who told me the story of Monica at the Northwest Gate, they wanted me to corroborate, and I hated those attorneys for it. I told them that we officers recognized we had made a mistake even discussing it, but I had put the snare on myself. We had discussed the story because we were tired, wound up, overworked, and frustrated at the corruption and the bullshit. We hated hanging tight and wading through the new culture that consumed the White House. We knew not to talk about that stuff, because it could implicate us in a legal fray. *I* was compelled to tell the truth, but why the hell was neither the president nor Mrs. Clinton ever really compelled to tell the damn truth? We had to get dragged through their mud for this. I didn't want to put another officer in the hot seat.

"Who was this?" asked the attorney.

"Do you—is it important? Do you need to know? I'd hate to disclose his name and—I mean, is it that important to you?" I asked. I pleaded.

He snapped back at me, unequivocally, "Yes."

"I know for a fact you've already talked to him about it. . . . I know we made a mistake and I, I prompted this onto him. We made a mistake. I do realize it's clear that you did need to know this but . . ."

I told him who it was. My fellow officer would be dragged back in to their damn office to be cross-examined yet again over the excruciatingly fine details. I was pissed at myself. It was all because of Monica. *No*, it was all because of Bill and Mrs. Clinton and the way they governed.

They asked me another question. I told them I needed to step outside.

Out in the corridor, I got my head straight. I returned and they asked me a few more questions, and I invoked privilege. Their attorney feared that they had pressed me too far and worried that I'd now stonewall behind privilege and foggy memory.

We took another break.

Many a time in my preceding interviews, I'd asked, "The director [of the Secret Service] isn't going to see this, right?" or "You guys aren't going to release this deposition to the public, are you?" I was being asked to provide very sensitive information pertinent to some higher-ups' careers. Some officers even had to divulge affairs not related to the president, snaring them into disclosing which directors or chiefs were having affairs with which staffers. It was all very bad. The stories got leaked to the press, and things got ugly for them. Again, lawyers conducting my depositions reassured me they wouldn't release my testimony, as the other lawyers did to other witnesses. It's what they told us all, those Justice Department and FBI bastards.

Not long after my video deposition, I was talking to a Secret Service colleague who worked the West Wing Lobby. He had just resumed his shift after returning from his own testimony. The president had just visited him. That was extremely suspicious—my associate was spooked.

"He just came out and came straight up to me like—like he was looking for me. Yeah, and he asked how I was by name. We chatted—like small talk—like normal. And then he asked how my wife and kids were. . . . We've never actually talked before."

Nothing about that was normal. It was obviously a subtle form of intimidation. The president was sending a message that he knew of the officer's recent testimony—and perhaps was sending an even more sinister message. I certainly was glad to be at JJRTC, away from them. It was all so wild, so bizarre. Prior to that, the president didn't seem to know my fellow officer by name. Someone—most likely the president's attorneys—advised him to make small talk immediately after the officer testified. The president's little "hint" spooked both of us. It confirmed to me what I suspected: That was indeed how they operated.

It was reminiscent of the stories we had heard of some of the women who alleged that the president, while governor, had either raped or sexually assaulted them. In one of the stories Mrs. Clinton had homed in on the alleged victim, despite having never met her beforehand, just as the president zeroed in on the West Wing Lobby officer. I was glad to be at JJRTC, but I feared that I was not far enough away.

Our Secret Service attorneys reassured us that our video depositions were supposed to be in lieu of actual in-person testimony. But that was never Starr's intention, and two weeks later Starr summoned us back to the courtroom for us to testify in person. It was insurmountably stressful. I remember the feeling of being trapped or drowning.

I, along with my fellow Secret Service staff, was still caught in the legal tug-of-war between the Treasury Department/Secret Service, who claimed protective privilege, and Ken Starr, who said that was pure hogwash. Not surprisingly, neither side would budge, and the issue went to court. In May 1998 Judge Norma Holloway Johnson (a Jimmy Carter appointee) sided with Starr, who said that USSS agents and UD officers could testify. The Treasury Department/Secret Service appealed. In early July 1998, a three-judge panel of the U.S. Court of Appeals for the D.C. Circuit unanimously sustained that opinion. The Treasury Department/Secret Service appealed again, this time all the way up to the United States Supreme Court. Now it was getting interesting.

Particularly for me.

Starr had already scheduled my appearance before the Whitewater grand jury.* But what was I free to say in front of it? Should I obey my bosses, who wanted everything hushed up? Or the appeals court, who wanted me to talk? If I listened to the appeals court and the Supreme Court ultimately ruled against it, I'd really be hung out to dry. Mark advised me to obey the law, tell the truth—and definitely not to "fall on my sword" for either Bill's or Monica's misdeeds.

Just as in the old Gary Cooper movie, the shoot-out would occur at high noon—or, at least, that was the deadline on July 18, 1998, by which the U.S. Supreme Court had to decide whether to take up the Treasury Department's appeal or to let the federal appeals court ruling stand—and allow me to testify.

---

* Ken Starr's investigation began with Whitewater Development Corporation scandal and under another special investigator, Robert B. Fiske. Though I testified before this so-called "Whitewater grand jury," my testimony had nothing to do with Whitewater.

The clock ticked.

Just four minutes before noon, word arrived from the Supreme Court: Chief Justice William Rehnquist had ruled. The Supreme Court would *not* grant the Justice Department's appeal. The D.C. appeals court ruling held. The Presidential Protective Function Privilege was bogus.

I could testify.

But to whom? The normal audience before whom I would testify—Starr's Whitewater grand jury—had been excused for a few days. I was sitting in the federal courthouse. They weren't. Starr grabbed another grand jury, completely unrelated to that one, from down the hall. I would testify before them.

The games would begin.

Another atmosphere of high drama, near panic, filled the room. It certainly consumed me. I was a wreck. In the past two weeks I'd gotten only three hours' sleep—*three hours*! I would run for seven miles a day trying to exhaust myself into some sleep. It never worked. I never slept.

I wanted to throw up. Reaching for a wastebasket to heave in, I struggled not to barf on a U.S. marshal. They hustled me out of the grand jury room.

I made it to the men's room just in time.

My grand jury testimony warred against everything that I believed in—and even against myself. No matter what I did, I could not escape a dreadful feeling of betraying someone or something: my fellow servicemen, my protectees, *the* protectee, and even my previous testimony! I've all but blacked it out of my mind, except for the horrible feeling of dread.

We servicemen completed our highly constrained testimony and waited for the other dominoes to fall.

Following a week of legal debriefing and further BS, I returned to my post at JJRTC's security unit. It was time to work on my career goal of becoming an instructor.

I kept checking in with my supervisor on my application to become an instructor. I wanted to teach others how to protect innocent lives and to halt bad guys.

When an instructor spot opened, however, I was repeatedly denied an opportunity even to test for it. I finally pressed my supervisor. Initially, she had trouble looking me in the eye. Then she sighed, folded her arms, and looked me *straight in the eye.* "Gary, I keep sending up the paperwork, but honestly, higher up the chain your name is mud. They all know who you are."

I wanted to scream. Long story short: I decided to short-circuit the chain of command by approaching someone I knew could help. He was as outraged as I was.

"I'm not asking that you give me the position," I told him. "Just give me the same chance as everyone else. Let me take the tests."

He agreed, and against the wishes of the higher-ups who had blackballed me I was allowed to test.

Meanwhile, the Starr investigation played out sordidly. Only half its drama, my part, transpired behind closed doors. The rest unraveled in full public view. The Clintons kept burrowing. Starr kept digging after them the way a dog digs a fox from its den. But I was ready to put the events of my Oval Office posting behind me and launch a new life of teaching men and women of character, bright apples picked right off the tree, how to defend not only their lives but the lives of others. I had a wonderful wife—and a healthy newborn baby girl. She was the great gift of our lives, a little ball of joy. We had survived the Clintons' hell and achieved something so victorious and so grand, our little firstborn, our baby girl.

I so much wanted to get on with the rest of the American dream.

On Monday afternoon, August 17, 1998, while still at the White House, President Bill Clinton became the first president to appear before a grand jury and testify regarding his own actions. It was videotaped just the way ours was, but he also appeared "live" (though remotely) to that grand jury via closed-circuit TV. Now *he* was cornered and finally had to pay the piper—or at least tell some portion of the truth. We all held our breath.

That night he spoke via television to the entire nation, furiously trying to stay ahead of the shit storm he himself had created when, on Saturday, January 27, he made a demonstratively false sworn statement—outright perjury—that the allegations about him and Monica Lewinsky were false.

He said emphatically and fervently, "I did not have sexual relations with that woman, Ms. Lewinsky." It was his word against ours with a titillated world watching. Only because of Linda Tripp, Monica Lewinsky's infamous blue dress, and Ken Starr could the truth set us all free.

Genny and I watched the president's four-minute performance as if it were a made-for-TV movie, albeit begrudgingly. It took our beautiful baby girl's hooting and hollering to break our stunned silence. That morning the president had presented his version of events to the Starr grand jury. We had stared at our TV as the president had commenced. He blinked twice. Someone behind the camera had delayed a few seconds too long to give him the wave signaling that they were on-air. It was a long, awkward, nail-biting two seconds.

"Good evening," he began. "This afternoon in this room, from this chair, I testified before the Office of Independent Counsel and the grand jury. I answered their questions truthfully, including questions about my private life, questions no American citizen would ever want to answer. Still, I must take complete responsibility for all my actions, both public and private. And that is why I am speaking to you tonight. As you know, in a deposition in January, I was asked questions about my relationship with Monica Lewinsky. While my answers were legally accurate, I did not volunteer information.

"Indeed, I did have a relationship with Miss Lewinsky that was not appropriate. In fact, it was wrong. It constituted a critical lapse in judgment and a personal failure on my part for which I am solely and completely responsible. But I told the grand jury today and I say to you now that at no time did I ask anyone to lie, to hide or destroy evidence or to take any other unlawful action. I know that my public comments and my silence about this matter gave a false impression. I misled people, including even my wife. I deeply regret that. I can only tell you I was motivated by many factors. First, by a desire to protect myself from the embarrassment of my own conduct. I was also very concerned about protecting my family."

The camera slowly zoomed in. I wondered why. Was the president poised to say something dramatic?

Nope. Just more bull.

"The fact that these questions were being asked in a politically inspired lawsuit, which has since been dismissed, was a consideration, too."

To which lawsuit was he referring? Whitewater? Paula Jones? Dismissed? His misconduct never was. He was deflecting from the *real* issue: his character and his lies.

He continued. "In addition, I had real and serious concerns about an independent counsel investigation that began with private business dealings twenty years ago, dealings I might add about which an independent federal agency found no evidence of any wrongdoing by me or my wife over two years ago. The independent counsel investigation moved on to my staff and friends, then into my private life. And now the investigation itself is under investigation. This has gone on too long, cost too much, and hurt too many innocent people. Now, this matter is between me, the two people I love most—my wife and our daughter—and our God. I must put it right, and I am prepared to do whatever it takes to do so. Nothing is more important to me personally. But it is private, and I intend to reclaim my family life for my family. It's nobody's business but ours. Even presidents have private lives. It is time to stop the pursuit of personal destruction and the prying into private lives and get on with our national life. Our country has been distracted by this matter for too long, and I take my responsibility for my part in all of this. That is all I can do. It is past time to move on. We have important work to do—real opportunities to seize, real problems to solve, real security matters to face. And so tonight, I ask you to turn away from the spectacle of the past seven months, to repair the fabric of our national discourse, and to return our attention to all the challenges and all the promise of the next American century. Thank you for watching. And good night."

My heart started to climb down to a normal beat. I rubbed my eyes and patted Homer. My wife turned to me and I to her. I so hoped we could now move on. I didn't want to see Secret Service guard Gary Byrne in the newspaper anymore, that was for damned sure.

We cleaned up the kitchen and made ready to start the day early tomorrow. I considered going out for another run to cool my nerves. We didn't know what he had said in the testimony, but later as I lay in bed, trying to translate the president's highly crafted words, I realized a few things—and I was pissed.

As I listened to his cunning, scripted message, I became even angrier. *He never apologized to us.* He never apologized for putting us in that position. He lied out of both ends of his mouth, blaming the Secret Service while saying he wanted to be forthcoming but couldn't—two lies in one! He and his staff created the Protective Function Privilege. He was the one who did the deed, committed the misconduct. He was the one who lied. Not only did he never apologize for costing the taxpayers, the Justice Department, the Secret Service, his staff, his constituents, or anyone for putting them through the ringer, endangering our careers, and our very lives. He wanted us to believe that he was sorry for embarrassing his family, Chelsea and Hillary. (I can understand about Chelsea.)

In typical Billary fashion, they claimed *they* hadn't created the problem. The media had, the Republicans, the lawyers—anyone but them. *He was sorry,* he said.

I couldn't stand it anymore.

I grew angrier, got out of bed, and went out for a run. I just hoped the president was right: I hoped it was time to get back to work. But why should any of his lies be different from the others?

August turned into September. Genny and I were still living in "the shitbox," a run-down rental home that sheltered us as we awaited the building of our new home. While driving there one day, I received a call from former UD colleague Sandy.

"Byrne," I said. Cops answer phones like cops even when they're home.

"They f—d us, Gary! They f—ed us!"

"Whoa, whoa. Calm down. Who f—ed us? What are—?"

"I can't believe it! I can't believe it! Are you watching? They f—ed us, Gary! They released the g-ddamn tapes! Our depositions are playing on the damn television. We're all over the g-ddamn news! They're showing our faces!"

She kept repeating herself frantically and angrily.

Get a call like that, and your mind races. Her voice resembled the intonation of a fellow officer calling for backup, one hand on the walkie-talkie, one on a drawn gun. Sandy sounded just like the K-9 officer who had called for backup when I had hopped the barricade and raced across the park to assist her against that knife-wielding suspect. But Sandy's trouble—and mine—was on television screens nationwide, on every news channel. I raced home and told Genny about it.

A neighbor appeared at our door. "Hey, Gary." He saw my expression, my nervous attitude.

I asked, "Everything okay?"

"Something's going on. Do you have cable?"

We didn't. He nodded. He led me down to his half-finished basement. His kids were watching cartoons and playing with race cars and Barbie dolls. I grabbed the remote and started flipping through channels.

There was C-SPAN. And there I was on it. This was only the second time I had seen my video deposition. The first was during my testimony when I'd been asked to confirm my testimony. But there I was on TV. I remember thinking, *The Justice Department and the FBI did f— us!* My neighbor's kids stopped pleading for their cartoons and sat speechless. They looked at the TV, the man on it, and then back at me, back and forth.

My neighbor was doing the same thing. He exclaimed, "Oh Gary, you're so f—ed!" and issued a nervous laugh. I was speechless.

A Justice Department lawyer soon explained to me that his department technically hadn't lied. Nobody *technically* lies in this game, it seems. The department *didn't* release the tapes to the public, but it knew damn well that it was going to release all its evidence to Congress, and once Congress got its own hands on the evidence, it would release as much or as little of it as it pleased. Congress released *our* tapes and more than three thousand pages of the Starr investigation's findings.

I wasn't out of the grinder yet. The media wasn't buzzing, it roared over every word. It was the ultimate game of he said/she said and fell right on American party lines. The Republican third of the country hated the Clintons, another third wasn't sure, the Democratic third vehemently toed the Clinton line. Folks in the middle waited for the smoke to clear—but kept lapping it all up.

Nothing was more embarrassing for this nation than the release of the president's grand jury testimony. Starr's investigators asked him to corroborate—or contradict—the sworn, often protected-by-immunity testimony of Monica, presidential staff members, Secret Service agents, and UD officers like myself. But his lies—and his earlier actions—trapped him in a painful, steel-strong web. Not even his elaborate legal weaseling could free him. For hours on end, a weasel did what weasels do, but a man was nowhere to be found.

For weeks and months, pundits debated its significance. They parsed the words and counted up the damage. The cost to President Clinton was incalculable. His character was laid bare.

The questions were relevant, though embarrassing, and often, when you got down it, obscene. News anchors prefaced accounts of the event by warning viewers that some of the language used was sexual, graphic, and vulgar, and that kids shouldn't watch. They kept saying it was "not for children" and "explicit." The world was glued to their sets and salivating to the drama.

The president swore to "tell the truth, the whole truth, and nothing but the truth," so help him God. He swore. They reminded him of his oath immediately after he took it and reminded him of his responsibilities. They couldn't have made it any clearer, but the independent counsel had to, because it was now President Bill Clinton's testimony against himself and what he had sworn before, and the word of others, including myself. I wanted vindication. But I also wanted this to go away. All of the USSS was watching, too, and they knew my part. Many were still pissed off.

They asked the president if he'd been truthful before, and he said he had. He was obviously, awkwardly, and painfully weaseling through a series of lies. They moved on to Monica Lewinsky, asking if he had been "physically intimate" with her. If he had lied about her—and he had—they'd shake his credibility regarding the Paula Jones case, Whitewater, and just about anything else, really.

The president got ahead of the line of questioning and asked to read from a prepared statement of his relationship with "Ms. Lewinsky." But right off the bat, he admitted that he had been alone with her on multiple occasions. One weight had been lifted from my shoulders and another had been placed on my chest. During this slow-motion train wreck, the president confirmed what I had said, that he had been alone with her, thereby contradicting his previous affidavit, the one he said was still somehow true. He then continued, saying he hadn't lied because he thought when asked about "sexual relations" he interpreted that phrase as "sexual intercourse," which he hadn't had. It was a huge stretch only a weasel with a law degree could make.

"If Monica Lewinsky says that you used a cigar as a sexual aid with her in the Oval Office area, would she be lying? Yes, no, or won't answer?"

"I will revert to my former statement."

Unbelievable! This is the man I was protecting? That's what I tolerated? I had tried and tried to prevent harm to this president, but he failed us all!

He and investigators tangled over the definition of "sexual" regarding intercourse. President Clinton introduced an entire generation to the concept of oral sex—and worse, provided them with rationalizations for risky behavior.

They asked him, "If Monica Lewinsky says that you had phone sex with her, would she be lying?"

He responded, "Well, that is—at least, in general terms, I think, is covered by my statement. . . ."

The lawyer, getting frustrated, went on: "Let me define phone sex for purposes of my question. Phone sex occurs when the party to the phone conversation masturbates while the other party is talking in a sexually explicit manner. The question is, if Monica Lewinsky says that you had phone sex with her, would she be lying?"

Jeez. That phone line was one of the reasons I had recommended to Evelyn Lieberman that Monica be transferred or moved, but I never knew what the hell she and the president did over that drop line!

The president again responded, "I think that is covered by my statement."

They followed that with a discussion of how the president ensured that Monica had an employment payback for her past "services" and maybe even for her future silence about the whole mess. The country would later gain more details of how the president had approached his friend, the influential Washington power broker Vernon Jordan, to assist Monica in securing private-sector employment. Jordan, who served on the board of directors of Revlon cosmetics, pulled strings to see that Monica got a look-see there. He did the same with another corporation on whose board he served.

Jordan was the president's pal, but he was no dummy. He was nervous about assisting Monica when she had been subpoenaed in the Paula Jones case, and he even quizzed Clinton on whether he'd had sex with Monica. The investigator brought that up. Clinton pathetically continued to bob and weave, obfuscating and deflecting left and right.

I heard them say:

QUESTION: . . . But isn't that why Vernon Jordan asked you on December 19th whether or not you had sexual relationships with Monica Lewinsky and why he asked her, because he knew it would be so highly improper to be helping her with a lawyer and a job if, in fact, she had had a relationship with you?

CLINTON: I don't know. I don't believe that at all. I don't believe that at all, particularly since, even if you look at the facts here in their light most unfavorable to me, no one has suggested that there was any sexual harassment on my part. And I don't think it was wrong to be helping her. . . .

They went on to discuss gifts exchanged between Monica and the president, gifts swapped with Betty Currie as a conduit, gifts I knew of—and was extremely wary about.

He finessed his way through it all, playing the "I don't recall" game. He played the same game when asked about how Betty and UD officers had inserted Betty's name on their official visitors' log when it was Monica who actually visited, so as not to betray the president. It was yet another obvious lie on his part. I knew that game. Everyone with eyes could see it.

He never recalled how she came to him with letters or papers. There was a back-and-forth on how the Clintons had garnered a lawyer for Monica so she could obfuscate matters and not implicate the president in his defense in Paula Jones's civil sexual harassment case. They discussed how unethical that was, and that's when the president had the nerve to blame the debacle *on the information's getting leaked,* not that it *actually happened.*

Finally it came down to blaming Monica.

The president was on a roll, employing the most time-tested tactic from the Clinton Machine playbook:

"After I terminated the improper contact with her, she wanted to come in more than she did. She got angry when she didn't get in sometimes. I knew that that might make her more likely to speak [to Paula Jones's lawyers], and I still did it because I had to limit the contact. And thirdly, let me say, I formed an opinion really in early 1996, and again—well, let me finish the sentence. I formed an opinion early in 1996, once I got into this unfortunate and wrong conduct, that when I stopped it, which I knew I'd have to do and which I should have done a long time before I did, that she would talk about it. Not because Monica Lewinsky is a bad person. She's basically a good girl. She's a good young woman with a good heart and a good mind. I think she is burdened by some unfortunate conditions of her, her upbringing. But she's basically a good person. But I knew the minute there was no longer any contact, she would talk about this. She would have to. She couldn't help it. It was, it was a part of her psyche. So, I had put myself at risk, sir. I was not trying to buy her silence. I thought she was a good person. She had not been involved with me for a long time in any improper way, several months, and I wanted to help her get on with her life. It's just as simple as that."

"It's time for a break," said his obviously frustrated interrogator.

The break failed to improve his memory. You had to wonder: If the man wasn't president, how would he find his car keys in the morning?

Or maybe, as Nebraska senator Bob Kerrey, a Democrat, once observed of him, he was just "an unusually good liar. *Unusually good.*"*

The note about how Monica missed him that was in the book she gave him for Christmas—can't recall. The conversations regarding her signing the affidavit—can't remember. His conversations with Betty Currie—ditto. *Weasel!* He had no right to embarrass someone as dedicated to the country as Currie. He had no right to do this to me or the rest of us.

The deposition continued. They literally couldn't agree on a definition of "alone," as if his statements were just a form of miscommunication. Hey! There were other people on planet earth last night—so maybe *I* wasn't alone with my wife.

It got worse, playing out on national television for all the world to see and devise its own judgments about. An attorney discussed with the president the semen on Monica's dress and how he would touch her, "arouse" her, and "gratify" her.

The testimony grew even more contentious. I wanted to switch it off. I couldn't. My head ached from all my head-shaking. On the screen before me they continued jousting regarding a conversation between the president and Betty that he told to jog his own memory, not to coach Betty, a potential witness, on what to say.

They discussed the president's statement and the line of questioning's scope, and how the investigation's intention was not to

* Gregory L. Vistica, *The Education of Lieutenant Kerrey* (New York: St. Martin's Press, 2013), p. 28.

embarrass the president and the office, but only to ask questions that pertained to his credibility and his perjury, and certainly not to delve into private details that would be kept for all of history and possibly released publicly.

That's when the president really pissed me off by saying, "And, so, I think I am right to answer all the questions about perjury, but not to say things which will be forever in the annals of the United States because of this unprecedented videotape and may be leaked at any time. I just think it's a mistake. And so, I'm doing my best to cooperate with the grand jury and still protect myself, my family, and my office."

It was far too little, too late.

They asked him, "Well, the grand jury would like to know, Mr. President, why it is that you think that oral sex performed on you does not fall within the definition of sexual relations as used in this deposition?"

The weasel responded in a sweaty yet matter-of-fact way, "Because that is—if the deponent is the person who has oral sex performed on him, then the contact is with—not with anything on that list, but with the lips of another person. It seems to be self-evident that that's what it is. And I thought it was curious— Let me remind you, sir, I read this carefully. And I thought about it. I thought about what 'contact' meant. I thought about what 'intent to arouse or gratify' meant. And I had to admit under this definition that I'd actually had sexual relations with Gennifer Flowers. Now, I would rather have taken a whipping than done that, after all the trouble I'd been through with Gennifer Flowers, and the money I knew that she made for the story she told about this alleged twelve-year affair, which we had done a great deal to disprove. So, I didn't like any of this, but I had done my best to deal with it and the—that's what I thought. And I think that's what most people would think, reading that."

What the hell does that even mean? Only the most lawyerly of weasels or the most weaselly of lawyers could concoct something so insane. This was our president. Still the suffering continued. Each awkward minute of this embarrassing back-and-forth mattered deeply to me. How hard we trained, how particularly we UD agents were selected to be "worthy of trust and confidence" was completely thrown away in his service.

Then things really got heated. The president tried employing his classic charm, but now it seemed more like venom than honey. Shifting sideways and forward and back, he two-stepped around each word and its definable wiggle room to lie some more, creating as much doubt as anyone might dare.

"Well, you're not telling our grand jurors that you think the case was a political case for setup, Mr. President, that that would give you the right to commit perjury?" the lawyer asked.

"No, sir. No, sir. In the face of their—the Jones's lawyers—the people that were questioning me, in the face of their illegal leaks, their constant unrelenting illegal leaks, in a lawsuit that I knew—and that by the time that this deposition and this discovery started, they knew—was a bogus suit on the law and bogus suit on the facts."

He went on, "In the face of that, I know that in the face of their illegal activity, I still had to behave lawfully. But I wanted to be legal without being particularly helpful. I thought that was what I was trying to do. And this is the—you're the first person to ever suggest to me that I should have been doing their lawyers' work for them when they were perfectly free to ask follow-up questions. On one or two occasions, Mr. [Clinton lawyer Bob] Bennett invited them to ask follow-up questions. It now appears to me they didn't because they were afraid I would give them a truthful answer, and that they had been in some communication between you and Ms. Tripp and them. And they were trying to set me up and trick me. And now you seem to be complaining that they didn't do a good enough job. I did my best, sir, at this time. I did not know what I now know about this. A lot of other things were going on in my life. Did I want this to come out? No. Was I embarrassed about it? Yes. Did I ask her to lie about it? No. Did I believe there could be a truthful affidavit? Absolutely . . ."

Again he was caught in another lie of his own making! I wondered if this was how I looked when I gave my statement, but then again I knew how I looked—I saw it on C-SPAN. I didn't weasel; I followed the rules that had been laid out for me by the Secret Service, the Justice Department, and my lawyers. It was simple: I didn't weasel. Until Chief Justice Rehnquist gave me permission I followed the rules that had been laid out for me by the Secret Service, the Justice Department, and my lawyers. It was why I had to preface so much with "Without revealing any privileged information, on the advice of my counsel . . ." But the president admitted that he lied only to save face. Investigators caught him on it.

"You're not going back on your earlier statement that you understood you were sworn to tell the truth, *the whole truth,* and nothing but the truth to the folks at that deposition, are you, Mr. President?" the lawyer asked.

I remember thinking, *Don't help him; don't feed his statements. Cut him down!* The president went on treading his own legal minefield as if he forgot where he placed the mines. He babbled on about how he deplored how Ken Starr and Paula Jones's lawyers, funded by his "political enemies," were trying to gather intel and then illegally leak it against him. In reality, it was Linda Tripp, his own former White House employee, who despised him for who he really was, who trapped him. It was Monica, his cohort, his mistress, who couldn't keep her mouth shut and made Tripp's involvement possible. How was this president so different from Richard Nixon when Nixon arrogantly claimed, "I'm saying when the president does something, it's not illegal"?

I watched Clinton continue: "So I will admit this, sir. My goal in this deposition was to be truthful, but not particularly helpful. . . ."

Oaths such as "the whole truth, and nothing but the truth, so help me God," it was clear to me, meant as much as "shall not be infringed," or "swear to uphold and defend," among others. For men of character, life is very simple. It's best to keep it that way. But clearly for the guy I was watching on television, life was just a sharp answer to woo a voter. Bill Clinton thought he had all the answers. But he never even understood the real questions in life.

I watched the rest of his proceedings in pieces, not being able to stand the deposition for more than a few minutes at a time. It was an embarrassment to me and the nation.

Later I watched it again, and that time I noticed how they discussed the witness list in the Paula Jones case and when the president had seen Monica's name on it. This was a part of the story I hadn't known about. I wasn't privy to such things.

That was December 6, 1997. And it was a date I knew very well but not because of Paula Jones, but because that was the day Betty Currie stalled Monica at the Northwest Gate.

Ken Starr's investigator continued: "Now, on the morning of the sixth [of December], Monica Lewinsky came to the NW gate and found that you were being visited by Eleanor Mondale at the same time and had an extremely angry reaction. You know that, sir, don't you?"

Holy shit. He was screwing with Eleanor in the Oval Office on that same day, the same day that the witness list for Paula Jones came out! You couldn't write this shit, I've always said, because these people were frankly so g-ddamn unprofessional.

Clinton responded flatly, "I know that," but underneath his cool demeanor I saw he was seething.

Bottom line, he couldn't keep his mistresses, where he saw them, and how he communicated with them, straight. I burst out laughing.

He continued: "What I remember is that she was very—Monica was very upset. She got upset from time to time. And—and I was, you know—I couldn't see her. I had—I was doing, as I remember—I had some other work to do that morning."

Another complete lie. The gall! He was seeing Eleanor, the B-list media star. I'd surprised them in the Map Room and had testified about it! I also testified to corroborate another Northwest Gate officer's testimony of what he told Monica when she just arrived, completely off schedule and off book, to the White House to see the president spontaneously, as if that's how things were—but then again, I knew that's how things were done. *Unbelievable,* but it was right there on C-SPAN. I'd seen his character firsthand. President Clinton saying he had work to do December 6 when he was seeing Eleanor Mondale: It was too elaborate a maze to navigate.

"And she had just sort of showed up and wanted to be let in and wanted to come in at a certain time. And she wanted everything to be that way. And we couldn't see her. Now I did arrange to see her later that day. And I was upset about her conduct."

He was upset about her conduct? What about his conduct?

"I'm not sure I knew or focused on, at that moment, exactly the question you asked. I remember I was—I thought her conduct was inappropriate that day."

It kept getting worse. Off camera, you could hear in the lawyer's voice that their nostrils were filled with the scent of blood. It must have been intoxicating. After all, this was the ultimate *A Few Good Men* moment they lived for.

The president continued, "I don't know whether I found out that day. I knew that they—I knew that somehow she knew that among— that—that Eleanor Mondale was in to see us that day. I knew that I don't know that I knew how she knew that on that day. I don't remember that."

"Pardon me. That leads into my second question, which is, weren't you irate at the Secret Service precisely because they had revealed this information to Ms. Lewinsky on that very day— so irate that you told several people—or at least one person—that somebody should be fired over this, on that very day?"

This was also absolutely true and he absolutely demanded it, with a heavy-handed insinuation, to "forget it ever happened." It was no different from the time I had turned Monica away at the Oval Office in trying to protect the presidency and frankly the Clinton brand. The president had immediately leaned out the door, stared me right in the face, as I stood next to the PPD agent, and said he was expecting someone to come with papers and that if I saw them to let them in.

For all the Clintons' repeated scandals, they blamed everybody except themselves. Every time I heard the Clintons blame the "vast right-wing conspiracy," the Uniformed Division, the agents on their personal details, their staff persons, the media, and others, I realized how glad I was to have gotten out of *their* White House when I did. I got out too late, but still mostly unscathed. I could still provide for my family, and by God's graces and a few men of real character, I remained on the job and became an instructor. That semen-stained blue dress saved our lives, one way or the other, in the media or from the Clinton Machine's ire.

I watched as the president continued to bash the Secret Service and the Uniformed Division on how "inappropriate" it was to reveal whom the president met with. Yes, we had, but he was so wildly beyond protocol and sowing discord among us for so long that he had no business judging an officer's character when his own mistress showed up to the White House for her booty call. The machine pushed me out, it pissed off Tripp, it pissed off the Fox, and it jeopardized the character and integrity of the presidency in so many ways. The Clintons never had our backs; they were on it. He demeaningly referred to us as "these uniform people."

I witnessed a funny little moment when the lawyer caught the president in a bind. He ended his question about the president's insinuating or directly telling officers and Betty Currie to make sure the Monica-becoming-irate story didn't get told out of school and he ended his question with "or anything to that effect?"

The president snapped, "What does that mean, 'anything to that effect'?"

"Well, Mr. President, you've told us that you were not going to try to help the Jones's attorneys, and I think it's clear from your testimony that you were pretty literal at times. So that's what I'm saying. I don't necessarily know the exact words. The question was, do you have any knowledge of the fact. . . ."

I enjoyed watching the man who still inhabited the Oval Office squirm. He looked as I did when I was trying to protect him in my own grand jury testimony.

Minutes went by and when I was done rubbing my eyes, my face and mouth muscles were tight from laughing, gritting, and fighting tears of despair. *His supporters had so much hope for this candidate and president. He promised so much.*

"Well, I have a question regarding your definition. And my question is, is oral sex performed on you within that definition as you understood it?"

"As I understood it, it was not, no," said the weasel.

When asked about the semen stain, he couldn't even give a straight answer.

Congress moved toward his impeachment—exactly what I had tried to save him from.

Impeachment proceeded. It was hell, but I wanted it all to go away. Either shit or get off the damn pot. Impeach him or don't, but I wanted it off the papers, and my face off C-SPAN and all the other cable news networks. I wanted Bill off the news, too. As long as he was on TV, I knew no work was getting done at the White House. And the impeachment proceedings damn near shut down, if not locked down, both the House of Representatives and the Senate. Two Republican speakers of the House forfeited their jobs after their own infidelities came to light. Unbelievable. But at least they had the decency to step aside.

The president was impeached on grounds of perjury before the grand jury and obstructing justice, which were both so demonstratively true. A count involving perjury in the Paula Jones case and an abuse of power charge failed.

Were his misdeeds sufficient reason to strip him from office? He'd perjured himself, ruined his own reputation, tarnished the presidency, and damaged if not destroyed the careers, reputations, and lives of a great many people, from myself to Monica to many of his staff. And for what?

The Paula Jones case wasn't a scam. President Clinton and his attorney, Bob Bennett, filed for dismissal, but her suit wasn't dismissed. It was real enough for Bill Clinton to fork over $850,000 in November 1998 to settle it. He admitted no wrongdoing. That's not his style. But he paid and got back to work.

In February 1999 the Senate acquitted President Clinton on both the perjury and obstruction of justice charges. He'd long been a lame duck; now so was Congress. President Clinton had squandered every chance of getting real work done for his own constituents and supporters. The Clintons didn't lose, but certainly no one won.

I hoped it was all over.

But I'd been disappointed before.

16.

"COMMENCE FIRING!"

At Beltsville, I finally got my instructor's test.
And I failed it.

I had studied as never before and knew every detail up and down. I failed badly. Failed! No amount of PT and self-abuse could push away the disappointment I felt in myself. After everything I had been through, I thought I had found a new calling in training others, but I'd failed the required written test.

I was either going to be pushed out into a lesser job further on the periphery of the agency, or some of the higher-ups (to whom I was mud anyway) would finally justify giving me the boot, citing my dyslexia and ADD. I'd be gone. The instructor who conducted and evaluated the tests called me in. I held my breath.

"What the hell happened, Gary?"

He was frustrated and couldn't understand how someone who soaked up the demonstrations and range instruction failed the written test. I was completely straightforward. I revealed my trouble with written tests, the "learning differences" I had hidden or compensated for over the years. My dyslexia was screwing me over, and it was terribly apparent from my written test score. My life was in their hands. A supervisor asked me a question that I'd answered incorrectly on the test, and I told them the answer—and I was right. He sighed and folded his hands, and I braced for the bad news.

"All right, Gary, here's what's going to happen."

Here it comes. I'm through.

But to my surprise they allowed me to take the test orally, asking me each question and then writing down my answer. They were as perplexed as I was elated. But they saw who I really was and I will always be eternally grateful to them. My test was no different from anyone else's except that it was read to me aloud, and I gave my answers verbally.

You know, that's what real diversity is: a diversity of the mind, which is absolutely apolitical as opposed to the politically correct version of diversity. My instructors recognized that I could recite all the answers and all the data (the same as I would have to with students), but I couldn't read and write it for a several-hour test—and when would an instructor ever have to do that with students? Never.

They knew the most crucial thing: Life in the real world (in this case gunfights and firearms training) doesn't correlate with written exams. Someone who could pass the written test with flying colors might be the last guy you'd want at your side when shit hit the fan.

I wanted to dance in the street or fire automatic weapons into the air—but I settled for a firm handshake.

As a JJRTC junior instructor, I considered how to act professionally and to really get through to the trainees. I had to find my style, be stern yet understanding, forceful but not pushy, and trusted and respected but never friendly. A good instructor is demanding, but a great instructor gets his students to be demanding of themselves. They have to push themselves to their own limits.

Fairy-tale notions of killing and training would be dispelled. Training opportunities had to move them to accurately evaluate their own abilities, diagnose their issues, and escape from the most impossible jams.

I taught, "If good guys aren't the best, then the good guys don't win. When you're engaged, it's going to be ugly. There is going to be blood everywhere: under your fingernails, seeping through to your underwear, and in your face. Your firearm will be slippery from it. They'll show pictures of it afterward and it won't look like the movies!"

Our training could be the difference between someone's retaining a firearm or being disarmed by an attacker, accidentally shooting a civilian, or being the marksman whom freedom counts on. Saving the Secret Service's top protectees and helping them retain their own lives and dignity would be won in training—*or lost.*

Training never stops. Training is worthless or even dangerous without the right character.

Abilities, like firearms, if not maintained, rust and become a danger, not an asset, in a pinch. With other law enforcement agencies, the first responsibility is to fight the attacker, but with the USSS, safeguarding the protectee comes first; killing or subduing some son of a bitch is a distant second. That's what an instructor ensures at JJRTC. Throw in fully armored vehicles moving at high speeds doing protection drills to teach students what they may be called upon to do, and things get really crazy. Honestly, it's like shooting fully automatic firearms to engage hostile targets while extracting a presidential protectee to a safe zone *and* administering serious first aid. The scenarios we ran at JJRTC were insane, but terrifyingly realistic.

The normal probationary period for a newbie instructor is one year, but I had my own classes in six months. We took puppy-eyed recruits and spit 'em out as Rottweilers. "Fight, shoot, move" was my motto.

I was pulling some OT at 0700 on a Sunday morning at JJRTC. The weather was nice. All was calm. It was going to be an easy day. The officer with me on the gate answered the phone.

"Uh, Gary, it's the SAC [Special Agent in Charge] of training. He wants to talk to you."

"Gary?"

"Yes, sir."

"Why the f— am I seeing your face on TV? Why are my kids watching you on HBO?" he asked, seething.

Here we go again, I thought.

"Well, those tapes got released along with the president's deposition," I explained, referring to the C-SPAN broadcast.

"Not that, Gary. This is something else."

So I ran to a break room, where I saw myself on HBO in a documentary called *American Anthem*. A documentary team had arranged a session with a presidential staffer and kept their video camera running as they passed through White House security. And who was the one officer who noticed their red light was on— and gave them a hard time about their unauthorized filming? *And* ended up on HBO acting like a hard-ass? Me! The video crew filmed exactly what happened to someone entering the White House from start to finish, and in the documentary I told her she couldn't go in—just before the staffer she was dealing with waved me off.

We obtained a copy of the documentary and battened down for a possible shit storm. Thankfully, no one ever made a big deal about it other than everyone in-house busting my balls over it.

The USSS was expanding. The lobbying every agency does for bigger budgets is like a competition, and our agency was doing well.

We trained larger and larger classes, but we were concerned that quality standards might fall to accommodate quickly expanding cohorts of servicemen. And greater funding meant more inspections to ensure that the taxpayers' money was well spent. That was fine. But in practice, that translated into more dog-and-pony shows.

And so it was that following the president's impeachment, I next saw Mr. and Mrs. Clinton during one of our dog-and-pony shows. I had my shades on and hoped my bald head wouldn't give me away. I really didn't want to be recognized by them and thankfully, I wasn't. They merely shook my hand along with everyone else's and thanked us all for our time. I wiped my sweaty bald pate in relief.

The First Lady took a surprising liking to firearms, especially a Thompson submachine gun, an original and an American classic, Al Capone's legendary "Chicago typewriter." When Mrs. Clinton let loose a spray of man-stopping .45 ACP rounds into the paper, dirt, and berms of our outdoor one-way range, I thought she'd erupt in a maniacal laugh. She just smiled ear-to-ear. Most newcomer women shy away, but not her. If not for the Assault Weapon Ban, she probably would've taken the Thompson home with her. Her next shots zipped right into the target's crotch. Everyone chuckled, turned away, or glanced at the president.

We also provided our visitors with a rifle, rested its stock on a sandbag, and sighted targets at fifty yards. The visitor just had to pull the trigger to hit the target. I was impressed that Mrs. Clinton pulled the stock of the rifle into her shoulder. Recoil can slam right into you, but she knew what she was doing. Higher-caliber rounds like the 7mm Remington Magnum can snap a collarbone, so we outfitted visitors with weakened, reduced loads. We also set the eye relief on the scope so the recoil didn't send it back into their eyes. If the First Lady got scoped, it could fracture her eye socket or eyeball or just leave a really swollen black eye—just like the one she gave Bill.

She sat on a ground-level shooting bench and fired, hitting her target on paper but high. She wanted a bull's-eye, so the instructor lowered the shot placement on her target. He adjusted her beanbag target rest, squeezing to raise the rifle's stock and lower its barrel, thereby lowering the bullet's point of impact.

She was looking through the scope, and he was squeezing the beanbag and asking her if the sights were lined up on the target. He kept asking if they were lined up and if the sights moved when he squeezed. It was some grand mystery to him why the sights weren't moving despite squeezing the beanbag.

He *wasn't* squeezing the beanbag; he had his hand on her breast! I was mortified and didn't know what to do. Eventually he caught on. We swallowed our laughter and were stoic. Our buddy was red-faced and apologized profusely, but in a low, serious tone so as to keep it just between her and him.

Thank God my fellow instructors honored my request to keep me at arm's length from the Clintons, because if I had accidentally pulled that shit—I could barely look at the Clintons regardless—I would be six-feet deep either in dirt, media headlines, or legal paperwork. But the show went on. I thought the incident highlighted many of the little awkward moments instructors have to worry about when teaching students of the opposite gender. We must ask ourselves five times a day: Am I about to be hit with a sexual harassment suit? Eventually you just move on. But the instructor with Mrs. Clinton was shaken at the thought.

In 1999, as I attained the instructor gig, we were summoned to run protective details when the USSS foreign missions branch required reinforcements with ambassador and foreign dignitaries' visits. We were increasingly called in to stem protection personnel gaps. We were a mix of agents and UD and even a few LEOs from other agencies. At least fifty of these security details floated around D.C. at any given time, protecting the who's who of the political and military world. These missions were fun and crazy. The fun depended on the mission specifics, but the craziness depended on the protectees, our principals. We didn't get to choose where they went, whether they visited a museum or strip club—we provided the ride. We just did our job, and I can tell you many stories of heroism regarding how these teams protected VIPs who weren't our president, the vice president, or the First Family.

We covered NATO's fiftieth anniversary. As everyone arrived for roll call at SSHQ, we all introduced ourselves. Hell, the last memorable time I was at SSHQ a damned FBI agent Mirandized me—that rat bastard. The shift leader realized who I was—one of the UD who testified against the president. Our protectee was Vaclav Havel, the first president of the Czech Republic. The communists had imprisoned Havel, a dissident and playwright, for many years before he emerged to lead a free Czechoslovakia. Unfortunately, he wasn't in good health and was going to keep a low profile during his stay in D.C. while he visited the NATO fiftieth birthday. I think he had one lung and some heart issues. The joke was that he was married to this blonde far younger than he, and our mission revolved around providing him with an AED (automatic external defibrillator) if he got too excited about her.

As usual, we traveled with an Uzi and a host of firearms handy, but our shift leader explained to everyone that our threat level was low. "As a matter of fact," he added, "our main driver, Officer Byrne, has a higher threat level than the protectee does." He left it at that. I wish he had explained a little further. It became the stuff of whispers and I had to keep explaining myself multiple times before the day was done. Everyone looked at me as if I had leprosy. I gave my big smile. My shiny red cranium tactical-operator Oakleys couldn't hide my embarrassment. When we walked outside to get everything set, a DEA agent gave me a pat on my bag and joshed, "Dude, how are you still alive?"

There was always an undertone under the joke. I always laughed it off. I didn't mind having enemies; I just wanted them in front of me.

This detail was easy. Life was good again. It was the new normal. Even walking back onto the White House grounds was a great feeling.

I was vigilant and alert. I told the lead agent to let me know if he wanted me to do anything differently and that I was glad to be a part of the detail. He told me to relax, but if he made a scissors motion with his hand, as if playing rock-paper-scissors, it meant he wanted me to close the gap with the car in front of us and leave little room for an attacking vehicle to ram us and knock us out of the motorcade.

Havel had requested that we have some Heineken beer ready so we wouldn't have to stop for any on the way to the hotel. That was cool with us: one less stop and one less risk.

We all exchanged cordial greetings with the president and his wife. She patted me on the shoulder.

"Heineken?" Havel asked. He had a great accent.

We were doing 85 mph on the highway—fast for a four-ton armored vehicle. I learned to appreciate it while training at JJRTC when braking suddenly around obstacles. The RA gave me the scissor signal—time to tighten up our convoy.

The park police pushed traffic out of the way. I kept thinking, *This is awesome!* The Czech president and his wife were pointing at everything as if they were at Disney World marveling at the sights as they downed beers. I was reminded about how great America was—even other countries' presidents got excited to see America! That night, President Havel explained he had an unscheduled meeting with another head of state in another hotel—that's how a typical shift could turn into a fifteen-hour one.

In April 2002, I saw the Bush family once again during a JJRTC tour similar to the one we had conducted for the Clintons. It was strange to see George W. Bush grown up and president. It took me back to when I first arrived at the White House—a rookie being cued in by old hats. I hoped President Bush could bring back what was so sorely missed and what once existed under his father. Dynasties made me nervous, but I sorely hoped Bush 43 (our forty-third president) would restore the White House to the level of dignity that Papa Bush had promoted. I thought of my own father, the life I led, and what my son might be like. Was I as strong as my father? Had I kept my promise to protect others? Would my children retain their character? I was honored that the new president remembered me and shook my hand, just as his father would have. I asked about Bush 41 (our forty-first president). It was blast.

A year passed and I was running my class. A fellow instructor warned me, "Hey, just a heads-up. A plane just flew into one of the skyscrapers in New York City."

I looked at him, puzzled. "Well, how'd *that* happen?"

He shrugged. I figured it was some jackass single-prop private plane pilot who screwed up. I knew that a B-17 dual-engine prop plane had once crashed into the Empire State Building on a foggy night. Shit happens, but that morning there wasn't a cloud in the sky.

Another instructor dashed in. "Second plane just hit another tower."

"No, someone already told me that."

"No, this was a *second* one on the *other* World Trade Center tower."

"Well, how'd that happen?" I was angry now.

"We're obviously under some kind of attack."

Not long afterward I received official notification. "All trainees head to your lanes," I barked through the loudspeaker. "Don't do anything. Don't say anything. All trainers meet me in the cleaning room."

My fellow trainers dismissed my edgy tone and busted me for it. I cut to the chase. "We're under attack. We think it's some kind of terrorist attack. Two airliners have flown into the World Trade Center. They think more are going to happen. Here's what we're going to do: Don't brief the students—have them put their guns away. Don't clear them, and I'll brief them here—all at one time. I don't want any rumors."

I directed our students to lock all their gun slides back, to "Check 'em, check 'em twice," and to return their weapons to the instructors. They weren't dumb. They knew something was seriously wrong. When professionals jettison protocol, that's a giant red flag. Good. They were, at least, learning that. We assembled in the cleaning room.

"Is anyone here heading to the New York field office?" I asked.

Three hands shot up.

"Do any of you have family members who work in the World Trade Center?" The same three raised their hands—although very nervously. I kept my own cool, but I wanted to throw up.

"You three, stand by."

An instructor waved me over for another phone call. "Here we go," I told myself.

I picked up the phone. It was this trio's class coordinator. Outside, in a parked and loaded Suburban, he wanted them *now*—pronto!

"And by the way," he added, "another plane crashed somewhere. We don't know where yet."

We managed to rig up a projector to our television and assembled to watch events transpire. The Pentagon. The World Trade Center. A jetliner crash in Pennsylvania. Where it would all end we didn't know. But we remained on high alert. Some of us talked tough. We were going to get "them"!

Them!

But most Americans didn't even know who "them" was, where "them" were, or how we would get back at "them." At least FDR and his radio audience knew who bombed Pearl Harbor. We could only guess who our attackers were—although our guesses weren't far off target. Islamic terrorists had tried to obliterate the World Trade Center once before, in February 1993, when they'd planted a 1,200-pound truck bomb in its underground parking garage. Back then they'd killed "only" six people, but they'd injured over a thousand.

But whoever our enemy was today, we at JJRTC stood ready to be part of a quickly summoned "send wave." We'd be part of our belated War on Terror.

We were tense. But at least we were alive. We saw other human beings plunging through the air from a hundred floors up, hurtling to their deaths on the pavement below. A nation watched that on TV. Some minds have blacked out that image, erased it from memory. I can't forget. It seared itself indelibly into mine. Through explosion-polluted air, reporters kept broadcasting from lower Manhattan. They had to be more traumatized than we were. But they kept going. I've had my problems with the press but not with those reporters that horrible morning.

We were *all* Americans.

In a very great sense, however, everyone in the Secret Service and in the other federal law enforcement branches knew exactly what had happened. Some group—whether foreign, domestic, or some diabolic combination thereof—had declared war on the United States of America. We knew our leaders—and our media— had shrugged off a grave threat. They'd focused on some small, stupid matter or other (like an intern or an E! Network host)—and our enemies had slipped past our weakest link. Someone messed up.

We packed two of our SUVs to the brim. Four officers volunteered to accompany the three students heading for New York. We feared civil unrest. This assault wasn't on mere buildings. It was an attack on our entire nation by targeting its chain of command, its military capability, its economy, and its civilian population. It obviously resulted from the highest levels of coordination and—however evil—professionalism. It was the sort of atrocity we always feared and always prepared for. Our forces couldn't be everywhere, but they could be anywhere. And not only that, they were *already* there. Close enough to sit next to you on a plane. But you'd never know. Danger-close.

We feared a second wave—more terror, more death. Maybe at the White House or the Capitol. And this September 11 morning, who even knew if there would be a third—or a fourth?

I stayed behind, but our two SUVs raced north to Manhattan, transporting as many first aid supplies, IFAK (Individual First Aid) and FAT kits, 12-gauge shotguns, 5.56 and 9 mm rifles as they could carry, *plus* extra batteries, fire extinguishers, food, water, and everything else we could think of to assist civilians and first responders. The New York City Police Department stood ready to guard against any criminal activity, but this was war. Our recruits wanted blood. Our minds ran wild.

I pondered how I'd carry off something like 9/11. *Shit*, at Chicago's O'Hare Airport in 1995, I'd even gotten *my firearm* past airport metal detectors.

We were furious and searching for answers to the smoking, twisted rubble that had once been sleek, twin 110-story steel-and-glass towers. Who was the weak link?

President Bush did us proud at Ground Zero. We hadn't even cleared the wreckage as safe, but he was there addressing emergency response workers and rallying a fearful nation. That's real leadership. That's actual character! But when all our United States senators peeked out of their fortresslike capitol to sing "The Star-Spangled Banner," hands over their hearts, I wanted to scream. I was furious. For all their committees, subcommittees, and special boards and the previous administration, I knew damned well that they shared part of the blame. Bosnia hadn't even been wrapped up. We had abandoned Somalia to become a hotbed of terrorism and fanaticism—a failed state. On television, the first person I watched on the news, alibi-ing that now was not the time for blame, was my old pal, now New York's junior United States senator, Hillary Rodham Clinton.

I was madder than hell.

They "volun-*told*" us instructors into forced OT but with a new limit on OT pay. The Secret Service erected more Jersey barriers on Pennsylvania Avenue. Weekdays I continued as an instructor. Each weekend I manned a post around the White House. Working three weekends in a row doing nothing more than watching slowly moving traffic—while holding down my full-time instructor's job during the week—exhausted and demoralized me.

Beyond that, Secret Service higher-ups used 9/11 to create more GS 14/15 pay-grade positions for agents "overseeing" us. It was all just a racket designed to manufacture pay raises for soft-handed, tie-wearing agents and to further demean the UD. Question management's moves and they said you lacked discipline and willpower. You lacked the "right stuff." A *new* new normal was growing, and it wasn't good.

What did any of it do to safeguard our planes and skyscrapers—our nation?

The Secret Service fosters an awful mentality. Everything is go-go-go. Fix every problem with more workload for bottom-rung guys *after* something goes bad. Before any disaster struck, however, we'd stand around with our thumbs up our asses. Afterward we said, "We told you so."

September 11 wasn't unique. That's why the Secret Service constantly hires so many people—you even see big posters for the Secret Service on Washington, D.C., Metro trains. Secret Service work became horrendous. People either left for the private sector or to take opportunities for less grueling work—and greater pay—at other federal agencies. Secret Service leadership just ran people into the ground. No human being could maintain a 24/7 alert for long. In the end, it was counterproductive. It was only an appearance of 24/7 vigilance, not a reality.

Overwork can lead to trouble, to potential mess-ups. "The mission is never so important that you f— it up" became my new saying.

While I was manning my post on Pennsylvania Avenue, a car pulled up on the curb and caught my attention. Big-time.

"Sir, you can't stop there!" I shouted.

"Oh, it's fine," the guy responded.

That pissed me off. No, it wasn't fine.

He exited his vehicle and moved toward his trunk. I grabbed my MP5 submachine gun, ready to go. *This is it,* I thought, calculating how many rounds it would take to put him down. He opened his trunk and put a box on the curb, then pulled out something else before walking up to me. I had my 9mm in ready possession. I didn't need this. I was tired, really irritated, and pissed off that he ignored my warning. A split second later and my training in action in the reflexive fire drills would swing into action.

He got closer still. Only then did he really notice my expression—*and* my poised firearm.

"Whoa, fella," he said and showed me what was in his hand.

It was a Bible.

I was mortified. I had almost wasted a man for trying to hand me a Bible.

We introduced ourselves. He was a very sweet man, a minister, and we chatted. On his off days he handed out Bibles to every law enforcement officer he passed. I was blown away, thanking him profusely for the gift. It meant a lot to me. I advised him on how best to safely complete his task without running afoul of understandably nervous law enforcement officers like myself. The blood of martyrs may be the seed of Christians, but there was no need for *us* to accidentally martyr him.

"Take it slow," I told him. "And make sure to tell them who you are."

We laughed off the tension. If he ever reads this book, I want him to know what he accomplished that day. He changed my life. We were all on a hair trigger, so amped up, so edgy. We hadn't enough sleep, food, and exercise for our tired, anxious, and overworked, undersexed bodies. We had zero time at home to balance and hack the small shit.

I learned how to back off.

I learned not to sweat the small stuff—and to remember that 99 percent of life *is* small stuff.

That man saved my life by shaking me out of my complacency, my rut. I knew I had to escape the Secret Service. I had loved it once, but it was no longer the life for me. A once-great agency had lost sight of its mission. It needed to stop protecting itself at so many others' expense.

Leaving the agency in disgust, one fed-up officer sent a public telex (a bit like a "reply all" email) equating Secret Service treatment of its lower-level employees to how Cherokee warriors ran their horses to death because they could replace them with others. It was a perfect analogy. I wanted to see my kids and my wife. I wanted to spend some time at home. Hell, I hadn't even had time to explain 9/11 to my own kids.

But we had an out. A new escape hatch.

Post-9/11, Congress elevated air security to a new level of strategic priority. Every U.S. flight, especially international ones, must be protected. The U.S. Federal Air Marshal Service (FAMS) expanded to better accomplish that and staffed up accordingly. A group of fed-up JJRTC instructors assembled at the ass crack of dawn and hopped into an agency Suburban heading for Atlantic City, New Jersey, where FAMS maintained its training center. They arrived so early they had to wait in the parking lot for someone from FAMS to show up. But when that happened, FAMS hired them on the spot— that very day! FAMS gave them their transfer letters, completed their paperwork, and not insignificantly, gave them better pay.

Word spread like wildfire. The Secret Service—particularly the UD—hemorrhaged personnel. But did Secret Service management learn anything from this? No. It kept a blind eye toward complaints. "You know what, if you're going to bitch about it, leave or go join another agency. Go join the Air Marshals!" they sneered at us.

By January 2003 the Secret Service had lost more than three hundred officers. At one point, three-quarters of all air marshals, from bottom and especially to the top, were former Secret Service personnel. The moral: Don't bluff. Don't arrogantly tell your men and women, "If you don't like it, quit." They insulted us and we did quit in droves. So many personnel went online to the FAMS employment application website while on duty at UD or at the training center, the Secret Service director had the IT guys for JJRTC block both the Federal Aviation Administration's and the Transportation Security Administration's websites! Guys walked up to their bosses' desks at SSHQ or the White House, dropped their equipment already folded and prepped, and said, "Uh, I'm transferring to the Air Marshals. Thanks for everything. Good-bye!"

At first the higher-ups laughed it off. They thought it was funny. They were ridding themselves of people around the edges whom they didn't value. Those who left, though, weren't all malcontents or losers; some were people who finally had their fill of bullshit and political correctness.

On January 12, 2003, I became one of them.

17.

NEW SKIES

The agency didn't want me to leave.

They didn't want anyone to leave. Not even me.

They thought they owned us.

I was pumping iron on a bench press. A special agent tracked me down.

"You're not going to be one of those [expletive-expletive-expletives] who ditch us and chase a bigger paycheck at FAMS? After all the money we spent on you, I'd be so pissed if you left!"

I kept lifting.

There was no way he knew about my application . . . but then again. I kept pumping. I told him straight out that management shouldn't force us guys into mind-numbing, chickenshit nonvolun-tary OT postings. Spending every weekend guarding Jersey barriers outside the White House wasn't my cup of tea.

I dropped my weights. "Didn't you transfer to JJRTC from some-where else?" I asked, toweling my neck. "Why didn't *you* stay *there*?"

He stormed off. I knew it would be bumpy when I gave my notice.

A lieutenant started to rag on me for the same thing in the JJRTC Control Center the first thing the next morning.

"Well, put yourself in my position," I said. "When I came on in 1991 we had a competitive shotgun team, rifle team, and pistol team. The UD would host an annual pistol match with police officers from around the world. It was a morale and pride booster and conveyed a sense of appreciation to local police departments across the country for their assistance. Everyone felt better. For a while, the Secret Service was the best. We couldn't be beat!

"Then they squashed that competition because the UD ran it. They ended Uniformed Division Benefit Fund and USSS director Brian Stafford even closed our gift shop. Kaput! They pulled elaborate strings and gypped us out of hundreds of thousands of dollars. They kicked us out of the White House to start their own gift shop. And this doesn't bother you? The agents treat us like shit. It's not typical government behavior. It's vindictive. It's designed to be demoralizing—and it's working!"

I was rolling, going on to tell of an internal agency audit of UD-acquired vehicles. Some were missing! Vanished! These weren't paper clips or file cabinets, these were cars. Missing! They turned up eventually—as take-home cars for agents (not officers) in Seattle.

The list went on.

"They could spin it any way they wanted to stay out of jail," I fumed, "and I don't expect the Federal Air Marshal Service to be any different—I don't. A shit sandwich is a shit sandwich, but for more money it goes down easier."

He stormed off too but came back furious. I had opened his eyes. "G-ddamn it, you're right!" he now agreed.

"We're like the frog in a pot of boiling water," I continued. "Turn up the heat slowly enough, and the frog never knows the difference until he's cooked." I let that sink in.

I showed my SAC (Special Agent in Charge) my FAMS contract. I asked him straight-up: "How could I refuse that?"

The SAC eyed its numbers, pored over its details: $72,000 a year *before* OT; $20,000 more to my annual retirement. He sighed heavily but couldn't help agree. "I can't believe they'll pay you guys agents' wages!"

I wanted to say, *Oh—you mean living wages.*

In the few days it took for my transfer paperwork to clear, he simmered down. He didn't hold a grudge; he even gave me *two* memorabilia plaques. Everybody posed for a group picture. My fellow UD instructors respected my decision and took me out to a Mexican joint. Lunch was great—and added a sombrero to my going-away stash.

Genny and I decided to max out our retirement payments. We'd move to a better neighborhood with better schools once I got the posting I wanted.

The president is still only one American. I was protecting hundreds—if not thousands. What good was any OT at the White House if our airlines remained unprotected, soft targets? The White House was only as secure as the weakest plane. What better way to serve the country than by going to FAMS?

International terrorists and even domestic criminals would still employ tactics dating from the 1960s and 1970s, when any number of planes were bombed or hijacked. Pre-9/11 there were plenty of attacks, bombings, and hijackings. Once one ended, the nation just clicked off its radios and TVs, went back to business, and forgot a crisis ever existed.

Shit happens. We can either learn from it or suffer the consequences. Some of my colleagues doubted that air marshals could do the job, no matter what they were paid. Air marshal tryouts demanded rigorous physical fitness standards, but the job required marshals to stay in a sedentary, seated position all the time—a potentially lethal assignment. The dramatic shift between extreme training and unending, repeated, hours-long inaction can cripple both body and mind and even cause a pulmonary embolism—a sudden, deadly blood clot.

NBC News' David Bloom died during the April 2003 Iraq invasion in Iraq just that way. As a frontline reporter embedded with the military, he spent most of his days confined inside armored vehicles. He developed a blood clot, deep-vein thrombosis, and pulmonary embolism. The human body is not designed to be restricted, reclined, confined, or prone for hours on end.

Most of us former UD officers turned air marshals didn't worry too much about that, though. We worried about a guy named Tom Quinn, a former U.S. Secret Service agent appointed to head the newly augmented FAMS. Quinn had a reputation for strongly disliking UD. Crazy stories circulated about him when he retired from the USSS in 1998. It gave many of us pause that they dug him up in 2001 to integrate FAMS into the newly formed Department of Homeland Security.

"If you think UD has gotten bad, Gary, with FAMS you're jumping out of the frying pan and into the fire with Quinn," many UD warned me.

I didn't listen.

No agency is perfect. Nobody's perfect. Bureaucracies certainly aren't. I learned that a long time ago. But I believed wholeheartedly in the FAMS mission. I also believed in FAMS because a few months after 9/11, as a JJRTC firearms instructor I got a call from the lead instructor that we were to recertify agents from the New York City field office. They were in New York during 9/11, and from a very frank discussion I knew it wouldn't be a normal certification.

Terrorists didn't just destroy the World Trade Center's north and south towers on 9/11, they also destroyed the forty-seven-story Seven World Trade Center, which housed a USSS field office. At JJRTC today, there's a display of a German-made Heckler & Koch MP5 submachine pistol and a revolver—or what's left of them—from 9/11. The inferno reached sufficient temperatures to melt the Secret Service's fire-resistant safe and twist the barrels of weapons inside like pretzels.

If only it was just metal that Osama bin Laden (whom Bill Clinton had a chance to capture) and his thugs destroyed.

A new technician at our Trade Center field office had just been assigned there a few days previously. On September 11 he raced from the safety of his room at the Marriott World Trade Center hotel into the fires of One Trade Center to tend to the injured. In the Army he had been a medic, and saving lives was his business.

We do not know how many lives he saved before he lost his own. A Port Authority Police officer was the last person to see him alive.

I wasn't at the Trade Center that day, but I was later one of several instructors tasked with recertifying agents from our vanished field office in regard to their service pistols. These men and women had been caught up in the chaos and buried alive for three hours under a pile of tower rubble in a wrecked New York City Fire Department truck. A fireman who helped pull them out was never seen again, one of the nearly three thousand persons who died that day.

Our people still looked traumatized from their experience. We saw it in their demeanor. It pulled at my stomach. Agents are masters of confidence, bravado, and tactical ability. These men and women weren't trainees; they'd confronted all sorts of New York criminals in the worst areas. But they were so visibly emotionally scarred.

Their hands shook noticeably—even before they picked up their pistols. Their bodies seemed frail, low, and bent. I had trouble keeping my composure because I never expected to see agents in this condition. What had they seen to render them so fragile? We avoided betraying our astonishment. *This was shell shock.* If these agents were ever to function again, they'd have to grab the bull by the horns, pick up their firearms, and master them again. It was going to be a long and painful day.

We violated normal protocol and checked and cleared their firearms *before* shooting commenced. Our supervisor had warned us to do that—and he was damn right! Each pistol was completely occluded with gray dust that came from 9/11's holocaust. Our armorer had to take each gun apart to clear it. Fire a gun in that condition, and it could explode and blow off your hand. The sorry condition of those handguns betrayed their owners' sorry mental state, perhaps even more than their haunted expressions and shaking hands did. With each round fired they actually shuddered, some a little, some a great deal. Each shot startled them. I'll never forget that day. But slowly they regained their confidence. We hoped so much that we had been helpful in reacclimating them to their old lives, their old selves.

When I started at FAMS, air marshals enjoyed a reputation as elite combat-pistol marksmen and experts in close quarter combat (CQC), in part because of incredibly high air marshal quarterly qualifications. Every law enforcement agency, from the most elite Special Forces down to local police, possesses special assets and abilities that others either lack or possess in more limited quantities. Instead of every agency reinventing the wheel, we needed to cross-train.

Law enforcement and the military finally stopped being selfish with specialized training. Law enforcement agencies and military schools held competitions and training events. They called each other to tap other's knowledge. For the USSS, I'd demonstrated the Uzi and the Belgian-made P-90 personal defense weapon to other law enforcement groups. In turn, for example, Navy Explosive Ordnance Disposal (EOD) technicians trained us. If a unit or agency needed to learn hostage negotiations (or how to run a press conference), they went to the FBI; for drug-related training, they turned to DEA; for protective details, they went to USSS.

Ultimately, we're all protecting Americans from harm.

For close-quarter pistol marksmanship on an airplane, the best were the original sky marshals who eventually turned into air marshals. They were respected by all agencies and military branches. But whenever an agency expands dramatically, a danger exists that standards may plunge.

As it expanded, FAMS contracted with a private firearms contractor and also recruited a cadre of retired mid- to high-level USSS agents to "modernize" FAMS training. It reminded me of when the Clintons wanted to make us more "user friendly." I always have to ask myself: Modernize and be user friendly for whom? I was apprehensive. At my age, would I be able to hack yet another training school and survive stricter physical, marksmanship, and classroom standards? If I couldn't—I didn't want to think about that. I had to commit everything I had to make it through.

Before 9/11 the Tactical Pistol Course (TPC) was the standard annual certification for in-flight air marshals. But when former USSS agents arrived, "modernization" translated into dumbing down and diluting established air marshal standards. The Tactical Pistol Course became the Practical Pistol Course (PPC), which remains a joke—but which is now the standard course for all federal law enforcement agencies. It might suffice for some agency's missions, but it's a far cry from what's required for qualifying competent air marshals. Not a sufficient standard to foil 9/11-style four-man hijacking teams at thirty thousand feet with no backup in a 530-mph flying aluminum tube! In fact, it's the same course that was used to qualify D.C.'s Federal Building Police forty years ago. We needed to heighten standards after 9/11, not lower them.

How could this have happened?

Simple. Arrogant agents became FAMS supervisors, and management all the way up the chain couldn't pass the TPC, so they just lowered the standards across the board. The PPC isn't much of a standard. With practice, just about anyone can meet it. And the physical standard? *I couldn't find anyone who knew about it.* It was all a mystery, which made me extremely nervous. But I didn't know that going into FAMS. (I did have a heads-up warning when I heard the name Quinn. But more on that in the pages ahead.)

Just before I left for FAMS training on December 24, 2002, a baby boy entered our world. The place hasn't been the same since. He's my little man, and if UD didn't appreciate how I wanted to spend more time with my wife, my daughter, and my son and raise them right, then they could find someone else. Even more, I was thinking of what kind of world I wanted my kids to grow up in; I wanted them to look up at tall buildings and say "Whoa," to look at airplanes and think of vacation and business trips, not how fast they could all come tumbling down. It inspired me to train and shoot harder.

While waiting for FAMS training to begin, I continued my JJRTC protective details at or near the White House. But I took time to prepare myself for whatever FAMS might have in store. I drilled and drilled, putting several hundred rounds of ammunition through my service pistol each day. Reloading during a training session, I noticed a piece of hot metal drop from its magazine well onto the cement. I knew exactly what that part was: the back end of the trigger bar. I reloaded, aimed, and engaged the next target. *BAM! Click. Click.* But I didn't miss a beat and unorthodoxly turned it upside down and fired with one hand.

"What the hell kind of gangster shit is that, Gary?" asked the armorer as I passed him the broken gun.

I explained that how on my reload, the trigger bar's back portion had fallen out of the gun—something just unheard-of. But I was pushing my firearm and myself to the limits even with my gun incredibly hot. Even with a piece of my service pistol AWOL I was going to take the fight to the enemy. I explained to the armorer how I immediately diagnosed and addressed the issue. I had learned it from a JJRTC range master. By turning the gun upside down, I could continue using it. I'd never tried that before, but it worked.

Good armorers love broken guns—broken from being worked so hard. "Damn, Gary, good job!" he said, and a little crowd of officers formed, ogling my broken firearm and learning for themselves.

I'd logged so many hours of advanced service pistol training that I knew it would work. I knew that firearm intimately because that's what professionalism requires. As the saying goes, "You won't know your limits until you push yourself to them." I was confident—or maybe just hopeful—that even at my age, even with older knees and eyes, I wasn't just going to meet FAMS limits, I was going to *push* them. The enemy wouldn't find a chink in the chain mail of any plane I guarded.

After I was accepted into FAMS, two experienced sky marshals grilled me in hypothetical scenarios before I packed for Artesia, New Mexico, and my first day at the Federal Law Enforcement Training Center (FLETC).

Part of our training involved a shoot house. A typical shoot house consists of a warren of thick-walled rooms and hallways lined with old tires, thick wood, and other materials to absorb live-fire bullets. Most shoot houses have furniture similar to that found in a house or drug den, a sofa and other furniture as obstacles with spaces like closets or hallways a suspect or even an innocent person could hide in or shoot from. A mix of noncombatants and bad-guy dummy targets are concealed or in the open, even behind doorways. The idea is that training should be as realistic as possible to best condition the tactical mindset and to ready trainees for real-life situations. When clearing an airplane or airport of Tangos (our lingo for terrorists), we have to be able to rapidly discern between Tangos, innocents, and our partners. Then we either issue verbal commands or engage Tangos with as little collateral damage as possible.

It may seem funny, but when thrown into a shoot house lots of guys end up concentrating on so many things that they trip over stuff, run into others, and do really dumb or dangerous stuff like freezing up and blocking doorways, obstructing their partners, or even pointing their firearms at corners of the room that are obviously no longer a threat. That's because they can't focus under the stress of absorbing so much stimuli while following the mission. Shoot house instructors keep changing the position and quantity of bad and good guys in each session. It keeps students thinking under stress as they move. After all, this is no written exam.

It can all be very dangerous. JJRTC training starts with dry fire—no one has live ammunition. Students slowly go through the drills, saying, "Bang!" Afterward, the instructor asks why you did the things you did. It's excruciatingly methodical. The next step is paintball rounds. Only after that do we employ live ammunition. If you can't do your job in a shoot house, you can't do it in real life—an absolute truth for an air marshal in midflight.

As an instructor at JJRTC, I understood when trainees told me they were nervous and had trouble concentrating; it's a lot for a rookie's brain to wrangle. I called them *distraction issues* but tried to keep instruction reassuring.

"Instead of remembering and thinking about all the different things all at once, just focus on the mission only. Let muscle memory and training kick in. Don't think—do! Ask yourself, 'What am I trying to do? What is my mission?' Then do that and think of nothing else. Focus on that and the rest will take care of itself. Don't sweat the small stuff, and ninety percent of life is small stuff. Don't focus on *not* failing, focus on succeeding," I would say. Sometimes I'd give them a minute to settle down. Sometimes I'd throw them right back in.

But for FAMS, the shoot house was, instead of a drug den, an airplane.

In a shoot house, there was trash and crap on the floor, tripping hazards, people everywhere, just as in real life. Tangos can use corners and doorways as fatal funnels, kill zones whereby it's easy to annihilate *you*. On a plane the whole thing is a giant funnel toward the flight deck. We could use fatal funnels to our advantage, too, especially since our job was to protect the passengers second, maintain control of the aircraft first. We aimed to be as clandestine as the enemy, but they had to reveal themselves first. Once they revealed themselves, we let them stab themselves with *our* swords; we used the fatal funnels against them.

But here, I noticed, these arrogant old fart instructors, former USSS special agent desk jockeys, were screwing it up for old guys and new alike. It was one of our first drills in the shoot house, and we jumped right into live fire. Many of these students had just handled a gun for the first time and were still concentrating on managing recoil. Not surprisingly, the first guy to enter the shoot house airplane bungled it badly.

The instructor, whom I'll call Timmy, started demonstrating how to "unf— ourselves." We sat in the passenger seats of the shoot house airplane. Timmy stood like a flight attendant giving a preflight safety briefing to passengers. Timmy, like many FAMS instructors, had never actually been an instructor before being hired here. Timmy gestured with his firearm as he was talking and then started *pointing his firearm at us,* as if we were the Tango targets or passengers on the plane! Even a little kid is taught when he's at the dinner table, he shouldn't gesture with a fork or knife. It's rude and potentially dangerous. A child given a BB gun knows the three basics of firearm safety. The very first is to never point a loaded firearm at anything you're not willing to kill or destroy.

Instructor Timmy chambered a round, demonstrating to us his movements, but he hadn't even de-cocked his pistol. It remained in single action and loaded as he lurched about, as if he were in dry practice. He continued gesturing toward us with his firearm. Our lives hung on his hair trigger, on less than two inches of movement from a crisp six pounds of trigger pull. One of us could be shot point-blank. A head would literally explode from the hollow-point bullet speeding through it.

You can believe I didn't hesitate to interrupt Timmy in mid-sentence.

"Sir, you realize you are flagging us with your firearm right now *and* you have a live round chambered in single action?" I said furiously, but still trying my best to be respectful.

My fight-or-flight response had kicked in big-time. Peering into the barrel of a loaded gun does that to a man. You might find it unfathomable that an instructor could get a student killed, but at JJRTC and elsewhere in the tactical community, we heard stories about training schools that played it fast and loose and someone got shot or killed. It happened. It was true. It resulted from complacency and negligence every time. There's an old military and law enforcement adage that was drilled into me in the Air Force: "Complacency kills."

Timmy responded sharply—and condescendingly, "Well, you're just going to have to get used to that, Gary. That's how things are done here."

"Well, no, I don't, because what you're doing is wrong. The gun's still loaded on single action, and I'm not going to watch you shoot one of us! Someone's going to get shot with *you* pulling that crap," I said, pointing my finger at him.

"Oh, you know what, Gary. . ." What followed was ludicrous, the lamest of excuses. Nothing short of repositioning himself to point his firearm in a safe direction, clear it, and make it safe would be acceptable—so I cut him off again. We had training firearms, blue plastic things for the purpose of practicing hand-to-hand combat with or for dry demonstrations, but there is never an excuse for an instructor to point a loaded, chambered, and live firearm at his students. It was beyond insanity, and it was going to get some poor student, father, mother, and good man or woman's head blown off. This instructor was in way over *his* head.

I turned to my class leader. "I'm not going to watch him shoot one of us. So I'm going to walk out. You should bring the rest of the class and leave with me."

He put his hands on my arm and grabbed me. "Gary, do you have your ducks in a row on this?"

"I do," I said, looking him straight in the eye.

He was a good man and was going to make a hell of an air marshal, but at that moment he was naïve and conditioned by the Army to trust blindly in authority. In the Army, just as in the Air Force, I'm sure that submission saves lives, but this wasn't the military— and FAMS had lowered its standards. I knew what our class leader didn't: He was about to watch his instructor shoot a squad mate in the head. My class leader didn't realize, at first, that we don't see ourselves as being individuals when we are part of a group or part of a team, but we *always* have the initiative to be a leader as individuals, wherever we rest on the food chain.

My class leader signed up for FAMS figuring the guy who would attack him would be shouting "Allah hu Akbar!" and wielding a box cutter. But sometimes bureaucracy and corruption make it so that the guy who shoots you square in the neck, leg, chest, or face could be your incompetent firearms instructor. Beyond the veil, sometimes the enemy is the one that's supposed to have your back, sign your paycheck, or shake your hand on graduation day. I learned that primarily from the Clintons, but the message really clicked once I had been threatened by the FBI for obstructing justice, withholding evidence of a federal investigation, and dereliction of duty. I was seasoned enough to know how to respond when bad character was going to get the wrong guy killed. Don't think. Act!

Everyone, including our team leader, knew that I risked being instantly kicked out of FAMS. I had called out a superior in front of our team, but every human being has the right to self-defense and dignity, to be a leader—that's the God's honest truth. Timmy should have swallowed his pride and admitted that he screwed up. Safety should always be number one in training, period.

I walked out alone.

No surprise there. Another instructor later followed me out of the shoot house—but only to give me grief. I anticipated being told to pack my stuff and go home. Waiting nervously by the tables of guns, ammunition, and gear, I readied myself for the tempers to flare and the human resources and legal shit storm to come, but whether you're facing armed terrorists or subpoenas, *what will be will be.*

Wishful thinking never saved a life.

Timmy's conduct had been immediately dangerous, so I handled it immediately. It would have been unsafe to hesitate or to file a grievance later. *The mission is never so important to screw it up.* That's why I couldn't be like my team leader or rest of the pack. Even the Service would never put up with that crap and would wipe the floor with a trainee or instructor who flagged (pointed a loaded firearm at) someone or was so wildly unsafe. I thought back to my FAMS interviewer. He had asked if I had any regrets from my time in the White House. Not really. Most nights I could rest my head squarely on my pillow and sleep soundly—that's the litmus test of character. My father had instilled in me that your odds of success don't create right or wrong. You fight for what is *right.*

At the classroom, maybe I saved a life that day. I could live with being shit-canned for it, but they would have to write me up on paper for it, and I knew they never would.

"Gary, do the right thing." Since the Clinton debacle, that saying always rang in my head.

The only way I was going to have a regret was if I hadn't walked out of that shoot house and someone got shot by an instructor's negligent discharge.

"You think for a second you're going to make it through training?" barked the self-assured instructor who followed me out. He thought he knew it all, even though he was junior to me in both age and experience.

"Listen," I told him, "if that's how you want to play this, I'm going to make a few phone calls. You make yours. We'll meet at the end of the day and we'll see who wins."

I was still choked up and flustered—partly from staring down an instructor's gun barrel, partly from staring down an unthinking bureaucracy's gun barrel. I didn't go back into the shoot house. The instructor made some calls.

So did I.

A few days later someone from FAMS headquarters came down and looked into it. It was clear neither I nor my instructors nor HQ was going to make a big stink about it. Just as in UD under the Clintons, I needed to keep my job *and* have my teammates keep our heads. Nothing was personal, but it was clear that a few instructors close to Timmy had it in for me. I had no trouble giving it back to them.

Cooler heads prevailed, but the head shaking didn't stop. The instructors, Timmy especially, should have drilled themselves in anticipation of teaching us. It sat poorly with a lot of students, including myself, that unqualified patsies were becoming overpaid power-tripping instructors only because they were friends with someone with pull. Many students were already so good, you wondered if their bullets were guided like unseen holy forces, like the ballplayers in the movie *Angels in the Outfield*. They fired with such quickness with their bullets so closely grouped on target. Some trainees were sheriffs, "staties," or weekend warriors who had some law enforcement and firearms experience. They weren't bad but needed to fill some gaps. But those who joined FAMS as their first law enforcement position struggled mightily.

They needed training badly.

And how could someone teach what he didn't know?

One instructor was messing with me, and it got too much. I had to get into his head as much as he was trying to get in mine.

"Listen," I said, daring to challenge him, "why don't we just put this to rest? You've got two choices. You and I can go out to the range and we'll have a shoot-off, and you pick whatever parameters you want—but I'm going to tell you right now you're going to lose because you can't even come close to my skill. Or we can take it to the mat room and we can *roll*. You're a former Marine and ten years younger than I am, so I'm sure you got all kinds of skills I haven't learned in the last twenty years, but even then, I'm going to win."

He responded, "Oh, well, I'm an instructor, so I can't really do that. . . ."

And I nodded at him. He knew he was a wuss, frankly. It told me everything I needed to know. An instructor has to be more knowledgeable and skilled than the students, otherwise *just certify me and put me on the airplane*. If he couldn't lay skills on the range or the mat room, then how in the hell did he have the confidence to teach anyone or put them into action on an airplane against terrorists? Our exchange told me two things: First, he wasn't confident in his own abilities and therefore was a fraud collecting a paycheck, an instructor in title only, and second, that he had weak character. Leaders should always demand more of themselves than those under their command; that is how you lead by example. A good leader issues demands of the men and women he's charged with, but a great leader gets the men and women under his or her command to demand from *themselves*. You have to know what the hell you're doing and be your own example—it's that simple. The rest will follow. That's something the Clintons, for example, never grasped.

Behind the instructors' backs in the parking lot after every training session, I was demonstrating and instructing new guys, and older ones, too, on what the instructors were *trying* to teach. I used a blue practice gun I purchased online. It was the best, and least, I could do. Many of my classmates were great people, and we all needed help in one area or another. A former Army medic and squad mate helped me manage my Motrin and other meds to decrease my muscle aches and the swelling in my shins, knees, and feet from all my running. Another was a real physical training guy. He showed me ways I could work on my cardio when we were on Weekend Morale and Rest (WMR), without running or using my feet, and he was my gym partner. Another person helped me with notes and in return I demonstrated what our instructors simply couldn't.

One drill the instructors were trying to demonstrate was the Six-Round Rhythm Drill. It's also known as the Six-Round Pistol Control Drill. It's a drill most anyone can do and is a staple for air marshals, Secret Service personnel, and competitive shooters alike. Just as at JJRTC, instructors have to teach not just proficiency, but also the ability for students to train themselves, maintain their abilities, and identify their own issues so they can correct them. We have to be able to keep our skills razor-sharp so when called upon, our reactions are second nature. The drill requires firing six controlled rounds within three seconds at seven yards and demonstrates the difference between rapid fire and controlled rhythmic shooting on target. That was the curriculum, and it's what air marshals would be expected to do, but *none* of our six instructors could fire the six shots in three seconds, period—let alone on target.

It was embarrassing.

"Well, you get the idea," said Timmy after he made some excuse why *he* couldn't do it but expected *us* to.

I raised my hand. "Sir, I think I might be able to demonstrate it."

After the shoot house incident, I was taking a stab at overt politeness. They brought me up to try my hand. It had been a few weeks since JJRTC and I was demonstrating in front of everyone, so I requested to do it dry a few times, then do it for real. I approached the line. As soon as the shot timer went *beep,* in the next three seconds exactly, my group was tight and that target silhouette was a dead man.

"Nice, Gary," said the one instructor recruited from Border Control. The instructors originally from USSS just stood there, shall we say, stoically.

Later, before everyone returned to the hotel, I explained the mechanics of how to accomplish the drill to the others. No one wanted to be *the guy* who just skidded through training. I began, "It's similar to what the instructors were saying, but forget all that. Here's what you do, and here's how it really works. . . ."

Still, the rift between our instructors and us got worse. Before class, one of the instructors slammed a stack of papers on my desk. "Here, Gary, hand out these papers. It's the perfect job for you."

"Anything, sir, to help out a fellow federal employee," I said like the brat I was.

If you give it out, you've got to be able to take it, and I handed out the packets to each student with a smile. Our instructor walked out, and I sat down and flipped through the packet. I gasped at the last page. It was a sheet with the names of every person in our class with our Social Security numbers and salaries.

"What the f—?" someone said.

"Do you see this?" I asked my friend Jimmy, who'd also transferred from UD. He nodded in astonishment as each person caught wind of the final page.

"Jimmy, grab those up. I'm going to go get this guy," I said, and I ran through the hallway.

"Excuse me, sir. Sir, do you realize what you just did?" I was trying to help him out so he could get ahead of his own jam.

"Mr. Byrne, get back in that classroom. I've had enough shit from you."

"All right. But I'm just trying to help you. Are you sure you don't want to hear me out?"

"I don't need *your* help," he said bitterly and looked me dead in the eye.

I returned to the classroom. Everyone was losing their minds. Some of the guys had entered FAMS at less than $50,000 from the Army after having served multiple combat tours, but guys from the UD, the Defense Department, and the Park Police had better leverage to transfer. They were already in the federal pay scale system and had rank. The military was a different system. Many of the guys were furious to be paid $20,000 less than both me and a former UD ERT sergeant, but we had twelve years or more in federal law enforcement. The sergeant earned $10,000 more than I.

Some were concentrating on the discrepancies in pay. Others saw this as a ploy for that instructor to trip us or divide our class into petty grievances. Each person had his or her cell phone out, contacting allies outside the chain of command. One Army veteran even phoned his congressman! Our team leader finally was catching on and marched us all to the Special Agent in Charge's office (technically we were skipping class). Though the instructor tried to hold us back, our team leader pushed us through. I'll never forget the SAC's face when he saw the final page. He turned ten sheets of red. The entire day of training was screwed over for HR damage control. Needless to say, it was a major disaster, dividing classmates for the rest of our training and deepening the wedge between us all and FAMS leadership.

Eventually we completed our training at Artesia, New Mexico, and it was off to Atlantic City's Federal Air Marshal Service Training Center for the next phase in training. The Atlantic City training center staff had its head on straighter, but it wasn't without drama. Of our starting class of forty trainees, some couldn't hack the physicality or the stress and washed out. I was forty when I went through the school. Some young guys thought they could take it, but they couldn't keep a steady pace for a two-miler or couldn't handle someone throwing them down on the mat room. No one washed out for marksmanship, which was astonishing (some of our class were terrible marksmen), but it was a serious blight on setting and keeping standards, the character of our leadership, and our piss-poor instructors. They were passing the buck to the field offices, which set a nasty precedent.

Yet one guy who didn't make it through FAMS was an inspiration, and I'll never forget him. I'll call him Barnett. He was on active reserve in the Marines, and his unit got called up. He could have finagled his way out of it, since he was in training for a federal law enforcement agency. But he had trained with his Marine unit, and to him they were family. He felt a great sense of loyalty to them, the Marines, our country, and the mission. He said he would go through school all over again after this next tour in the War on Terror. Men like that don't do it for the money; they do it for the mission. When I was working alongside him he reminded me of situations where commitment was either 100 percent or not, even with no guarantee of either success or of life itself.

I graduated from Atlantic City's training center and even took home a marksmanship and shooting award. I was among the top five shooters, but the four guys above me, Barnett included, were far beyond my skill level. Those four trainees were so lightning fast that we couldn't see them move. When you looked at their shot timers, they all read less than a second. Their paper targets were hit in such a tight group—they looked like a single .410-bore shotgun hit—that you thought they had missed their follow-up shots. These guys were some former Special Forces pros, true warriors because they had been on the two-way range in the War on Terror and in other conflicts. I'm proud of my marksmanship award; it's a memento of my skills. But so many of my colleagues humbled me by their service and heroism. They gave me great strength and kept my ego in check.

By my August 2003 graduation, 40 percent of new air marshals going to their field offices were failing their first qualifier, the Practical Pistol Course (PPC), and therefore couldn't fly—and we shrugged it off as if it were normal. And even the PPC was heavily dumbed down from its former standards. My fellow qualifying air marshals would sarcastically say, "But hey, fly safe" no differently than an Army vet might raise an eyebrow when witnessing similar bad policy and cynically say, "Safety Number One." Worse, our field offices were under too much pressure and were having the failing FNGs (freaking new guys) fly missions while still on probation.

Never is the mission so important to screw it up!

After our transition from training school to our field office we stood ready to deter and to combat hijackings, bombings, and attacks on our commercial air traffic by all means possible that don't hinder or deter Americans from traveling and maintaining a healthy economy. After all, the 9/11 attacks were as much an attack on our economy and way of life as they were designed to inflict mass casualties or destroy command structure and real estate. The president and Congress agreed on that policy. FAMS leadership was to implement the policy and we, the boots on the ground (or in the air), were to make it actuality.

I was flying missions just a few days later from the field office covering Philadelphia International Airport. Tensions ran high. We were sure—we felt it in our bones—that more attacks, bombings, and hijackings were coming our way. Most laypersons think it's been all quiet since 9/11. They're dead wrong. That myth drives us crazy. It's the great irony of our national security personnel, from the swords to the shields, that if we do our jobs right, no one hears about it. The best umpire in the league is one you never notice. But if we don't do our jobs right, it's the USS *Cole,* Beirut, Oklahoma City, or even Benghazi all over again. Today we're doing a tremendous job, but we're at a crossroads.

Since—and even before 9/11—the United States has been constantly probed for weaknesses, from both terrorist groups and full-bore state-run attacks. I initiated my FAMS duty with domestic Return over Night (RON) missions, typically two-day missions. Fly, stay, and then fly back. I had negotiated my transition to FAMS to be based out of Philly International. I wanted to raise my family where I grew up and to have my kids' grandmother be part of their lives. When I was starting out, the usual trips were Philly–Miami (with D.C. in the middle), Philly–Charlotte, or Philly–Los Angeles, followed by an office day, then a day off. The day after that, I was back flying missions. Sometimes we'd have two office days in a row or an occasional training school for explosives detection and disarmament, in case I ever had a Jack Bauer–style moment disarming a ticking time bomb. These training schools were always amazing because our tactical renaissance development was moving so far, a development that gets the bad guy dead and the good guy home with fewer casualties. As the old military adage goes, "If you're in a fair fight, you're doing it wrong."

At forty-one, as a new air marshal, I was high-strung and eager, for two reasons. Genny and I had sold our house in Maryland and were, as if college kids, living with our parents until we could acquire a house to raise our family. Further weighing on my mind, even in 2003, were our country's three wars: Afghanistan, Iraq, and the less defined but equally crucial Global War on Terror. In Iraq we had just shifted from invasion to policing and counterinsurgency. I still hated the image in my mind of Congress, along with Hillary, standing on the Congress steps singing the national anthem, knowing they had f—ed us with petty BS that left us so vulnerable leading up to 9/11.

In Tom Quinn's infinite wisdom, FAMS policy mandated we wear a suit and tie. We also preboarded the aircraft in our positions ahead of all passengers. For most jobs, dressing professionally is a great thing—*but not for undercover work*. Board before the first first-class passengers and it was extremely obvious who the undercover air marshals were: the A-holes who looked like Secret Service agent wannabes. Being undercover was supposed to thwart the same terrorist threat that fought to the cockpit on 9/11. They were clandestine operators, too, after all, and they dressed subtly. They didn't go around wearing "I Love Radical Islam" T-shirts.

But with Quinn's goal of *appearance* of strength rather than *actual* strength, we would be easily identifiable to terrorists. They'd take us out and then take our weapons. It endangered not just our lives, it endangered the entire mission. It made it easier for a 9/11 to happen again.

We even had passengers thank us for our service when they boarded and as they stowed their bags overhead. Normally getting thanks as a cop or military guy is great, but for us as air marshals, it made us feel as though we had a giant target on our backs, throats, and major arteries for any contraband razor blade, garrote wire, sleeper hold, or sharpened toothbrush shank hastily crafted in the bathroom. Our protection plans worked only if we could maintain our cover identities as just other passengers. It was a farce. FAMS's micromanaging policies jeopardized everything. It was all about appearances and portraying air marshals like hotshot agents. It was moronic.

Sometimes when we were preboarding, flight attendants and pilots would give us the rundown of the plane and show us the under-areas and nuances of the specific aircraft. That was great and helped foster the bond of our being in this together to maintain international air traffic security. But on one preboarding, our pilot (a retired Air Force pilot) pulled me aside and gave me a piece of his mind about how unprofessional and stupid the air marshals were. He referred to us as "you guys." I just bit my tongue until he ran out of breath—or I could get a word in. I appreciated the old-school military-style critique—made me a little nostalgic even. I knew he wasn't going to stop until he got winded.

"You g-ddamn air marshals are costing us millions!" he exclaimed, berating us for checking everything and holding up flights an extra thirty minutes. "You're not bomb-sniffing dogs! What the hell are you searching for?"

I didn't know, either. Some planes had their nuances, but this was clearly a policy adapted by the Secret Service for prechecking hotels. The pilot continued bitching about how obvious we were to everyone, and in reality how we didn't do a damn thing to keep anyone safe.

He took a breath.

"Are you done?" I asked, letting him wipe the sweat off his forehead and breathe.

He was, so I leveled with him. "I hear you, and I agree with you. I'm just the air marshal. I don't like the policy, nor do I set the policy, any more than you do. I just follow it. Believe it or not, I'm actually a new guy here. Yeah, I've only joined just recently, and all I can say is the air marshals are trying to work through it. It'll get fixed, but it's going to take a while."

I didn't mention a reason but gestured upward so he could read between the lines. It was all so ridiculous, and it ruined my agency. Many air marshals sidestepped agency brass to air their complaints to legislators and even to anonymously leak stories to the press. If it took embarrassing FAMS management to save its mission—and lives—then guys would do that.

Behavioral detection was one policy that did get adapted eventually and I loved that. It became just like what the USSS UD did at checkpoints. "Nervous?" I'd ask someone with a smile as I watched their posture to see if it stayed the same or fluctuated, if they went into some elaborate story, if they got defensive for no reason at all, or if they were consistent within their cultural or religious norms.

The 9/11 hijackers were divided into groups of four with one trained pilot and three other terrorists armed with crude melee weapons, some hand-to-hand training, and the will to kill and succeed at the expense of their own lives. I was looking for someone like myself, someone who was mentally and physically prepared to succeed in his or her political mission by killing and even giving his or her life, if necessary. The difference between them and me is that if I succeeded, everyone who boarded the plane would walk off alive. If they succeeded, three hundred plus people would be dead.

I harbored no Snow White illusions of what the plane was going to look like if a hijacker and I tangled. It was going to be ugly, and bloody, and it would make passengers want to vomit. If I did exactly what our protocol and training dictated, it was going to be a mess. I'd conditioned my mind for it. I did that as I trained at CrossFit. I did it each morning as I reminded myself why I had my firearm in the first place. But I'd be lying if I said that the mental conditioning didn't take a toll. Premeditating to kill someone places a ghastly burden on the mind and even on the body.

The "underwear bomber" and the "shoe bomber" failed because they sweated through their bombs. The underwear bomber was so incredibly nervous that he decided to wear the bomb three weeks before his mission, and that's how he ruined it. He was willing, and he tried to kill a plane full of people—but what he actually did was burn his crotch off. There happened to be a Swedish documentary filmmaker several seats over. When he saw the fire and the bomber fiddling with his explosive, the Swede hopped over seats from the other side of the plane and beat the crap out of him. Other passengers joined in. Those passengers didn't have to be embroiled with the fatigue and stress of mentally preparing for a fight, because they never planned on it. They didn't think—they acted. But the underwear bomber was thinking and emotionally compromised—and failed.

I wish I could tell you that it was some FBI mosque undercover agent, cyber team, or TSA or FAMS agent who stopped him. Nope, it was his own sweat because of the emotional burden of his mission. In 1991 a Tamil Tiger (radical Sri Lankan terrorist), the "bra bomber" (actually it was a belt), didn't sweat through her bomb, though, and she accomplished her goal, assassinating Indian prime minister Rajiv Ratna Gandhi. She was ruthless.

My partner and I once homed in on a passenger and we were so keyed on him that when he entered the bathroom I took my in-flight magazine and placed my gun underneath it. When everything panned out without incident, I figured no harm, no foul. Many air marshals at the time were similarly hyperaware; we believed a hit was coming any damn day.

Since 2003 we started to refocus and retrain. I've heard stories, though, of how after 9/11 higher-ups were basically handing firearms to those transferring to FAMS and saying, "Get on the plane." Things have greatly improved since then, but I fear the pendulum is swinging both ways. I believed in the FAMS mission—*and* we needed to stay vigilant.

In the years that followed, many air marshals like myself, who still held the mission-first mentality, knew we had to pick and choose our battles carefully; otherwise midlevel management was going to stick *its* neck out to put *ours* on the chopping block. We couldn't be the guys who were always saber-rattling and rocking the boat. But when we did, they knew to take us seriously. One guy—bless him—pushed management's micromanaging back into their smug faces. Our dress code was professional coat and tie, but as in the movie

My Cousin Vinny, one air marshal bought a very old red formal suit with coattails!

"But I'm still in dress code," he retorted to management—and he was.

No one likes a stink, but sometimes stinks have to be made. Management was either going to have to fight him, citing protocol; change the protocol to let us dress undercover; or make the dress code *worse* so that we really would look like U.S. Secret Service or FBI G-men, with the typical *Men in Black* monochrome suit and tie, shades, earpiece. But if they wrote him up, they were going to have to air grievances on paper.

Eventually, after several other air marshals banded together in a series of hilariously dressed stunts, management caved. We no longer preboarded and could finally dress the way we best deemed fit the mission. Our dress code became to simply blend in. A suit from Philly to Boston may have been fine, but from Philly to Miami? It garnered attention.

It was clear at both our training schools, at our Philly field office, and from hearing from my old classmates and other field offices that FAMS pervasively discriminated against women and minorities. It created a crossfire. Management at every level pledged to wipe that shit up and out, but management's solution was the constant political-appearance-based solution. They created "protected classes," as we called them, while routing out diversity of thought- and performance-based competition. Instead of leadership's digging deep, creating tough standards, and holding everyone equally accountable, they played games.

The worst game was making our qualifications pass-fail rather than score based—because management could not pass the older sky-marshal standards of marksmanship and physicality. If an air marshal can't do a pull-up or thirty-five push-ups in a minute, will they really be able to fight to the death against someone committed to dying to succeed in taking down a plane? Hell, no.

I have to say it: For some middle management and a select few, the federal air marshal program has become a shining example of the worst government welfare I can think of. Former Secret Service special agents used FAMS as a way to pay into and collect on a second pension from the same U.S. Treasury—double dipping because they came from the old D.C. police and fire retirement program before President Reagan instituted the Federal Employee Retirement System.

What made matters worse is that so many former SAs treated their new full-time FAMS jobs like part-time gigs. Supervisors often clocked in late and left early. FAMS's system of pay and timekeeping was designed to leech hours for employees so that more personnel had to be hired. I flew on a plane! I had a ticketed flight and set schedule that they gave me at a set hotel that I had to get approved, so why was it necessary that I logged my hours and got them approved on the back end, too? It was not only unnecessary, but it was made far too complicated purposely. If you've seen the NBC television series *The Office* or Jennifer Aniston's movie *Office Space,* you've seen what our office days looked like. I'm dead serious. It was criminal, but I was mandated to play the game.

Here's how ridiculous it got: I was on an overseas mission, and what did I see proudly displayed on my hotel wall? "Customer of the Month: The Federal Air Marshal Service." *What the hell?* Could you imagine an undercover law enforcement officer being outed because of that? Who bought into that? Meanwhile, an air marshal who put his schedule on his family fridge got fired over it.

To politicians the problem was actually perception—not the problem itself, not what actually jeopardized the mission. For me on an airplane and in any undercover work, it was true that I didn't want operators who looked like cookie-cutter slimmed-out Caucasian-only men. But it was just as damned dangerous to hire people based on gender and skin color. Performance standards and accountability applied to everyone.

We needed FAMs worthy of trust and confidence to complete the mission. It was the only way to *fight* crime and terrorism. Character for us had no appearance except for a look of general athleticism. On the flip side, there were air marshals who needed seat belt extenders because they were too obese to use the regular airplane belts. One air marshal nagged management so much that they allowed him to carry a SIG P239, a much smaller version of our pistol, which meant our cartridge magazines weren't compatible. Management at HQ were complaining that the SIG P229 made them "look fat." *Right, blame the gun.* So they instituted the SIG P239 for *themselves.* Then they had to accommodate all other the whiners, too. Then anyone who was overweight or inconvenienced by carrying the standard issue got to carry the smaller pistol with half the amount of standard ammunition—not that the original whiner could shoot the broad side of a barn, no matter whether he had a bandolier full of ammo.

If you can't raise the bridge, lower the water. If you can't meet the standards, well, just lower them.

Another air marshal couldn't stay awake in a meeting, let alone on an airplane. (I'm no doctor, but. . . .) He had horrible sleep apnea, to the point where even the flight attendants found it irksome. Management refused to bench him or hold him accountable. It was like having a lifeguard who couldn't swim. If we didn't laugh, we'd cry. But I finally had to shut up about it, even though I was fuming.

The ugly truth is that so much of middle management had lost sight of the mission. They truly didn't believe another attack on a plane would happen. That was their mentality. They often used "check ride" flights that are made to verify in-flight air marshal performance as transparent excuses to visit friends or for family events like weddings or vacations.

While many air marshals were hard chargers, management had a created an "everyone's a winner/everyone gets a participation trophy" mentality. Protected classes were a lost cause. Management was so worried about HR grievances that I knew an air marshal who refused to get the quarterly physical.

FAMS actually hired an independent review board to create a minimum standard for us. They spent thousands of dollars on it. The board settled on three pull-ups, a mile and a half in fifteen minutes, and thirty-five push-ups in a minute. That was abysmally low. Does that level of fitness indicate someone's being able to fight four 9/11-style hijackers? No. But FAMS didn't even enforce this standard—so we really didn't have any. And there was zero incentive for an individual air marshal to comply, other than one's own self-respect and sense of duty. I couldn't live with myself if I let a tragedy occur.

We had a protected-class female air marshal who weaseled her way into a promotion to become an "airport liaison" by insinuating (really threatening) to file a discrimination lawsuit. I'm just glad I didn't have to fly with her often, because she wasn't on my team.

I discussed her with the air marshals I knew from other countries. Foreign air marshals could spot our flaws from a mile away and laughed at us (the Germans, for example, had an excellent program). They were impressed by her case.

"Don't even get me started," I'd say.

"Don't you have fitness standards?" they'd ask in their various accents.

And I'd shake my head, and they'd laugh and shake theirs. "I can't talk about it—she'll file a grievance against me. So just drop it."

Foreign air marshals could sense our own marshals' disdain for our system's abusers. FAMS management's lack of professionalism stemmed from persons of weak character attaining key leadership positions. Lower level slipups occurred when higher-ups junked the principle of leading by example. It led to misconduct such as marshals' hiring prostitutes on foreign trips, wasting tax dollars, and overlooking outright corruption. FAMS recently made the papers after a pilot kicked an air marshal off his plane; the marshal had threatened to sue over not being offered the same meals as others and groused that a drink was *deliberately* spilled on him.

As time passed, even expert instructors who had been active combat Army Rangers, Navy SEALs, Delta Force, and other Special Forces–type operations abandoned FAMS. They could no longer stand the pattern of constant administrative back-and-forth and broken promises. It had become routine for us, but they, as private contractors, could work anywhere—and soon did.

FAMS simply couldn't retain anyone with their level of craftsmanship, not with FAMS's slipshod character and too-often scrambled priorities. Just about anyone can learn to shoot and to teach others to shoot—at least, in ideal conditions—but the know-how to shoot and fight under the worst imaginable situations (gun jams, taking fire, injuries, dynamic positioning) is incredibly difficult. You can't put a price tag on it. Those experts who departed FAMS in disgust taught from hard-knock, real-life experiences—and FAMS tried to nickel-and-dime them while wasting precious resources on free college tuition for anyone in FAMS who wanted it. Leadership frankly treated those expert outside contractors like shit, trying to insult them as much as possible. It was damned upsetting, to say the least, to see qualified people like that move on.

FAMS management's "thrift" with outside instructors was exacerbated by its wastefully piling on the paperwork and make-work during marshals' office days.

FAMS played catch-up for a long time. It wasn't all FAMS' fault. For too long Congress—and the nation itself—failed to recognize the terrorist threat facing us. It shouldn't have taken a 9/11 to wake us up, but it did. But the appointment of Tom Quinn as the modernized FAMS's first director only worsened matters. His misplaced priorities and featherbedding for old Secret Service cronies turned an essential program into an almost-instant national laughingstock. A hasty get-it-done mentality didn't work for FAMS any better than it worked for Hillary Clinton.

Tom Quinn resigned in early 2006. His absurd dress code and preboarding policies caught up with him. In June 2015, acting TSA director Melvin Carraway resigned after reports that agency undercover "red teams" assigned to several airports had failed to detect bombs and guns in a frightening 67 out of 70 tests conducted by the Department of Homeland Security's Office of the Inspector General. I had to ask myself: So why were the people who failed at that rate getting paid to begin with? But the go-to congressional solution was to do two things: Dump more money into the problem and send a cosmetic message that the problem would be solved by a high-level resignation. I wish it were that simple, but the next director will be part of the same in crowd.

Healing in this case requires an enema, not a Band-Aid.

I joined FAMS to accomplish a vital mission. I joined to halt terrorism in its tracks—hopefully, even before a situation unfolds. I wanted to exceed the level of commitment displayed by four-person-plus teams of trained and committed hijackers. Anything short of that just wasn't good enough. Why should Americans pay me—or anyone else—for anything less than that?

Let me tell you exactly what it would look like if a trained committed air marshal had to do their job on an airplane against a four-person-plus hijacking team.

The human body pumps blood incredibly fast, and 9/11's hijacking team cut into a few people to make examples of them. They killed the pilots because the terrorist trained as a pilot could assume control of the flight deck. Imagine the smell, the blood-soaked carpets, the screams, the volume of noise in the airplane, the panic as nearly three hundred people were scared stiff and hopping over their seats and running as best they could in a crowded airplane to get away from people killing other people.

Now imagine that you're an air marshal with an obese, asthmatic, sleep apnea–ridden partner. Now imagine that you're an air marshal who's been outed by agency dress code and preboarding policies and who, because of that, has had his or her firearm stolen. Imagine what it would take to be an air marshal who has to retake the flight deck. Imagine the marksmanship and brutality it would take to battle those four or more hijackers—fanatics all—and accidentally shoot one or more of the passengers or flight attendants or pilots fighting for their lives and trying to barricade themselves in the cockpit.

Imagine the concussive force of firing a weapon in a pressurized tube at an altitude of 30,000 feet at 530 mph—except that maybe you're really not at 30,000 feet and 530 mph, you're losing altitude rapidly while gaining immense speed as the copilot puts the plane into a dive and swerves to thwart the attackers as he or she tries to make an emergency landing anywhere—no matter how dangerous it is—possible.

Imagine that the terrorist pilot is armed and firing down the aisles, using them as fatal funnels. Imagine the level of fitness, situational awareness, and yes, violence that you would need to hold the flight deck. Terrorists use women and children because sometimes *they are* women and children! By the time the threat reached the aircraft, we air marshals would have at best maybe seven seconds to identify the threat for what it was and to take action. I knew that I was going to want to vomit. I knew that my adrenaline was going to give me the highest dosage immediately, but the airplane was going to go from complete calm to complete hell in an instant.

That's what each federal air marshal is hired to face.

FAMS was created to be an onboard shield against a terrorist spear. Terrorists know that they only have to get it right once for their mission to succeed. But the Federal Air Marshal Service leadership and middle management had so obviously lost sight of their agency's mission. September 11 wasn't the first attack on airplanes, not by a long shot, and it hasn't been the last, not by a long shot, either. Any air marshal who falls short of matching that threat shouldn't be an air marshal. It's that simple.

Otherwise passengers would be better off knowing that it's up to them, just as Todd Beamer knew when he retook United Flight 93 on 9/11 on the intel that he and his fellow passengers had received that their terrorist attackers had embarked on a suicide mission. Beamer, a regular American, an exceptional American hero, spoke up before retaking that airplane and taking it down in Shanksville, Pennsylvania, saving thousands of lives at the terrorists' still-unknown target.

"Are you ready? Okay. Let's roll," were Todd Beamer's last words before storming the deck.

Are we ready to roll?

Think of Navy diver Robert Stethem, who stood up to terrorists when they hijacked TWA Flight 847 in June 1985. He took that risk because he knew his fellow military hostages were all married and he wasn't. His captors pummeled him and shot him in his right temple before dumping his dead body from the plane and then shooting him again for good measure. Think of Flight 847's German-American flight attendant Uli Derickson, who, after trying to protect Stethem, stood up to the terrorist who had just killed him. When the terrorists demanded she identify the several Jewish passengers on board, she refused and hid their passports. I thought of heroism like that when I was training or at work to focus my thoughts and recall just why I did what I did. We've been there before. We shouldn't have to be there again.

Let's also acknowledge this: Despite all the crap from our top-heavy, lead-from-behind management, the boots on the airplane floor, the air marshals, have succeeded since 9/11 in safeguarding American air travel. And because of that, terrorists have had to change their playbook. FAMS has made our domestic and international airplane travel a hard target. They have succeeded again and again in thwarting attacks.

Can another 9/11 happen?

It *will* happen, but because of air marshals dedicated to their mission—and your safety—the next catastrophic terrorist hijacking attempt won't go without a major fight at thirty thousand feet.

But—and this is a big but—we know exactly what the terrorist threat has evolved into: Al Qaeda, ISIS, Boko Haram, or even a crazy "lone wolf"—I hate that term; they're not wolves, they're jackals—or a four-person-plus coordinated assault.

The enemy selects a target based on two criteria: First, it's soft; it *can* be attacked. It is *attackable*. Second, attacking that target will wreak the most psychological havoc on our population to influence its national leadership in an intended political direction.

It's that simple.

They will absolutely select public places such as malls. We saw that in the September 2013 Westgate Mall attack in Nairobi, Kenya, by Al-Shabaab, which killed sixty-three persons, injured over 175 more, crippled the Kenyan tourist economy, and locked down the city of Nairobi entirely. Attacks may resemble the six highly coordinated simultaneous attacks in November 2008 in Mumbai, India, most notably at the Taj Mahal Palace Hotel. One hundred and fifty seven innocent souls were murdered. More than six hundred people were injured by the series of gunfights and bombings.

Any country is vulnerable to mass murder from radical Islamic terrorism. That was proven once again in Paris in January 2015 as terrorists attacked the weekly satirical magazine *Charlie Hebdo* as well as a kosher deli. That November, terrorists coordinated six more attacks on the French capital, striking at a major concert hall, a stadium, bars, and restaurants. They massacred 146 innocent human beings. The attacks crippled French tourism.

Why did these attacks happen? Why were those targets chosen? Simply because they fit the two criteria I just listed: 1) they were soft targets and 2) they created a psychological impact followed by a policy impact.

Think of it as Murphy's law—or Byrne's Law on Security: Any attack that *can* happen *will*.

But an attack in the United States will so obviously include schools and public arenas because we still haven't gotten our act together in protecting what matters most. It's happened before, yet we still don't learn. It will happen at the White House because we still haven't learned. I know from the "We Hate You" book in my FAMS field office. It's the latest intel, basically a list of the latest threats. I know it all too well.

Yes, I believe in the FAMS mission, and I believe it's working, but the agency has to update its counterterrorism techniques to meet terrorism's evolving tactics. We must harden our targets at home and take the fight to the enemy abroad. But when terrorists turn on our news, what do they see? A man lands a gyrocopter on Congress's lawn without interference. A knife-wielding man runs unchecked into the White House, right past all its beefy security. In Atlanta a man carrying a gun is allowed onto an elevator carrying President Obama. Those last two incidents cost Secret Service director Julia Pierson her job in October 2014.

I have high hopes for her replacement, Joe Clancy, since I worked with Joe many times for many hours in USSS UD. Leadership doesn't come from the bottom up or the top down; leadership with character comes from the top-down after someone has served from the bottom-up. I think Joe Clancy can turn the mentality around.

Terrorists can recognize the difference between actual security and its mere appearance. You think they can't see past a gun-free zone sign? It might as well say: "Terrorists welcome! Ready access to undefended scores of innocent children!" Please, get over the gun control distraction. Ask yourself what stops four men from going into a school with knives or bombs. I know that by the time a threat reaches me on an airplane there's no time for hesitation, talk, quarter. I want to win more than I can tolerate losing.

In 2016, federal agencies are training their law enforcement personnel to respond to active-shooter scenarios. Concealed-carry permits for civilians are going up—that's great. But we need a more honest discussion. By the time a terrorist or criminal boards a plane with ill intentions we're past the time for obfuscating their plans or negotiating them down. Either FAMS personnel is on the plane when it takes off, or its passengers and crew are marked for death, and they better know it.

The federal air marshal, the passengers, the flight crew, and the pilots are truly the last line of defense. American public spaces and schools need the same approach. Let's cut the feel-good politics and recognize that by the time someone with dangerous plans reaches your doorstep, it's too late to ponder root causes of antisocial behavior—it's time to act! All of the thinking should have been done beforehand. And the level of commitment to stop grotesque violence in its tracks—stone cold dead—has to exceed theirs if protecting the principal is going to succeed.

Have no misconceptions: Any outcome at that point will be bloody, ugly, and lowdown. It's like nothing you've seen in a Hollywood movie, and it's going to be bad-breath and fingernail close. But it's a fight that's coming our way whether we get ready for it or not.

Let's get ready.

My father passed away on December 21, 2007, and as I flew at thirty thousand feet I felt closer and closer to him. It wasn't because of the altitude or the puffy clouds, but because I was keeping my promise to him that I would protect others. Our federal government and agencies have also made that promise to the American people.

It's time they dug deep, took the harder, character-driven road, and protected what matters most—the Americans who can't protect themselves.

18.

CYPRUS

Halfway across the world someone dug a tunnel under a tank guarding a border. For a moment, all remained still. Why would that day be any different from the last? Soldiers clad in their flat green-and-tan uniforms awoke each day and went to work just as they always had. Still, they knew what I knew: It may be rare for an attack to hit *me,* but it's guaranteed to hit someone. They were Israeli tank personnel guarding the tinderbox Gaza–Israeli border.

BOOM!

It was June 26, 2006, and seven or eight Hamas operatives detonated an improvised explosive device—the beginning of a highly coordinated raid. They killed two twenty-year-old Israelis and claimed to have captured three more. For years Israel authorities had those captured men on their minds and wanted them back desperately. They didn't know that two of the men who were taken that day were actually killed during the raid. Still, Hamas used them as bargaining chips in a prisoner exchange two years later. A third solder, Corporal Gilad Shalit, had actually been captured and was still alive.

The incident preceded a full-blown Israeli Defense Force incursion (Operation Summer Rains) into the always fractious Gaza

Strip. New fighting erupted on Israel's northern border with Lebanon as well. Israel called it the 2006 Israel-Hezbollah War. The Lebanese called it the July War. In the Middle East people can't agree on anything.

The raids and the rockets threatened to ignite even wider fighting in the world's powder keg. Word went out from our State Department: Get our people out now! From Lebanon, Hezbollah rocketed Ben Gurion Airport, locking down all air traffic in and out of Israel. The State Department contacted the Defense Department. U.S. military forces shipped out to Israel and Cyprus. American citizens and numerous refugees also raced to Cyprus. Two years previously the Republic of Cyprus had joined the European Union, and its three airports were suddenly the only routes for refugees fleeing the Mideast's fast-growing turmoil. Americans, Europeans, and people from all over the world, finding themselves trapped in Israel and Lebanon, used any method they could to get to Cyprus. Boats of every kind were suddenly and haphazardly commissioned to ferry desperate refugees across the Mediterranean from Israel to Cyprus.

The call came in, but it didn't surprise us. We had been following the story closely. Even before FAMS requested volunteers, a good many air marshals had already stepped up to the plate. "I want in," I emailed my superiors.

I was formally on board almost immediately. It felt good to be back in the action. I felt as if I'd returned to the old helter-skelter days of last-minute Secret Service details covering Clinton campaign events or protecting NATO summits—when events came down to the wire, and we had to trust our own instincts. But this was 2006. Yes, the road had given me some weather, but I was just as eager as ever.

Whenever a war erupts, no matter in what part of the globe, Americans somehow get caught in its figurative or literal crossfire. All flying FAMS (the guys who fly and don't sit behind a desk) went on alert. FAMS was the perfect agency to safely transport Americans out of a hot zone and to ensure that terrorists couldn't take advantage of whatever panic and chaos festered to seize control of a plane or even to sneak operatives or intel past our country's borders.

The plan was simple—it usually was. Our Philadelphia-based team—Mark, who was our team leader (TL), Jim, Bill, and I—would board a rent-a-plane flown by three pilots and an engineer and head from Philly to Haan, Germany. A sixteen-woman flight crew awaited us. We'd refuel before landing at Larnaca International Airport on Cyprus's southeastern coast. We were ordered to remain at Larnaca for no longer than four hours—it was even printed on our mission orders. Customs and TSA personnel would screen everyone thoroughly before anyone boarded. The Americans would be ready to board when we got there. Our task was to behaviorally profile everyone as they boarded. Then it was back to Haan for refueling and then on to Philadelphia, where Customs and FAMS security would process our refugees.

After that, it wasn't my business.

Both this war-created refugee crisis and Cyprus itself were hotbeds for terrorist activity. I knew that well enough. When four Popular Front for the Liberation of Palestine terrorists hijacked Lufthansa Flight 181 in October 1977, they demanded the plane be diverted to Larnaca International before heading for Bahrain, Dubai, Aden, and then Mogadishu. Commandos from German Special Forces executed a daring rescue (Operation Feuerzauber—"Fire Magic") and rescued all eighty-six passengers. But the operation bore the earmarks of every antiterrorism operation, even the successful ones: It teetered a hair trigger away from complete catastrophe.

We departed late that night. When it's a red-eye I either try to sleep beforehand or hang with Genny and the kids after school, but in an anxious situation like this, I simply couldn't settle. My brain wouldn't switch to off-duty mode. I departed around 10 p.m., driving through the empty suburban streets and sparsely trafficked Philly highways before reaching the airport.

When we saw our mode of transport, the four members of our team groaned, "Oh, *great!*"

Our charter plane was an old DC-10, a McDonnell Douglas jetliner largely phased out of commercial fleets. Our particular plane was just fresh from flying the NBA's Charlotte Hornets. Delta Air Lines was aware that our last-minute chartering of this aircraft was for our nation's emergency humanitarian airlift and graciously volunteered a space for it on Philly's runways and hangars—but the plane was a mess, and that held us up. Cleaners struggled to get it in shape. We didn't have a minute to spare and pitched in to help. It was a 260-seater, so it was a big job—and an unwelcome holdup.

For these kinds of missions we weren't undercover or even close to it. We wore the range gear that we used on training days: tan cargo pants, our vests that made us look from afar like fishermen or photographers, agency ball caps, and dull blue T-shirts that said U.S. Federal Air Marshal Service on the back. I couldn't avoid mentally associating wearing my range clothes with a full day in the shoot house and live-fire training. Instead, I was heading for Cyprus. That attire served another purpose as well. I wasn't undercover, and being undercover is a strain. You worry about drawing attention to yourself. You worry about a holster bulge giving the game away. There was none of that tonight. We were dressed as if were ready for anything, though we didn't know what "anything" meant. We had no idea what to expect from a State Department–ordered airlift.

Once we were airborne, our TL, Mark, ordered us to put our heads together and concoct scenarios of what we might confront in Cyprus. We started with the standard ones. Air marshals protect the cockpit first, then the plane as a whole, from hijacking or anything else. But this mission was different. Maintaining control of the aircraft remained priority number one, but we'd be lucky if even a few refugees spoke English—and if *any* part of our mission transpired according to plan. We agreed that controlling infighting, maintaining general order, and protecting the flight attendants would be our close seconds. We reviewed our basics and trusted our strategy (what we had of it), training, individual instincts, and teamwork to see us through.

Training remained paramount because there were events in every law enforcement officer's career where the only certainty is uncertainty. This was clearly one of those moments. We had no idea what we'd confront on the ground in Cyprus or what our passengers would be like, but we'd handle it. We had six hours to kill on the way to Germany and let our imaginations run wild.

Except for the crew, we were the only people on that 260-seat jet. None of us were very familiar with the DC-10, and our pilot and his engineer were helpful in revealing its nuances. They even showed us how to put on movies, which sounds frivolous. But it was knowledge that might later assist in calming agitated passengers. More important, they showed us each compartment and where food was kept in the galley, which we could reach only by elevator. The plane was eerily empty *and loud*. People absorb sound, whether in a theater or a restaurant—or a plane. And we were the only folks taking up that slack.

Having learned the DC-10's ropes, the four of us swapped stories before finally curling up and catching as much sleep as we could. But sleeping was tough, at least for me, and I suspected for the others as well. It provided more unwelcome time to mull things over—and not just our current mission, but all the ones that had preceded it.

The thought crossed my mind: Maybe I should write a book.

Nah!

After seven hours airborne, we landed in Haan, refueled, and picked up our crew—so far, so good. Six hours later our landing gear touched down in Cyprus. I looked out the window. The airport was overcrowded and awash with panic and refugees. The flight tower wasn't sure where to put us at first and we circled for some time. On landing, we saw hordes of anxious refugees. Somewhere in those throngs were the Americans we were tasked with rescuing. But corralling our approximately three hundred refugees would not be the end of our problems.

We had good reason to fear. The Americans we were charged with protecting and taking home would be either from Israel or from Lebanon, the two countries at war. We didn't relish mixing civilians who had resided with (and most likely sympathized with) both warring sides in one tightly packed and tense airplane. We didn't even have a really reliable estimate of how many souls we were picking up to take home, because another FAMS mission had arrived in-country a day before us. We were eager to check in with them, but then again, they should have taken off already but hadn't. If all had gone according to plan, they would have left before we arrived. Even the best-laid plans go to shit, and we feared our plans were halfway down the bowl.

We peered out of the tiny passenger cabin windows and from the cockpit. Families of all ages huddled everywhere around the airport and behind fence lines, carrying whatever they had been able to pack together. Larnaca International was clearly understaffed in manpower, especially in security. Regular airport manpower, even at full staff, was nowhere near enough to sort, process, and adequately secure the hundreds and thousands of people who had fled to Cyprus hoping to head home, wherever that was. Rarely are airports state-of-the-art. Larnaca wasn't that old, but it had been hastily thrown together when Cyprus itself blew apart into Greek Orthodox Christian and Turkish Muslim in the early 1970s. Neither it nor most airports were built to facilitate modern security measures like screeners and magnetometers, let alone accommodate this exodus of thousands of refugees.

Seeing the situation, our pilots grew very nervous. As we deplaned, one pulled us aside. Struggling to be heard, we shouted at each other over the roar of incoming airliners. One pilot said, "I need assurances from you guys. I get what we're doing and it's important, but I'm not sacrificing my crew. We don't know who these people are! I gotta give my crew some kind of . . . you know?"

"We got you. We get it. We're not going to let anything happen to your—*our* crew. You and this plane are our top priority. We're always going to have an air marshal with you at the front, too. No matter what happens in the rest of the aircraft you'll always have at least one of us by you—and we are going to look after your crew," we reassured him.

I added, "You're how we got here, you and the crew. So you and the crew are our priority."

He said he understood that, but I could tell he'd been around the block enough times to know that like dreams, assurances don't always hold. But he needed us to come through. He was going to have to trust us.

I shouted, "Listen, whatever ends up happening, we will be on here, too!" The pilot nodded. It was the best we could do for each other at the moment.

American security personnel were on full alert to get our citizens, but the airport remained clogged with people wanting so desperately to board flights off the island. The situation was getting worse—as so often happens in war zones. Collateral damage in lives and livelihoods is difficult for anyone to quantify or fathom. Civilians rarely take heed of war until it's too late, and the 2006 Lebanon–Israel border seemed not so very different from New York City in September 2001. Panic-stricken civilians wanted out any way they could go: running, walking, driving, flying, you name it.

We didn't know whom we were picking up. We didn't know whom among them we could trust. And our flight crew wasn't sure they could trust *us*.

Perfect.

And in typical United States Secret Service and United States Federal Air Marshal Service fashion, our phones starting alerting us to voice messages from our supervisors. "Crucial" messages of FAMS HR bullshit.

"This is [I'll call him Ryan]: I just wanted to let everyone know that *we are only paying the usual eight hours plus two paid hours for this mission*."

Unbelievable.

Thank you for caring.

The rest of our voice mails and emails were updates and confirmations and repeats! Half of us were pissed. I was fuming, too, but not about the pay. I wanted to tear Ryan's head off once I got back. We saw the multiple alerts on our work phones and thought the message had to be serious—some sort of actionable intel of an enemy attack that we needed to be aware of. Nope. We didn't care about the damn pay! We could yell about that afterward. Ryan had no clue what he was sending us into but he made sure, as usual, to screw with our heads as soon as we hit the ground running.

While in flight, we had talked of rumors of hazard pay because this mission was stretched so thin and was so important. But our supervisors, cushy and comfy behind their desks, instead sent us a message that they hadn't secured even overtime for us yet. The over-budget expenses associated with our mission hadn't been allocated from FAMS, the State Department, the Defense Department, or anywhere else. So we were in financial limbo for our added time in-country. This wasn't actionable intel! There was nothing we could do about it. Ryan's rash of messages served only to take our minds out of the mission.

The plan was to be there four hours—no more.

Instead, another FAMS team switched with us.

Shit.

They took our DC-10 and filled the plane to the brim with passengers and headed back to Haan. We were left in airlift limbo. Our team leader grabbed someone with an airport ID patch and had him drive around the airport in a little taxiway car to gather what intel we could. We scurried to locate the airport's FAMS HQ—and found it in, of all places, the food court: just a few guys with cell phones, radios, and laptops sitting in plain sight by a pizza counter. They coordinated everything from there.

I had to laugh. I respected *these* guys: They were actually working, and under trying circumstances, but I couldn't respect top-heavy stateside management, people like Ryan, who was probably

busy typing another stupid email informing us that we weren't getting paid for being stranded in Cyprus. Our duty day so far was
twenty hours *plus*, and now we didn't have a plane back!

Mark got the real sit-rep (situation report) from other air marshals at ad hoc FAMS HQ from a guy who hurriedly waved him
directions as he spoke to someone else on his cell phone. It was that
kind of a day.

We made our way to a hotel right on the Mediterranean. It was
beautiful, an old but timeless inn that reminded me of *Casablanca*,
except it was live and in color! Somehow everyone could tell we
worked for the American government. (Could it have been our "U.S.
Federal Air Marshal Service" T-shirts?) We had our T-shirts but not
our weapons. We'd been disarmed as both FAMS and normal host
country policy.

Well, not *every* host country. Israel insisted that we carry our
firearms. Our government still vehemently insisted they be locked
up at any Israeli airport. I'll never forget the eighteen-year-old Israeli
female who questioned me about the policy.

"You're trained, yes?" she asked in her thick accent, referring to
my tactical ability.

"Sure am," I said. I didn't want to explain the "logic" behind our
leadership disarming us.

"Then I don't understand why we have to take this from you,"
she said as she took my SIG pistol to lock it up.

Yet I have to concede that in many countries, I actually preferred
to temporarily surrender my service pistol because I didn't feel that
toting it everywhere was necessary. But not in Cyprus. Not today. I
wanted my lifeline, my service pistol, and not because I thought I
might need it while on alert at the hotel—though kidnappings and
targeting had occurred. I needed to retain it to absolutely ensure I'd

have it for the mission home. In all the chaos, a real possibility existed that it might get "misplaced" in the shuffle, and we'd be screwed. Administrators we turned our gear over to weren't nearly as scrutinized as we or even our LEO (law enforcement officer) host-country counterparts were.

We had hailed a taxi to get to our hotel and were fortunate that Cypriot taxis were familiar with tourists. On this mission our government rate for hotels was adequate. At the hotel I ran into a fellow air marshal I had known from the Secret Service. It was good to see a familiar face, someone who knew the Secret Service wear-and-tear the way I did. He was one of our schedulers and he filled me in on just how crazy the situation was. He informed me that everyone was playing catch-up, though he also insisted that everyone was doing all that could be done—they understood the importance of the mission. I appreciated everything he was doing. We needed more people like him, the kind who lead and delegate from the front. They harbor no misconceptions or illusions. When leadership like that hands you a shit sandwich, they don't call it by another name. They're eating it right there with you.

Our team lodged two to a room, so I shared a room with Mark, the TL. Having been awake for nearly twenty-four hours, we were both exhausted. Immediately we plugged our one room key into the air conditioner to get it going. The beds were two youth beds squeezed together and we laughed.

"I've served in the Navy, but even I have my limits," Mark said.

We separated the beds, and Mark went out to get a baseline on the rest of the hotel and the surrounding neighborhood. I showered and finally caught some Z's. I awoke to the sound of Mark banging on the door. I was very groggy and buck-naked, and I felt hungover. I looked at my full water bottle next to me and hated myself for not remembering to chug it before I let myself fall asleep. We were still technically on alert. I grabbed my FAMS shirt and covered myself as I opened the door.

"Damn, dude. I told you I served in the Navy, but even I have my limits," he said again.

I made sure to chug my water bottle before we passed out. It was ninety-some degrees *at night*, and the air conditioner was blasting out air at a still very uncomfortable *eighty-seven* degrees. The locals tolerated their summers far better than we did. Air conditioners were clearly mere tourist amenities that they didn't quite grasp. The nighttime view, however, was truly beautiful—a real job perk.

We were supposed to be there for four hours, but soon we'd been there four days. The restaurant across from the hotel accepted us as family. We went from strange American guys to tourists to regulars, and by the end of the second day they had us sitting at the family table and eating with them. They were great! So was the Cypriot cuisine, a mix of Greek and Mediterranean food: fried cheese, tomatoes, lamb, yogurt, and pita.

On our fourth morning in Cyprus, we reunited with our original flight crew. The pilot gave us the same speech: They wanted to do it, knew it was important, but he, his crew, and his plane had to be safe and secure. We got the rundown of the DC-10 again and were happy to have it. With the stress of a crisis on everyone's shoulders, everyone either works together or falls apart, but we were in sync. They told us to treat it like it was our plane.

We were almost glad for the major delay between our original flight plan and our new charter because we got to see the "screening process" or lack thereof. Screening? There wasn't even ticketing. But in a few short hours, between 250 and 300 refugees would descend on us. We had as much intel as we would get.

We still needed a plan.

We huddled. Our TL ordered to pat down everyone, no exceptions. Men should be seated in the rear of the plane separated from families, with women and children in the front in first class, no exceptions. From our reconnaissance we knew the majority of the people on our plane would be seventeen- to thirty-five-year-old military-aged males (MAMs). That term flew under the radar more so than the term I had learned in the service: combat age. If any man moved toward the front of the aircraft, he would immediately be a red flag.

The crew was pleased with our assessment, and the horde of American refugees moved toward the plane. They were a sorry sight. My eyes went right to their feet. Many were shoeless and had traveled the last few days from Lebanon and Israel across the Mediterranean, only to wait for days on end at Larnaca International. The boats they arrived on were often improvised. Many suffered from bruises, untreated cuts, abrasions, and rashes caused by the blazing summer sun, hot asphalt, or any number of other reasons.

We began our screenings. Initially, many opposed our patting them down. It gave us an opportunity to establish our authority—how this flight was going to play out. "If you don't like it, then you stay here. And if you cause any problems, we will kick you out!"

Air marshals aren't concerned with excuses. We were focused on checking for weapons. As usual there would be no exceptions to our pat-down policy, even if the person was a Muslim woman. They had a choice like everyone else: Submit to being checked—or don't board. They quickly acquiesced.

We homed in on English-speakers and pulled them aside to let them know that we would need their help once everyone had completed boarding. We were just four American air marshals surveilling three hundred desperate and immensely frustrated passengers—plus a sixteen-member crew, three pilots, and a flight engineer. Our most suspicious passenger was a well-rested Caucasian young man with clean skin, clothes, and shoes. He stood out like a giraffe among lions. I spotted him standing apart from the long line of other refugees. He was of combat age, but there was nothing combatant about him. He looked like a small-framed college boy. Mark approached me.

"Hey, this State Department guy says he needs to get on board for some important assignment," Mark said, obviously agitated.

Mark and I went back and forth. I didn't want him on board, but there was supposedly an agency behind this guy. Still, I wasn't convinced a refugee should lose a seat for some State Department guy. If I was wrong we'd surely hear about it later.

"I want to talk to this guy," I told Mark.

"Be my guest."

I approached the State employee. "Look, don't bullshit me. You're what, a GS-9?"

"Uh, yeah," he said. Then I really thought he was full of it, but I wasn't going to get into his pretext.

"And you're here on behalf of the State Department?"

"Yeah, I represent the State Department."

He didn't even refer to it as *State*, which is how *everyone* refers to it in shorthand.

"And what is it that you do for State?"

"I was helping set all this up," he said, gesturing to the people and aircraft.

"Yeah, sure. *You're* a GS-9. Now why is it you need to get back to the United States? Why're they sending *you* home? If you're 'helping set all this up,' your job's not *done* yet."

He got frustrated and raised his voice: "Well, it's my parents' anniversary."

I laughed angrily. "So you lied to my team leader. You're probably still lying to me now to get a free ride home."

"Well, look, my supervisor said it would be all right."

"Oh yeah? What's his name and number?" I asked, pulling out my phone.

"Well, look, he's not available."

I looked him over. He did have credentials and had been patted down, so I figured, *This is gonna be great.* We let him on board and sat him in the rear with all the other men. I took note of his credentials and got back to work helping real people. If that State guy wanted a taxpayer-funded trip, he was going to get a lesson in karma.

As soon as we got everyone loaded, we gave the cue to get into the air and get us to Haan, then back home to the states. Medical care became our biggest issue on takeoff. People were falling asleep. They'd take their seat and immediately pass out *hard,* and rousing them to make room for other passengers was an issue. One woman who had been running for days was so exhausted she couldn't sleep. She had cuts all over her and was so withered that one passenger gave her pain medication while another provided her with some sleeping medication. Her heart rate dropped to a point where we had trouble finding a pulse and it was difficult to rouse her. We grabbed another female passenger to monitor her and made a note to keep checking on her once we got in the air.

But that wasn't the half of it.

A fight erupted at the demarcation between the women-and-children section and the men's. An entire family was shouting and shoving against another man. Soon other passengers were either involved or trying to get a hold of flight attendants—or us. We had to squash it immediately. We physically got involved and let everyone know that we would restrain everyone if we had to.

"Translate for me," I said to an English-speaking passenger. She nodded. "I don't give a shit what your issue is. You are not my problem. I am not stopping this plane for you. But if you continue, when we land in Germany I will open the door as we land and toss you the f— out without your passport. Now sit down and shut up!"

I didn't think we needed a translator after that. We later figured out from another English-speaker that the two men involved were business partners who operated a chain of restaurants. Once fighting broke out near their home, one partner opened a safe the partners had embedded in the floor of one of the restaurants. He was supposed to retrieve their cash to bring it with both families to America. He either claimed that it was too chaotic to reach the safe or that when he arrived someone had stolen their cash—maybe he claimed both things. Either way, his partner's family accused him of stealing their share of the money and stashing it somewhere. Whatever the truth of the matter, they had had enough and just snapped. I felt sorry for them.

Meanwhile, our State Department friend ended up seated next to someone who I think also smelled the lies on him. Fearful of this "very angry-looking man" next to him, he ended up begging for one of the air marshal or flight crew's seats—which was fine. We were by then nearing Haan and still hadn't gotten a chance to sit down.

The flight crew had a powwow and included our TL in it. He spread the word. He didn't know why, but we weren't flying into Philly. None of us questioned the decision because at this point we didn't care. We weren't going to let any news from Ryan and the higher-ups like him destroy our focus. We had work to do.

Our flight attendants were fantastic and didn't stop moving, distributing as much water as they could. Soon even their water ran out and they handed out every can of soda they still had to our desperately dehydrated passengers. Their suffering tore my heart. Still, we always had an air marshal posted by the flight deck. We were in constant eye contact with passengers. I never lost sight of the priority of the cockpit or the vulnerability of the young female flight attendants going above and beyond the call of duty to pass out as much food and water as they could.

I've used *shit show* to describe a great many things in my twenty-nine years of service, but on the plane it got literal. Babies and infants and children had shit themselves during or before this flight, and no one had any way of changing them or cleaning their mess. Swollen diapers remained on each infant. Shit ran down legs and onto the floors. Everyone was piling into the bathrooms, which damn near started overflowing even before we took off. I suspected that many passengers didn't know how to use the airplane toilets. I watched one kid leave the bathroom, and brown turds followed him out in a blue stream. We didn't have time to think about that. I really tried to not think about all the bare feet aboard. But I did know that every aircraft's nose points upward, which meant everything that overflowed flowed toward the back of the aircraft.

I kept returning to my personal bag, and it wasn't long before every snack and meal replacement bar, wet wipe, Band-Aid, and first-aid supply had been handed out or administered. It was the same with every other air marshal and attendant. Genny had packed plenty extra of everything, but no amount was enough today.

We needed to get to the ground—*quick*.

We landed at Haan, and the captain made it clear: We were there to refuel. No one was getting off. We couldn't waste the time. The question was, would the plane be able to refit for water, medical supplies, and food? The answer was no. It was the same with the air marshals. No matter how many supplies we restocked and administered, these people needed too much help for us to realistically provide. We had to look them straight in the eyes, even every mother and bleeding and feces-covered child, and sternly level with them. It was a hard choice but the right choice: We weren't stopping for anything—we were going home.

As we refueled, we didn't even open the doors other than to communicate with the ground crews. Aside from that single open door, we never enjoyed a single lungful of fresh air. We knew if we gave an inch, we could start a panic. As in a sports game, everyone had to be patient and run out the clock.

Back in the air and still not one air marshal had gotten off his feet. Thirty minutes from the States our pilot popped out of the flight cabin. Our destination had changed again! Then again! Our pilots weren't even told why. We finally reached a point of no return and mercifully touched down . . .

At Philly International!

The doors opened, and I've never been so thrilled to be back in the USA. Every air marshal, along with any returning federal agent or military man, is accustomed to being screened by Customs when returning from a foreign country on assignment. World War II GIs ruined it for all of us with their often-deadly, often just contraband "souvenirs." But our airport liaison Warren Griggs waited alongside the lead Customs official. He went the extra mile for us and pointed each of us out—we weren't difficult to spot. Customs agents stamped us and funneled us through without checking any of our gear or luggage.

I phoned Genny. My whole body ached as if I had run a marathon. I stumbled to my truck like a zombie—and passed out. I awoke sometime later and somehow made it home.

I awoke once more and chugged a full two liters of water. I felt great. My body didn't feel great, though—it throbbed. But my soul swelled with the feeling of accomplishing exactly what my father instilled in me so long ago. Of all the things I've done professionally in my twenty-nine years of law enforcement service, serving in that airlift was perhaps the greatest mission of my life. No, that airlift wasn't exactly what I had signed up for in joining the Air Force, but I couldn't shake the memories of my father scolding me and asking what choice I would make. Would I be someone who protected others?

I had helped rescue nearly three hundred fellow Americans, and I couldn't be more thankful for the opportunity.

Ryan phoned us the next day, informing us that the three days off that had been promised to us for taking the volunteer mission couldn't be allowed. And . . . we needed to come in for an office day.

I went into work the next day, stayed for an hour, then left. There was nothing to do, so why stay? I made my appearance, chatted with some other in-flight air marshals trapped in an office day, and learned that a few air marshals had served though two of these Cyprus missions. God bless them.

I went home.

But I made a conscious effort not to focus on the minutiae. No overtime—*fine*. No days off—*fine*. Maybe I'd skip CrossFit for the next few days. I reminded myself of my motto; it's how I find what's most important in my life: Don't sweat the small stuff and 90 percent of it is small stuff! No, it is *bullshit.*

When I cleared out the distractions and reflected on the mission, I swelled with pride. I had a sudden realization.

I served to protect others who couldn't protect themselves.

I did it, Dad.

AFTERWORD

It was 4:26 p.m.

It was good to be stateside, back from Amsterdam. The weather wasn't much different here, the same cold, gray rain. Soon Genny and the kids would be home, but for now the house was calm. I lingered in the kitchen and jettisoned my nine pounds of official gear: a collapsible baton, cuffs, gloves, two phones, credentials, keys, badge, blade, holster, a large-frame SIG P229 pistol (my lifeline), and two extra ammo magazines.

The clanking of my air marshal hardware on the kitchen table, the patter of rain on autumn leaves, the fizz of my first beer—these were among the most welcome of domestic sounds. I checked my work phone—no notifications yet, thank God. I checked my personal phone—no news was good news. With a glorious first sip, I felt that this was heaven on earth.

It sure beat Cyprus.

I loved being home, and I love this country. I'll be here for thick and thin.

But I know the average American's focus is often blurry, their attention span short, their memory so short-term that's its scandalous.

On 9/11 we vowed "Never forget." But we always somehow do.

And because I was there—in the spotlight, in the crosshairs—I realize better than most Americans that we have pretty much forgotten what an amateur-night, three-ring circus the Clinton White House was.

But *I* haven't forgotten.

I remember Monica, sure. But I remember Hillary, too: the shortcuts she took, the methods she employed, the yelling, the screaming, her disdain for "the little people," Bill's black eye—*the country's* black eye.

You want to know something? I *wanted* to forget it all *myself*. I *needed* to forget it all. I'd had enough of the whole damned mess— the sleepless nights, the Protective Privilege bullshit, the lawyers, C-SPAN . . . the cuddling up at night with a loaded pistol *just in case.*

Satchel Paige said: "Don't look back, something might be gaining on you." I didn't want to look back. I wanted to move forward, to shut the door on the Clintons and their whole sordid operation.

To *never* look back.

But there's another saying: "It ain't over till it's over," and now it's 2016, and Hillary's running for president again. I faced a choice in 1998: Would I keep silent? Or tell the truth about what I knew, what I saw?

I spoke up. I testified truthfully.

Not everybody did. Some people's memories got really faulty. Maybe you can't blame them. They got scared. They had mortgages and careers. They had kids.

People who swore an oath to the Constitution and the law, people who pledged to lay down their lives for principle, people who strapped iron on their hips . . . *got scared.*

And they conveniently forgot things.

That was almost two decades ago, and yes, a lot of people have now forgotten what a Clinton White House was like. Millennials were too young to watch it firsthand. Their parents had to make them leave the room.

Their parents had to make them leave the room. *Think about that.*

Our collective amnesia about the Clinton White House is dangerous because it could happen again—maybe with a different Clinton dealing the cards, but with the same stacked deck.

So I had to answer the same question I faced in 1998: What am I going to do about it?

I knew the answer even before I asked the question. I *have* to speak up about Hillary—and a mess of other things well.

She's a problem, but she's not the only one.

The media notices—I *won't* use the words *focuses on—*pervasive, deep-rooted problems only once they're bubbling over the frying pan. They skip from crisis to crisis, scandal to scandal, never adequately analyzing anything. We never get a chance to solve anything before we're off to the next horse race. More often than not, we find an easy answer, breathe deeply, and move on to our own private fun and games. That's all President Clinton did each morning (or night) when I was at the White House. Why shouldn't *we*? Or least that's what we ask ourselves.

So what's the solution? Usually, we just offer up scapegoats to our media gods. Don't change the system; change the nameplate on the door.

Headline: "Madman Jumps White House Fence, White House Secret Service Chief Jumps Ship"—or something like that.

Secret Service director Julia Pierson's resignation was a shame. I liked working for her. She was kind. But America feels as if it "did" something about the protection flaw.

Just wait. The president, the White House, the First Family, the Secret Service aren't better off without Julia Pierson, and neither are we Americans safer without her. She wasn't the problem. The culture was the problem. I recognize the pattern because I was there, and I still see it. Beware the hucksters. The guys and gals with easy answers, anyone who's claiming to have all the answers—who says he can solve *all* the problems: People like that raise a giant red flag. They are trying to sell you something. Beware the "As Seen on TV" candidates.

March 2016. There comes a time for all good men to . . . *retire.*

Yes, retire.

I'm getting ready for my last official air marshal flight. This time it's to Brussels, and when I touch back down again, that's it. I'm over-and-out. I lay down my sword and shield.

Right now I feel like Mel Gibson in *Lethal Weapon,* griping, "I'm too old for this shit." I'm not, but I'm getting there. But unlike some of my colleagues, some young, some not so young, some higher paid, I'll be at CrossFit tomorrow at 5 a.m. I'll be the oldest one there, but I could still get the cuffs on most any of them.

So my time really isn't done. I'll lay down my sword and now I've picked up my pen because I was there with the Clintons. I could not keep silent then, and I can't keep silent now.

You and I have to do our jobs and take the heat when we mess up. If I so much as accidentally use my government credit card on a personal purchase, I immediately take the hit. Why do we expect any less from our leadership? From Clinton Inc.?

Just last year, Mrs. Clinton claimed that as secretary of state she didn't carry a work phone. It was too cumbersome and inconvenient for her to carry two phones. She didn't have room for them.

Then we learned she carried an iPhone and BlackBerry, neither government issued nor encrypted.

Then we learned she carried an iPad and an iPad mini.

But she claimed she didn't do email.

Then we learned she had email—on a private server.

But then she claimed her email was for personal correspondence, yoga, and wedding planning.

Then we learned her email contained government business as well—lots of it.

Listen, nobody transmits classified material on the Internet! Nobody! You transmit classified material via a closed-circuit, in-house intranet or even physically via courier. You can't even photocopy classified data except on a machine specially designed for hush-hush material, and even *then* you still require permission from whatever agency and issuer the document originated. So the only way for that material to be transmitted over an email is for her or someone in her office to dictate, Photoshop, or white-out the classified material in question, to remove any letterhead, or to duplicate the material by rewriting it in an email.

Government email accounts are never allowed to accept emails from nongovernment email accounts. We're supposed to delete them right away. Exceptions exist for communications with private contractors, but those exceptions are built into the system.

I *repeat*: To duplicate classified material without permission or to send it over an unsecured channel is completely illegal. That's why every government agency employs burn bags, safes, and special folders for anything marked Confidential, Secret, and Top Secret. People have lost their careers and gone to jail for far less. Yet Hillary Clinton transmitted classified material by the figurative ton. No one else can operate like that in government. But she takes her normal shortcuts and continues to lie about it.

There is no greater example of double standards in leadership than First Lady, Senator, and Secretary of State Hillary Clinton. Is it too inconvenient or cumbersome for her to follow the same rules that agents in the field have to follow? Maybe it would make morale too high? Clinton's behavior harkens to the old motto: "The beatings will continue until morale improves."

Once when my encoder to log in to my work email malfunctioned, I couldn't even file my invoice to get paid for the month through my personal email, because it wasn't protected enough. I was told that a potential enemy could use my invoice against the country, and I believe that's the truth. It's truer for a secretary of state and the material he or she handles. Still, we're asked to believe nothing inappropriate happened, no slip-ups, no wrongdoing.

It all reeks of "I did not have sexual relations with that woman."

Controversy followed the Clintons even when they were leaving office and purchased a $1.7 million mansion in Chappaqua, New York (so Hillary could carpetbag to the U.S. Senate from New York). Per its normal procedure, the Secret Service maintained a detail at their residence to continue to protect the former First Family as Hillary prepared and ran for Senate. Nothing out of the ordinary there. Perfectly proper.

To protect the Clintons, Secret Service personnel were stationed at a former garage on the property, and I had the chance to spend some time there on protection details myself. Rumors have since swirled that the Clintons receive $1,100 per month rent from the Secret Service.

That doesn't appear to be the case.

But what I heard from other Secret Service personnel on the scene was this: The Service paid $7,000 per month rent on an adjacent house to serve as their unit headquarters from a rental company. Again, nothing wrong there. But what was also well known and what I also heard was that—at least for a while—the Clintons were charging the identical amount for that small garage of theirs to the Secret Service to basically have the Service cover the cost of their mortgage as Hillary ran for office.

I can't verify that (I'm former Secret Service—not Ken Starr), but it's interesting to once again contrast the Clintons with Papa Bush. The USSS did, in fact, cover the costs of *renovating* former president Clinton's garage, which was mostly space heaters and meager basic utilities. When Papa Bush was still president, the Secret Service needed to construct a facility on his Kennebunkport, Maine, property. President Bush said fine—but on two conditions. One, make it bigger, so you guys aren't cramped. He cared about the little guys. Two, you'll be protecting me after I leave office—so *I'm paying for it.*

The Clintons are *crass.* Papa Bush is *class.*

Hillary Clinton's email scandal has garnered a lot of attention. Every week we learned something so startling that we weren't even shocked anymore. I guess Americans stopped being shocked by the Clintons one blue dress ago.

But here's the scandal that's gotten dwarfed by her email scandal: the Clinton Foundation.

Suspicious financial deals are nothing new for the Clintons. Long before there was a Monica there was a Jim McDougal and Whitewater. Not long afterward, there was the Clinton pardons scandal. Today it's outrageous speaking fees running into the hundreds of thousands of dollars for her and Bill and for the multi-, multi-, multimillion-dollar Clinton Family Foundation.

In 2015, author Peter Schweizer published a meticulous investigation of the Clintons and that foundation. He called it *Clinton Cash: The Untold Story of How and Why Foreign Governments and*

Businesses Helped Make Bill and Hillary Rich. In it he detailed "a pattern of financial transactions involving the Clintons that occurred contemporaneously with favorable U.S. policy decisions benefitting those providing the funds."

Schweizer noted questionable donations from such places as Colombia, Haiti, and Kazakhstan. His information was so strong it even earned the respect of such papers as the *New York Times.* London's *Daily Mail* noted:

> The *Times* reported that *Clinton Cash* lists examples of the pattern including a free trade agreement in Colombia that benefitted a donor with industrial interests there.
>
> It also cites development projects in Haiti after their devastating 2010 earthquake, and a $1 million payment to Bill Clinton made by a Canadian shareholder in the Keystone XL oil pipeline while it was being discussed by State Department officials.

Pretty serious stuff. But not really very unexpected by veteran Clinton watchers.

In her article "Stuck in Scandal Land," published in the *Wall Street Journal*, Peggy Noonan nailed it:

> As long as she is in public life, Hillary will protect and serve herself. . . . Doesn't the latest Hillary Clinton scandal make you want to throw up your hands and say: *Do we really have to do this again? Do we have to go back there? . . .* Do we really have to return to Scandal Land? It's what she brings wherever she goes. And it's not going to stop.

I'm constantly asking myself the same questions because I know Hillary's embroiling more Gary Byrneses, people who signed up to serve this country (or maybe just to install a server) and ended up before grand juries, all because of her self-serving motives for power. Right now she's involving more and more government employees in her crisis of character. Even those who share her party affiliation should ask themselves: Is there no one else better here to serve our party, our nation, or his or her own sense of honor? Her supporters seem genuine—I can give them that. But all along the way the Clintons have continually hamstrung their own objectives, embarrassed their followers, and compromised their associates, men and women of character like Leon Panetta.

Now let's take a minute to discuss the recent spate of active-shooter scenarios. Even these tie into the Clintons.

Active-shooter scenarios are really nothing new, whether they occur in Paris or halfway around the world in San Bernardino, California. They're just the latest tactic of radical Islamic extremism, which has moved from flying planes into buildings to suicide bombers to *improvised explosive devices* (*IEDs*) to active shooters, with a multitude of iterations between. Even in dealing with IEDs, we moved from confronting detonations by triggermen to mine-like IEDs to IEDs thwarting metal detectors by containing very little metal. It's a dance of death. We constantly maneuver, but you have to know your enemy, keep pace with him, anticipate his next move—then make yours.

History never ceases to repeat bitter lessons, but the media doesn't have the time to connect the dots. I watched the aftermath of an active-shooter man and wife infiltrate the country and massacre fourteen Americans in San Bernardino using our Second

Amendment rights against us. To some political showboat artists the answer is to decrease American's rights. It's not mine.

San Bernardino didn't come out of the blue. Neither did New York City on 9/11. Both were soft targets. So was Virginia Tech. And if you're Indian you know about 26/11 (the Mumbai attacks of November 26, 2008). If you're British, it's 7/7 (the London attacks of July 7, 2005). If you're French, it's *Charlie Hebdo* and 13/11 (the Paris attack of November 13, 2015).

But you should also know about Garland, because it *doesn't* fit that pattern. On Sunday, evening, May 2, 2015, in Garland, Texas, an active-shooter incident *didn't* end in a massacre. It ended when an *armed* police officer took the fight to the enemy, literally pushing toward them and killing the duo before they could massacre innocents in a crowded event center. Forget politics. Forget before and after. When the attack is initiated there is no negotiation, no thinking—only fighting, pushing, and close killing. The event in Garland wasn't quite the soft target the terrorists thought it would be. They didn't have the access to the defenseless civilians they thought they'd have.

Defend yourself—now rather than later. Strength stops strength. Overwhelming strength stops massacres in their tracks. The principle we saw demonstrated in Garland is the same principle that has thwarted hijacks since 9/11.

Benghazi: We, and the Clintons, have been there before—and on the same continent. In 1993 we called it Somalia and Black Hawk Down. Not wishing to look like invaders, the Clinton White House moseyed a company of Rangers and a team of Delta operators into a city of hostiles where they had to shoot their way in and out, killing thousands. Because the administration denied armor support, we lost some of our men. They did not have to die. Our mission failed entirely. Somalia ended up as a classic failed state, just as Libya now turns into yet another haven for ISIS murderers. It's the same pattern. The Clintons treat running the free world like a damn part-time job.

U.S. ambassador Chris Stevens and State Department Foreign Service officer Sean Smith should never have gone to Benghazi—and shouldn't have stayed once they got there. We were woefully unprepared at every single angle to protect them. We created a classic soft target and didn't bother to think, *What if?* When U.S. Global Response Staff (GRS) had to bail everyone out of Benghazi in September 2012, Secretary of State Hillary shifted blame from Islamic terrorism and the Obama administration's deadly lack of foresight to American freedom of speech and an obscure YouTube video.

I don't care if Hillary Clinton watched caskets come home behind Secret Service protection at Andrews Air Force Base. That's not leadership. Character in leadership comes down to two questions: Would you trade places with anyone under your command? Do you hold yourself to the same level of accountability as those for whom you bear responsibility? Would Mrs. Clinton have been willing to trade places with Chris Stevens and Sean Smith? No. She was too busy swapping gossip and classified information with Clinton loyalist Sidney Blumenthal.

I scratched my head at the deadly irony. Why do the lowest security threat places in D.C. have the most security, yet a consulate—in reality an embassy—in one of the most dangerous cities in the world—*on the anniversary of 9/11!*—is protected by a mere handful of agents armed only with pistols? Our security personnel's safe room even lacked standard-issue Emergency Escape Breathing Devices (EEBs). Contrast that with the security cocooning Secretary of State Clinton when she traveled.

And here's what everyone missed: Benghazi shattered military and federal law enforcement morale. We all wondered, *Will they come for us if we're attacked? Will they stand by us? Does "no man left behind" mean a damned thing? Will they even tell the truth after I'm gone?*

How do I explain Benghazi to my children? How do I use Hillary Clinton as a role model in leadership? It drives me mad, so I don't. I shake my head.

Let's say it straight out: Hillary Clinton lied about the reason for the Benghazi attack. She lied about it to the nation as a whole and she lied right to the faces of the grieving family members of those who died there—and then lied about her lying. And she keeps telling Americans one huge, disgusting lie after another. As I wrap up writing this book, Hillary has claimed that we "didn't lose a single person" in Libya. Really? Try telling that to the families of the four men we lost on September 11, 2012.

Not too long before Mrs. Clinton committed that amazing, bizarre falsehood, the late Sean Smith's mother, Pat, broke down on national television, exclaiming, "Hillary is a liar! I know what she told me." Pat went on to say that she wanted to "see Hillary in jail" for her misdeeds at Benghazi. "She's been lying. She's turned the whole *country* into a bunch of liars."

Two decades ago the late *New York Times* columnist William Safire wrote: "Americans of all political persuasions are coming to the sad realization that our first lady—a woman of undoubted talents who was a role model for many in her generation—is a congenital liar."

The lies change.

The liar doesn't.

I don't know where the future will lead, but I know enough of history and I know my own personal experiences. I trust in the Constitution. I know who I am, what I do, and whom I'm doing it for. My God, my family, and my country are my riches. I'm not looking for a fight, but I don't run from one, either: I walk softly and carry my standard-issue stick. I'm proud of my legacy, but it's not over, not yet. No matter what, I never stop hearing Genny in my ear: "Just do the right thing."

That's why I told you my story. Me, I'm not important. But what I learned about the Clintons firsthand—the hard way—is very important.

It's 2016, but with Hillary Clinton again running for president, it feels uncomfortably like the 1990s again—as if America were trapped in some great, cruel time machine hurtling us back to the land of Monica and Mogadishu and a thousand other Clinton-era nightmares. Fool me once, as the saying goes—your fault. Fool me twice . . .

The bottom line: My job in the 1990s was to lay down my life for the presidency. My obligation today is to raise my voice, to help safeguard the presidency *from* Bill and Hillary Clinton—to remind readers like you of what happened back then.

We all remember—or should remember—what a Clinton White House was like.

If we board that time machine for a return trip—*it's our fault.*

ACKNOWLEDGMENTS

"All gave some, but some gave all." This book would not be possible without others whose memory and example of heroism and sacrifice to country continues to inspire.

A special thank-you to Grant Schmidt of Flim Films LLC, David Pietrusza, and the unnamed couple without whom this project would not have been possible. And of course to all those who always said, "Damn, Gary, you should write a book!"

Thank you to Keith Urbahn and Matt Latimer at the Javelin Group and our publisher, Center Street, for taking us on and believing in the project.